# Fundamentals of Securities Regulation, Fifth Edition

## *by Louis Loss and Joel Seligman*

*Fundamentals of Securities Regulation* is a concise one-volume treatise that provides essential information covering a wide array of topics concerning securities law. This compendium reviews the most significant aspects of securities regulation.

The Fifth Edition of *Fundamentals of Securities Regulation* incorporates the statutory changes provided by the Sarbanes-Oxley Act, officially codified as The Public Company Accounting Reform and Corparate Responsibility, including the creation of the new Public Company Accounting Oversight Board and new Section 15D, which addresses Securities Analysts and Research Reports. The Sarbanes-Oxley Act also has led to substantial changes in the federal securities rules and regulations.

### 2007 Cumulative Supplement Highlights

New legislative, regulatoty, and case law developments are analyzed in the 2007 Cumulative Supplement.

Highlights include:

- The SEC's proposed amendments to the disclosure requirements for executive and director compensation, related party transactions, director independence, and securing ownership of officers and directors (Chapter 2, §D.2.f), which were substantially adopted in August 2006.

- The SEC's revised shelf offering process, including the significant changes to the shelf registration process that concerns the automatic shelf registration for well-known seasoned issuers (Chapter 2, §A).

- The SEC's amendments to its accelerated filer deadlines for large accelerated filers (Chapter 6, §B.1.a).

- Steps the SEC intends to take to improve §404 implementation (Chapter 2, §B.4.b).

- The SEC's approval of the application of the Nasdaq to become a national securities exchange (Chapter 7, §A).

- Comprehensive amendment of the SEC's *penny stock* rules (Chapter 9, §C.3.a).

- The SEC's proposed amendments to Rules 14a-2, 14a-3, 14a-4, 14a-7, 14a-8, 14a-12, 14a-13, 14b-1, 14b-2, 14c-2, 14c-3, 14c-5, 14c-7, Schedule A, Schedule C, Form 10-K, Form 10-KSB, Form 10-Q, Form 10-QSB, and Form N-SAR to provide an alternative method for issuers and third persons to furnish proxy materials by posting them on the Internet. Shareholders would be given notice of the availability of the proxy materials and could obtaincopies at no cost (Chapter 6, §C.2.c).

- The SEC's proposed amendments to the tender offer best price Rules 13e-4 and 14d-10 (Chapter 6, §D.2.c.iv).

- United States Supreme Court decisions in *Merrill Lynch, Pierce Fenner & Smith v. Dabit* and *Kircher v. Putnum Fund Trust.*

- SEC's Statement Concerning Financial Penalties in the context of an announcement of the settled actions against corporate issuers, *SEC v. McAfee, Inc. and Applix, Inc.* (Chapter 13, §B.1).

This cumulative supplement contains an updated Table of Cases.

**11/06**

For questions concerning this shipment, billing, or other customer service matters, call our Customer Service department at 1-800-234-1660.

For toll-free ordering, please call 1-800-638-8437.

Wolters Kluwer
Law & Business

FUNDAMENTALS
OF
# SECURITIES
# REGULATION

## 2007 Supplement

ASPEN PUBLISHERS

# FUNDAMENTALS
## OF
# SECURITIES
# REGULATION
## Fifth Edition

### 2007 Supplement

## LOUIS LOSS
Late William Nelson Cromwell Professor of Law
Harvard University

## JOEL SELIGMAN
President
University of Rochester

## TROY PAREDES
Professor of Law
Washington University
School of Law

.Wolters Kluwer
Law & Business

AUSTIN   BOSTON   CHICAGO   NEW YORK   THE NETHERLANDS

© 2007 Estate of Louis Loss, Joel Seligman, and Troy Paredes
Published by Aspen Publishers. All Rights Reserved.

ISBN 0-7355-6083-8

Printed in the United States of America

1 2 3 4 5 6 7 8 9 0

# About Wolters Kluwer Law & Business

Wolters Kluwer Law & Business is a leading provider of research information and workflow solutions in key specialty areas. The strength of the individual brands of Aspen Publishers, CCH, Kluwer Law International and Loislaw are aligned within Wolters Kluwer Law & Business to provide comprehensive, in-depth solutions and expert-authored content for the legal, professional and education markets.

**CCH** was founded in 1913 and has served more than four generations of business professionals and their clients. The CCH products in the Wolters Kluwer Law & Business group are highly regarded electronic and print resources for legal, securities, antitrust and trade regulation, government contracting, banking, pension, payroll, employment and labor, and healthcare reimbursement and compliance professionals.

**Aspen Publishers** is a leading information provider for attorneys, business professionals and law students. Written by preeminent authorities, Aspen products offer analytical and practical information in a range of specialty practice areas from securities law and intellectual property to mergers and acquisitions and pension/benefits. Aspen's trusted legal education resources provide professors and students with high-quality, up-to-date and effective resources for successful instruction and study in all areas of the law.

**Kluwer Law International** supplies the global business community with comprehensive English-language international legal information. Legal practitioners, corporate counsel and business executives around the world rely on the Kluwer Law International journals, loose-leafs, books and electronic products for authoritative information in many areas of international legal practice.

**Loislaw** is a premier provider of digitized legal content to small law firm practitioners of various specializations. Loislaw provides attorneys with the ability to quickly and efficiently find the necessary legal information they need, when and where they need it, by facilitating access to primary law as well as state-specific law, records, forms and treatises.

Wolters Kluwer Law & Business, a unit of Wolters Kluwer, is head-quartered in New York and Riverwoods, Illinois. Wolters Kluwer is a leading multinational publisher and information services company.

# ASPEN PUBLISHERS SUBSCRIPTION NOTICE

This Aspen Publishers product is updated on a periodic basis with supplements to reflect important changes in the subject matter. If you purchased this product directly from Aspen Publishers, we have already recorded your subscription for the update service.

If, however, you purchased this product from a bookstore and wish to receive future updates and revised or related volumes billed separately with a 30-day examination review, please contact our Customer Service Department at 1-800-234-1660, or send your name, company name (if applicable), address, and the title of the product to:

**ASPEN PUBLISHERS**
**7201 McKinney Circle**
**Frederick, MD 21704**

---

### Important Aspen Publishers Contact Information

- To order any Aspen Publishers title, go to *www.aspenpublishers. com* or call 1-800-638-8437.
- To reinstate your manual update service, call 1-800-638-8437.
- To contact Customer Care, e-mail *customer.care@aspenpublishers.com*, call 1-800-234-1660, fax 1-800-901-9075, or mail correspondence to Order Department, Aspen Publishers, PO Box 990, Frederick, MD 21705.
- To review your account history or pay an invoice online, visit *www.aspenpublishers.com/payinvoices.*

# CONTENTS

## CHAPTER 3

### COVERAGE OF THE SECURITIES ACT OF 1933:
### DEFINITIONS AND EXEMPTIONS

## CHAPTER 4

### PROTECTIVE COMMITTEE REFORM:
### THE TRUST INDENTURE ACT OF 1939 AND
### SEC FUNCTIONS UNDER THE BANKRUPTCY
### CODE

CONTENTS

CHAPTER 6

REGISTRATION AND POSTREGISTRATION
PROVISIONS OF THE 1934 ACT

CHAPTER 7

REGULATION OF THE SECURITIES MARKETS

CHAPTER 8

## REGULATION OF BROKERS, DEALERS, AND INVESTMENT ADVISERS

CHAPTER 9

## FRAUD

CHAPTER 10

MANIPULATION

CHAPTER 11

CIVIL LIABILITY

CHAPTER 12

GOVERNMENT LITIGATION

# CONTENTS

## CHAPTER 13

## SEC ADMINISTRATIVE LAW

# PREFACE

Recent publication of a Fourth Edition of *Securities Regulation* began with a new coauthor, Troy Paredes. Troy also will be the coauthor of *Fundamentals of Securities Regulation*, beginning with the 2007 Annual Supplement. For me there is an extraordinary significance to this continuity. Louis Loss started Yale Law School in 1934, the year the Securities and Exchange Commission itself began. He started a 15 year career at the Commission in 1937. His career and scholarship stretch back to the very dawn of modern securities regulation. When I began work with Louis as coauthor in 1984, I was very much his junior and benefited immensely from the chance to learn from the master in the field. He remarked to me more than once that our interest in codification and in treatise scholarship had begun at roughly the same point in our lives. Now, decades later, I am the senior coauthor and joined by an extraordinary new scholar in securities regulation who also started at approximately the same age as I did. Troy Paredes, who graduated from the Yale Law School like Louis, has already begun to make his mark as a securities and corporate scholar with significant articles such as Blinded by the Light: Information Overload and Its Consequences for Securities Regulation, 81 Washington University Law Quarterly 417 (2003); A Systems Approach to Corporate Governance Reform: Why Importing U.S. Corporate Law Isn't the Answer, 45 William & Mary Law Review 1055 (2004); and On the Decision to Regulate Hedge Funds: The SEC's Regulatory Philosophy, Style, and Mission, 2006 University of Illinois Law Review (forthcoming).

Let me acknowledge my gratitude to Lynne Hasman, who is responsible for the typing of this Annual Supplement, and to Beth Cross-Wilhelm for her cite checking.

## PREFACE

This Annual Supplement speaks generally as of June 1, 2006, although there are occasional references to later materials.

*JS*

August 2006

CHAPTER 1

# BACKGROUND OF THE SEC STATUTES

## B. STATE REGULATION OF SECURITIES

### 1. THE UNIFORM SECURITIES ACTS

*P. 24, after 1st par.* Where does the combination of NSMIA and the new Uniform Securities Act leave coordination of federal and state law today?

After NSMIA the federal securities laws employ three separate methods to coordinate federal-state securities laws:

(1) Specified aspects of the registration and periodic reporting of covered securities, broker-dealer regulation, and investment adviser registration and regulation are *preempted* in full or in part by NSMIA.

(2) Enforcement remains subject to *concurrent federal and state regulation* under express provisions preserving the jurisdiction of state securities commissions. The Securities and Securities Exchange acts, for example, specifically save "all other rights and remedies that may exist at [state] law or in equity." See Sec. Act §16(a); Sec. Ex. Act §28(a); *accord:* Sec. Act §18; Inv. Adv. Act §222; Inv. Co. Act §50.

(3) Section 19(d)(1) of the Securities Act of 1933 authorizes the SEC to cooperate, coordinate, and share information with "any association composed of duly constituted representatives of State governments whose primary assignment is the regulation of the

securities business within those States," an elaborate way of refer-
ring to the North American Securities Administrators Association
(NASAA) that operates in both Canada and the United States.

The harmonization of these different types of United States
federal-state securities coordination methods functions differently with respect to policy development, enforcement, and regulatory flexibility.

### Policy Development

Sections 19(d)(2) and (3) of the Securities Act stress a federal
policy that emphasizes "maximum uniformity in Federal and
State regulatory standards." In particular cooperation is encouraged by §19(d)(3) between the SEC and NASAA in three specified
areas:

> (A) the sharing of information regarding the registration or
> exemption of securities issues applied for in the various States;
> (B) the development and maintenance of uniform securities
> forms and procedures; and
> (C) the development of a uniform exemption from registration
> for small issuers which can be agreed upon among several States
> or between the States and the Federal Government. The Commis-
> sion shall have the authority to adopt such an exemption as agreed
> upon for Federal purposes. Nothing in this Act shall be construed
> as authorizing preemption of State law.

In recent years, cooperation has been a mantra of both United
States federal–state securities policy development and efforts by
the states to harmonize state policies.

The 2002 version of the Uniform Securities Act includes §608,
a reciprocal provision to §19(d) of the Securities Act of 1933.
Section 608(b)(2) of the 2002 Act provides that the securities
administrators "shall, in its discretion, take into consideration
in carrying out the public interest ... maximizing uniformity in
federal and state regulatory standards."

Consistent with the intent of such provisions as §19(d) of the
Securities Act of 1933 and §608 of the 2002 Uniform Securities
Act, the SEC and NASAA have adopted uniform forms (for
example, Form BD for broker-dealer registration; Form ADV

for investment adviser registration); cooperated with the NASD on one stop filing procedures for broker-dealers (the WebCRD or Central Registration Depository) and investment advisers (the IARD or Investment Advisers Registration Depository); and worked jointly to adopt the Uniform Limited Offering Exemption (by 2003 adopted in 50 of 53 U.S. state jurisdictions), which works in tandem with the SEC's Regulation D securities registration exemptions.

Critical aspects of joint policy development are less formal. Section 19(d)(4) further specifies that "in order to carry out these policies and purposes," the SEC "shall conduct an annual conference as well as other meetings to which, among others, NASAA representatives shall be invited to participate." Since 1984 these annual conferences on federal securities registration have addressed a wide array of mutual concerns.

The NASAA has been a particularly frequent and influential commenter on SEC rule and form proposals. NASAA is a membership organization of United States state and Canadian province securities regulators, with a centralized staff in Washington, D.C., that holds annual and other meetings and frequently adopts statements of policy and resolutions, as well as provides comment letters to the SEC and testimony to the United States Congress.

The degree of federal–state cooperation in securities regulation should not be overstated. There are important policy differences on occasion between the SEC and the NASAA or among the states themselves. As significant as policy differences has been the enthusiasm of the SEC Chairmen for working with the states. To cite a significant recent illustration of both points, in October 1995, SEC Chair Arthur Levitt announced his opposition to the initial version of what became the 1996 NSMIA Act in a speech to NASAA that urged cooperation in six areas: investment advisers, investment companies, registration of brokers, examination of brokers, registration of corporate securities, and enforcement authority. NASAA representatives were disappointed both by the substance of what Levitt urged and with the lack of prior consultation. From NASAA's point of view Levitt appeared to be compromising traditional areas of investor protection. Levitt viewed NSMIA itself as a compromise between the initial bill earlier introduced and the NASAA position. J. Seligman, The Transformation of Wall Street: A History of the Securities and Exchange Commission and Modern Corporate Finance, 674–681 (3d ed. 2003).

To put this in different terms, the SEC has not acted as if constrained by the statutory emphasis on cooperation when responding to emerging market needs when they are time sensitive. But as a general matter the Commission is required by the federal Administrative Procedure Act to employ notice and comment processes before adopting new rules. The statutory emphasis on federal-state cooperation has generally become part of this analysis. While states' comments are taken seriously, so are those of other federal agencies, industry, and investors.

For the most part the SEC has largely deferred to the states on intrastate and local policy issues. It was striking, for example, that the SEC did not participate in the 1978–1985 unsuccessful effort to rewrite the Uniform Securities Act and did not attempt to impose any policy position not required by federal statute in the 1998–2002 effort to do the same.

### Enforcement

Enforcement remains the area of federal and state securities law that contains the most complete degree of concurrent regulation. While the United States Congress in the Private Securities Litigation Reform Act of 1995 and the Securities Litigation Uniform Standards Act of 1998 limited private securities class actions at both the federal and state level, NSMIA expressly preserved state securities commission authority "to investigate and bring enforcement actions with respect to fraud or deceit, or unlawful conduct ... in connection with ... securities transactions." Sec. Act §18(c)(1). Indeed §102(a) of the Securities Litigation Uniform Standards Act of 1998 attempted to augment state enforcement power with a hortatory provision calling for reciprocal subpoena enforcement.

The major issues with respect to federal–state securities enforcement have been at the level of lore rather than law. There is an implicit nonstatutory assumption that the states will largely enforce intrastate and smaller claims and that the SEC will primarily enforce interstate and larger claims. States bring a larger volume of enforcement actions than does the SEC, but these actions tend to be smaller (in terms of the dollar amounts), involve individual defendants, and often relate to failures to register securities, individual broker-dealers, or individual investment advisers. SEC enforcement actions tend to be larger (in terms of dollar amounts), involve multiple defendants, and relate to a wider range of claims. Occasionally there has been frustration with this nonstatutory assumption either because particular states have been inadequately funded to perform a meaningful enforcement role, or when the SEC has expressed concerns about *interstate* claims such as the 2002 settlement that New York State Attorney General Eliot Spitzer negotiated with Merrill Lynch concerning its research analysts' misconduct. Merrill Lynch, Spitzer Reach Interim Deal; New Securities Research Disclosures Ordered, 34 Sec. Reg. & L. Rep. (BNA) 647 (2002). As a general matter the two most serious ongoing enforcement issues have been inadequate enforcement budgets in many states and periodically at the SEC. When there are significant increases in fraud, as there appeared to be in late 1990s, many states and the SEC can be overwhelmed. This can lead to inconsistent policy with respect to interstate cases.

At the same time, the New York State criminal case against research analysts is a useful illustration of a key virtue of concurrent enforcement. Precisely because the states also had investigatory and enforcement powers, one state was able to take up the slack and initiate what became a $1.4 billion settlement with ten leading broker-dealer firms. Wall St. Agrees to $1.4 Billion Payment, Broad Reforms, Resolving Conflict Charges, 34 Sec. Reg. & L. Rep. (BNA) 2037 (2002). Ultimately the SEC worked with the NASAA, NASD, and the State of New York on the Global Research Analyst Settlement. SEC Press Rel. 2003-54 (Apr. 28, 2003).

5

## Regulatory Flexibility

At a statutory level there is a sharp distinction between topic areas where federal law preempts state law (such as merit regulation standards applied to covered securities) and concurrent regulation where state rulemaking authority is largely unfettered.

In practice the distinction is somewhat less sharp. Under §18(b)(3) of the Securities Act, for example, the SEC could significantly expand the categories of securities preempted from state merit standards by adopting a rule defining the term *qualified purchaser*. NASAA opposed an initial SEC proposal that would have reached natural persons with net worth of $1 million *or* income of $200,000 because NASAA believed this would increase the risk of defrauding natural persons. To date the SEC has desisted in either adopting the proposal or reproposing it.

On the other hand, when states are not subject to NSMIA's preemptive provisions, the states have often taken, as an SEC report explained, "significant actions to enhance uniformity in regulating offerings of securities that are both 'covered' and 'not covered.'" These included coordinated review of filings, a uniform registration statement for offerings that are exempt at the federal level, and statements of policy on a number of review issues that enhance uniformity of review in the states. SEC Rep., Uniformity of State Regulatory Requirements for Offerings of Securities that Are Not "Covered Securities" (1997).

The basis for this dulling of the state rulemaking authority distinction between preemptive and concurrent statutory provisions seems threefold.

First, implicitly both federal and state securities laws share common purposes to maximize investor protection while minimizing interference with capital formation. Cf. Sec. Act §19(c)(2)(B) & (C); Unif. Sec. Act (2002) §608(b)(1) & (3).

Second, at least since the 1956 Uniform Securities Act, most of the states have recognized that support for uniform state standards and coordination with federal law further reduces the likelihood of federal preemption. Cf. Unif. Sec. Act (1956) §415; Unif. Sec. Act (2002) §608(a). This point was powerfully illustrated when the failure of the states to agree with the securities industry on a common approach to merit review and securities registration exemptions prompted Congress in 1996 to enact NSMIA. Before NSMIA, but after the 1994 congressional elections, NASAA did create a Task Force on the Future of State and Federal Securities Regulation (including the author), whose primary implicit purpose was to find compromise positions acceptable to both NASAA and proponents of federal preemption and to discourage the United States Congress from acting. The political landscape was so significantly changed by the 1994 United States congressional elections that this effort at compromise failed.

Third, pivotal aspects of state securities law, particularly with respect to novel products or practices, repose in NASAA statements of policy, which can be adopted at the state law level as state rules or guidelines. See NASAA Rep. ¶¶351–3841. Currently there are over 60 such NASAA statements. The flexibility that these statements provide in the rapidly changing securities marketplace has been recognized as essential to securities regulation not only by NASAA, but also by such industry representatives as the Securities Industry Association (SIA) and the American Bar Association (ABA). Both the SIA and the ABA endorsed the new Uniform Securities Act (2002), including §203, which authorizes the securities administrator to grant additional exemptions and waivers and §204(a), which in specified instances, authorizes the administrator to deny, suspend, revoke, condition or limit existing exemptions.

While the United States federal–state system of securities regulation may appear reticulate, if not byzantine, a core reality is that it generally has worked well. Both the SEC and the states perceive advantages to having more, rather than fewer, regulators involved, particularly to review filings, conduct examinations, and bring enforcement actions. Both the SEC and the states have usually recognized that contradictory state policies or conflicts with the SEC may deter investment in the United States and strengthen the case for federal preemption. Both the SEC and the states take pride in the growth of the U.S. securities market and the number of direct and indirect investors under a regulated federal–state system.

Given these institutional realities, both the SEC and NASAA have emphasized consultation, whether formally through periodic conferences, or less informally through NASAA comments on SEC rule and form proposals, or meetings or telephone calls on specific topics such as enforcement cases. It is the informal shared values and coordination that is pivotal to making the U.S. system work as well as it does.

To be sure there are costs to the concurrent system of regulation. There can be redundant regulatory efforts including multiple fees for securities issuers and professionals. Federal and state policies can also be contradictory as they were with respect to state merit regulation of securities issues or the initial different enforcement strategies with respect to investment analysts. Both the federal government and the states can rationalize under-financing securities regulation on the logic that it is addressed by a different layer of government. This has been a particularly challenging question with enforcement actions in states that have inadequate enforcement budgets. Coordination with 50 states can delay federal rule or form adoption and may be complex given different state policies. The significance of these types of costs varies over time. But, on balance, even with these costs, the United States federal–state model of securities regulation has generally been perceived to work well. See generally Donaldson Reinforces Message: State Enforcement Welcome, with Caveats, 35 Sec. Reg. & L. Rep. (BNA) 1559 (2003); Donaldson Reassures State Regulators that SEC Not Looking to Diminish Powers, 35 id. 1560.

By 2006, nine states beginning with Missouri in 2003, as well as Idaho, Iowa, Kansas, Maine, Oklahoma, South Carolina, South Dakota and Vermont, as well as the Virgin Islands had adopted the Uniform Securities Act (2002). To date the major debate over enactment concerns whether variable products should be excluded from the definition of security. Variable Annuity Industry under Scrutiny for Exchange Sales, Market Timing Abuses, 36 Sec. Reg. & L. Rep. (BNA) 425 (2004).

## 2.  NEW YORK AND CALIFORNIA

*P. 28 n.32, end note.*     After enactment of the Sarbanes-Oxley Act of 2002, California amended §1502 (subsequently amended further and adding §1502.1) and §2117 (subsequently amended further and adding §2117.1) of the California Corporations Code to require publicly traded corporations to file an annual statement disclosing, among other things, their independent auditor; any nonaudit services provided by the auditor during the two most recent fiscal years; the annual compensation paid to each director and to the five highest compensated officers who are not directors; and a description of any loans made to a director at a preferential rate during the two most recent fiscal years.

California also adopted §2207 of the California Corporations Code, requiring a corporation to notify in writing the state attorney general or the appropriate government agency, as well as the corporation's shareholders, if the corporation has knowledge of certain acts, including "actual knowledge that any officer, director, manager, or agent of the corporation" has made or issued in any report or prospectus any "material statement or omission that is false and intended to give the shares of stock in the corporation a materially greater or a materially less apparent market value than they really possess."

California further adopted new §25,404, making it "unlawful for any person to knowingly alter, destroy, mutilate, conceal, cover up, falsify, or make a false entry in any record, document, or tangible object with the intent to impede, obstruct, or influence the administration or enforcement of [the Corporate Securities Law of 1968]." California also stiffened the penalties under §25,540. Other states similarly adopted so-called "mini-Sarbanes-Oxley Acts." See generally French & Soderquist, State Responses to Corporate Corruption: Thirteen Mini Sarbanes-Oxley Acts, 32 Sec. Reg. L.J. 167 (2004).

# D. A TELESCOPIC PREVIEW OF THE SEC STATUTES

### 4. PUBLIC UTILITY HOLDING COMPANY ACT OF 1935

***P. 47, end 1st par.***    The Energy Policy Act of 2005, 119 Stat. 594, repealed the Public Utility Holding Company Act of 1935. The Energy Policy Act replaced the 1935 Act with the Public Utility Holding Company Act of 2005. The 2005 Holding Company Act substantially overhauls the regulation of public utility holding companies, with the effect of easing the regulatory burden on the electric industry, and transfers authority from the SEC to the Federal Energy Regulatory Commission, which will administer the 2005 Act, and to relevant state commissions.

### 6. INVESTMENT COMPANY ACT OF 1940

#### c. Registration and Regulatory Provisions

***P. 59, new par., after 2d full par.***    In 2003, Eliot Spitzer, the New York Attorney General, settled State of N.Y. v. Canary Capital Partners, LLC, in which a hedge fund agreed to pay $40 million after civil allegations were filed alleging an unlawful trading scheme involving several leading mutual funds. N.Y.A.G. Launches Probe of Fund Industry; Hedge Fund Pays $40M to Resolve Claims, 35 Sec. Reg. & L. Rep. (BNA) 1505 (2003).

Subsequently, several instances of improper trading by mutual fund executives or favored customers and failure to give customers appropriate discounts were widely reported. See, e.g., Labaton, SEC's Oversight of Mutual Funds Is Said to Be Lax, N.Y. Times, Nov. 16, 2003, at 1. The SEC was further criticized by Spitzer for a rushed settlement with Putnam Investments. Spitzer, Regulation Begins at Home, N.Y. Times, Nov. 17, 2003, at A23.

Chairman Donaldson testified to a House hearing in late October 2003 that market timing and late trading abuses by mutual funds were "quite widespread ... more widespread than we originally anticipated." Donaldson Says Improper Trading in Mutual Funds "Quite Widespread," 35 Sec. Reg. & L. Rep. (BNA) 1806 (2003).

In December 2003 the Commission proposed amendments to Form N-1A to require open end management investment companies to provide enhanced disclosure regarding breakpoint discounts on front end sales loads. Inv. Co. Act Rel. 26,298, 81 SEC Dock. 2581 (2003) (proposal).

Separately the Commission circulated a concept Release requesting comments on several mutual fund transaction cost issues. Inv. Co. Act Rel. 26,313, 81 SEC Dock. 2600 (2003).

In 2004 the Commission adopted amendments to Forms N-1A, N-3, N-4, and N-6 to require mutual funds to disclose their policies with respect to frequent purchases and redemptions of fund shares. The Commission also adopted amendments to Forms N-1A and N-3 to require specified variable annuities to explain the circumstances and effects of any use of fair value pricing. Inv. Co. Act Rels. 26,287, 81 SEC Dock. 2553 (2003) (proposal); 26,418, 82 SEC Dock. 2357 (2004) (adoption).

In Inv. Co. Act Rel. 26,288, 81 SEC Dock. 2553 (2003) (proposalto amend Rule 22c-1), the Commission proposed a time limit on the purchase of redeemable fund shares to prevent the receipt of an order after the time that the fund establishes for the calculation of its net asset value to prevent unlawful late trading in fund shares. Cf. Key Groups Oppose SEC Proposal on Providing Same-Day Price to Fund Shares, 36 Sec. Reg. & L. Rep. (BNA) 296 (2004).

In July 2004 the Commission adopted several new Investment Company Act governance rules. Inv. Co. Act Rels. 26,323, 81 SEC Dock. 3414 (2004) (proposal); 26,520, 83 SEC Dock. 1384 (2004) (adoption). Collectively the rule amendments would require that the covered funds usually have a board with at least 75 percent independent directors; that an independent director be chair of the fund board; that the board conduct an annual self-assessment; that the independent directors meet at least once each quarter without any interested persons present; that the independent directors be authorized to hire staff to help fulfill the

11

board's fiduciary duties; and that the board retain copies of written materials that directors consider in approving advisory companies under §15 of the Investment Company Act. Commissioners Atkins and Glassman dissented from the requirements that 75 percent of the board be independent and that one independent director be chair.

The District of Columbia Court of Appeals later granted in part the Chamber of Commerce's petition for review. Chamber of Commerce of United States of Am. v. SEC, 412 F.3d 133 (D.C. Cir. 2005). The Court agreed with the SEC that it had authority to adopt the requirement of 75 percent independent directors and an independent Chair, but agreed with the Chamber that the SEC failed to adequately consider the costs that mutual funds would incur in complying with the new standards or alternatives to the independent Chair requirement. The Commission subsequently readopted the Rule on a 3-2 vote.

In August 2005, the court stayed the 75 percent independent director and independent chair requirements pending court review. Chamber of Commerce of United States of Am. v. SEC, Order No. 05-1240 (D.C. Cir. 2005).

In early April 2006, the District of Columbia Circuit again ruled against the Commission. The federal appeals court found that the Commission did not follow proper procedures in readopting the mutual fund governance rules requiring more board independence. See Chamber of Commerce of United States of Am. v. SEC, Order No. 05-1240 (D.C. Cir. 2006). The court, though, allowed the Commission a limited opportunity to address the procedural shortcomings by reopening the record for comment on the cost of the 75 percent independent director and independent chair requirements.

The Commission also adopted new rules and other rule amendments to require broker-dealers to provide their customers with point of sale information regarding the costs and conflicts of interests that arise from the distribution of mutual fund shares, unit investment trust interests, and municipal fund securities. Inv. Co. Act Rel. 26,464, 82 SEC Dock. 3441 (2004) (adoption).

In March 2004, the Commission settled the largest market timing and late trading case to date with Bank of America and two FleetBoston Financial Corporation subsidiaries. The settlement aggregated $675 million in a combination of disgorgement and civil penalties. BOA, FleetBoston Agree on $675 Million to Resolve SEC, N.Y. Charges over Abuses, 36 Sec. Reg. & L. Rep. (BNA) 513 (2004). See also Putnam to Pay $110M to Resolve Charges Its Employees Engaged in Marking Timing, 36 id. 663.

In 2003, total mutual fund assets were equal to $7.414 trillion and invested in 8,126 mutual funds. $3.685 trillion were invested in 4601 equity funds, $1.241 trillion were invested in 2043 bond funds, $437 billion were invested in 509 hybrid funds, and $2.052 trillion were invested in 973 money market funds. ICI, 2004 Mutual Fund Fact Book at 1, 13. In 2003 for the only time since 1990, mutual funds had a net cash outflow (of $43 billion). Id. at 56. 2003 mutual funds owned 22 percent of United States corporate equity and 18.4 percent of household financial assets. Id. at 59. In that year 91 million individuals in 53.5 million households (47.9 percent of all households) owned mutual funds. Id. at 79-80. In all, United States investors owned 53 percent of a world total of $13.958 trillion in mutual fund net assets. Id. at 141.

In 2004, the Commission adopted amendments to Forms N-1A, N-2, N-3, and N-CSR to identify portfolio team managers, disclose potential conflicts of interest, and disclose the portfolio manager compensation structure and securities ownership. Inv. Co. Act Rels. 26,383, 82 SEC Dock. 1149 (2004) (proposal); 26,533, 83 SEC Dock. 1802 (2004) (adoption).

In 2005, the Commission further adopted Rule 22c-2 to permit mutual funds to impose a two percent fee on the redemption of shares purchased within the previous seven days. Inv. Co. Act Rels. 26,375A, 82 SEC Dock. 1419 (2004) (proposal); 26,782, 84 SEC Dock. 3664 (2005) (adoption).

In 2004, the Commission, on a three to two vote, adopted new rules requiring that hedge fund advisers register under the Investment Adviser Act. Inv. Adv. Act Rel. 2266, 83 SEC Dock. 1124 (2004) (proposal); 2333, 84 SEC Dock. 1032 (2004) (adoption).

As of 2004, there were approximately 8000 registered investment advisers who managed more than $23 trillion in client assets. Id. at 1125. While the diversity of investment advisers was strikingly broad, it did not include hedge funds.

Under the Investment Advisers Act §203(b)(3), *private* advisers (i) with fewer than 15 clients during the past 12 months, (ii) who do not hold themselves out generally to the public as an investment adviser, or (iii) who are not advisers to a registered investment company are exempt from registration under the Investment Advisers Act.

Hedge funds have often claimed exemption under §203(b)(3) by creating pooled investment vehicles, such as limited partnerships, business trusts or corporations (each of which the Commission counted as a single client), even when a substantial number of natural persons invested in the investment vehicle.

The Commission adopted Rule 203(b)(3)-2 to require investment advisers to count each shareholder, limited partner, member or beneficiary of a *private fund* to determine the availability of the §203(b)(3) exemption. *Private funds* are defined in Rules 203(b)(3)-1(d)(1)–(3) to mean a company:

> (i) That would be an investment company under section 3(a) of the Investment Company Act of 1940 but for the exception provided from that definition by either section 3(c)(1) or section 3(c)(7) of such Act;
>
> (ii) That permits its owners to redeem any portion of their ownership interests within two years of the purchase of such interests; and
>
> (iii) Interests in which are or have been offered based on the investment advisory skills, ability or expertise of the investment adviser.
>
> (2) Notwithstanding paragraph (d)(1) of this section, a company is not a private fund if it permits its owners to redeem their ownership interests within two years of the purchase of such interests only in the case of:
>
> (i) Events you find after reasonable inquiry to be extraordinary; and
>
> (ii) Interests acquired through reinvestment of distributed capital gains or income.

(3) Notwithstanding paragraph (d)(1) of this section, a company is not a private fund if it has its principal office and place of business outside the United States, makes a public offering of its securities in a country other than the United States, and is regulated as a public investment company under the laws of the country other than the United States.

Rule 203(b)(3)-2 is, in effect, an exception to Rule 203(b)(3)-1, see infra at 334-335, which is a safe harbor that provides only a corporation, general partnership, limited liability company, trust or other legal entity will be counted as a client when the investment adviser provides advice based on the investment objective of the entity, rather than individual investment objectives of the beneficial owners.

The Rule 203(b)(3)-2 exception to Rule 203(b)(3)-1 is based on three characteristics shared by virtually all hedge funds. First, the private fund must be an investment company required to register under the Investment Company Act but for the specified §§3(c)(1) and (7) exceptions. This condition would exclude advisers to many business organizations such as insurance companies, broker-dealers, and publishers.

Second, a company would be a private fund only if it permitted redemption within two years of the purchase or an interest. The redeemability requirement would exclude investment advisers who advise private equity and venture capital funds, as well as other funds that require long term commitments of capital. Unlike hedge funds, funds with longer term temporal commitments have not been a major enforcement concern for the Commission.

Third, private fund interests are offered on the basis of the ongoing investment advisory skills, ability, or expertise of the investment adviser.

The Commission also adopted amendments to several other Investment Advisers Act rules, including relief from a record-keeping requirement in Rule 204-2; application of the performance fee exemption in Rule 205-3 for earlier established hedge funds; Rule 206(4)-2, the adviser custody rule, and Form ADV.

Commissioners Atkins and Glassman dissented from the hedge fund registration requirement, writing in part:

> Our main concerns with this rulemaking can be broadly divided into the following categories:
>
> - There are many viable alternatives to this rulemaking that should have been considered. . . .
> - The pretext for the rule does not withstand scrutiny. . . .
> - The Commission's limited resources will be diverted.

Id. at 1087–1088.

In June 2006 the District of Columbia Court of Appeals in Goldstein v. SEC, 451 F.3d 873 (D.C. Cir. 2006), vacated the SEC Hedge Fund Rule as an arbitrary rule, criticizing among other things the Commission's failure to adequately justify departing from an earlier interpretation of §203(b)(3).

## F.  THE SECURITIES AND EXCHANGE COMMISSION

### 2.  THE COMMISSION'S STAFF

**P. 68 n.7, end note.**    In 2003, the Commission made fiscal year 2004 adjustments under §6(b) under the Securities Act of 1933, as well as §§13(e) and 14(a) under the 1934 Act, raising the rate to $126.70 per million and raising the rate to $39.00 per million under §§31(b) & (c) of the 1934 Act. Sec. Ex. Act Rel. 47,768, 80 SEC Dock. 147 (2003).

Early in 2004, the SEC sought a $913 million budget for FY 2005, as part of the President's budget, 12.5 percent above the SEC's recently enacted FY 2004 budget of $811.5 million. In FY 2004 the Commission anticipated adding 842 positions. The FY 2004 budget would add 106 additional staff. SEC Releases FY 2005 Budget Information, SEC Press Rel. 2004-2011; Bush Asks 12.5 Percent Increase for SEC in a Vote for Strong Wall Street Presence, 36 Sec Reg. & L. Rep. (BNA) 234 (2004).

The fiscal year 2005 adjustment to §§31(b) and (c) changed the fee rates to $32.90 per million. Sec. Ex. Act Rel. 49,634, 82 SEC Dock. 2613 (2004).

In the fiscal year 2005, the fee rates applicable under §6(b) of the 1933 Act and §§13(e) and 14(g) of the 1934 Act were changed to $117.70 per million.

Separately the Commission adopted Rule 31 and Form 31 to govern the calculation, payment, and collection of fees under §31. Sec. Ex. Act Rel. 49,928, 83 SEC Dock. 502 (2004) (adoption). Under the Accountability of Tax Dollars Act of 2002, P.L. 107-289, 31 U.S.C. §3515, beginning in the 2004 fiscal year, the SEC is required to prepare financial statements audited by an outside auditor. The new Rule and Form facilitate the ability of the SEC to calculate §31 fees and assessments consistent with the 2002 Act.

In 2004 the Commission published a 2004–2009 Strategic Plan. The Plan began by generalizing about Commission resources:

> The agency's staff of almost 4,100 monitor and regulate a securities industry that includes SROs (including 13 securities exchanges, 11 clearing agencies, NASD and the Municipal Securities Rulemaking Board), more than 7,000 broker-dealers, 900 transfer agents, and almost 500 municipal and government securities dealers. In 2003, the volume traded on U.S. exchanges and Nasdaq exceeded $22 trillion and 850 billion shares.
>
> The Commission also regulates more than 35,000 investment company portfolios (including mutual funds, closed-end funds, unit investment trusts, exchange-traded funds, and interval funds, and variable insurance products), more than 8,200 federally registered advisers, and 28 registered public utility holding companies.
>
> Each year, the Commission accepts, processes, and disseminates to the public more than 600,000 documents from companies and individuals that are filed through the agency's Electronic Data Gathering, Analysis, and Retrieval (EDGAR) system. These filings include the annual reports of more than 12,000 reporting companies, which comprise up to eighteen million pages annually.

Id. at 9.

C H A P T E R   2

# FEDERAL REGULATION OF THE DISTRIBUTION OF SECURITIES

## A.  DISTRIBUTION TECHNIQUES

### 2.  FIRM COMMITMENT

*P. 85 n.10, end note.*  The SEC announced that, beginning in August 2004, it would publically release comment letters and filer responses to disclosure filings reviewed by the Divisions of Corporation Finance and Investment Management. SEC Press Rel. 2004–89 (June 24, 2004).

### 5.  SHELF REGISTRATION

*P. 89, end 3d par.*  In 2004, as part of its Regulation AB Release, Sec. Act Rel. 8518, 84 SEC Dock. 1624 (2004) (adoption), the Commission adopted Rule 15d-22 to require annual and other reports with respect to asset backed securities registered under Rule 415(a)(1)(x).

As part of the public offering reforms the Commission adopted in 2005, the Commission revised, and in many respects relaxed, the shelf offering process. The SEC, for example, relaxed the two year formula. In particular, for shelf offerings under Rule 415(a)(1)(x) and for continuous offerings under

Rule 415(a)(1)(ix) that are registered on Form S-3 or F-3, the Commission eliminated the provision in Rule 415(a)(2) that limits the amount of securities registered to "an amount which, at the time the registration statement becomes effective, is reasonably expected to be offered and sold within two years from the initial effective date of the registration." This limit remains in place, though, for business combination offerings under Rule 415(a)(1)(viii) and for continuous offerings under Rule 415(a)(1)(ix) that are not registered on Form S-3 or F-3.

The SEC did adopt a new sort of three year formula, though. Under new Rule 415(a)(5), the shelf registration statement for offerings under Rule 415(a)(1)(ix) and (x), as well as the shelf registration statement for mortgage related securities offerings under Rule 415(a)(1)(vii), can only be used for three years after the initial effective date of the registration statement under which the securities are being offered and sold. In other words, a new registration statement must be filed every three years. The three year period is subject to a limited extension, however. Securities covered by the old registration statement may still be offered and sold until the earlier of the effective date of the issuer's new registration statement or 180 days after the third anniversary of the initial effective date of the old registration statement. Also, a continuous offering of securities covered by the old registration statement that started within three years of the initial effective date may continue until the effective date of the new registration statement, so long as such offering is permitted under the new registration statement. (Filings of a new registration statement with respect to automatic shelves, discussed below, are effective immediately under Rule 462(e), so the 180-day extension period does not apply.) Rule 415(a)(6) further provides that even though a new shelf registration statement must be filed for shelf offerings under Rules 415(a)(1)(vii), (ix), and (x) every three years, unsold securities under the prior registration statement and any fees already paid in connection with such unsold securities may be carried over and included as part of the new registration statement that is filed.

When originally adopted, Rule 415(a)(1)(x) covered securities registered on Form S-3 or F-3 "which are to be offered and sold on a continuous or delayed basis." The Commission's 2005 amendments to Rule 415 relaxed this provision to allow primary offerings on Form S-3 or F-3 also to occur "immediately" after effectiveness of a shelf registration statement. Rule 415(a)(1)(x), accordingly, now covers "[s]ecurities registered (or qualified to be registered) on Form S-3 or Form F-3 ... which are to be offered and sold on an immediate, continuous or delayed basis by or on behalf of the registrant, a majority-owned subsidiary of the registrant or a person of which the registrant is a majority-owned subsidiary." In practice, this change allows for immediate take-downs of securities off the shelf.

Another relaxation of the shelf offering process included in the Commission's 2005 public offering reforms concerns so-called *at the market offerings*, which Rule 415(a)(4), prior to the 2005 amendments, defined as "an offering of securities into an existing trading market for outstanding shares of the same class at other than a fixed price on or through the facilities of a national securities exchange or to or through a market maker otherwise than on an exchange." Under Rule 415(a)(4) as in effect prior to the 2005 amendments, an at the market offering had to satisfy a number of requirements, including (i) the offering must come within Rule 415(a)(1)(x), (ii) where voting stock is registered, the amount of securities registered must not exceed 10 percent of the aggregate market value of the registrant's outstanding voting stock held by non-affiliates, (iii) the securities must be sold through an underwriter or underwriters, and (iv) the underwriter or underwriters must be named in the prospectus included in the registration statement. Under the amended Rule, the restrictions on primary at the market offerings have been eliminated, except that the offering still must come within Rule 415(a)(1)(x). The amended Rule also revises the definition of *at the market offering* to mean "an offering of equity securities into an existing trading market for outstanding shares of the same class at other than a fixed price."

The most significant change to the shelf registration process concerns automatic shelf registration for well-known seasoned issuers, a new category of issuer included as part of the 2005 SEC public offering reforms. Rule 405 defines a *well-known seasoned issuer* (or *WKSI*) as follows:

[A]n issuer that, as of the most recent determination date determined pursuant to paragraph (2) of this definition:

(1)(i) Meets all the registrant requirements of General Instruction I.A. of Form S-3 or Form F-3 and either:

(A) As of a date within 60 days of the determination date, has a worldwide market value of its outstanding voting and non-voting common equity held by non-affiliates of $700 million or more; or

(B)(1) As of a date within 60 days of the determination date, has issued in the last three years at least $1 billion aggregate principal amount of non-convertible securities, other than common equity, in primary offerings for cash, not exchange, registered under the [Securities] Act; and

(2) Will register only non-convertible securities, other than common equity, and full and unconditional guarantees permitted pursuant to paragraph (1)(ii) of this definition unless, at the determination date, the issuer also is eligible to register a primary offering of its securities relying on General Instruction I.B.1 of Form S-3 or Form F-3; and

(3) Provided that as to a parent issuer only, for purposes of calculating the aggregate principal amount of outstanding non-convertible securities under paragraph (1)(i)(B)(1) of this definition, the parent issuer may include the aggregate principal amount of non-convertible securities, other than common equity, of its majority-owned subsidiaries issued in registered primary offerings for cash, not exchange, that it has fully and unconditionally guaranteed, within the meaning of Rule 3-10 of Regulation S-X in the last three years.

(ii) Is a majority-owned subsidiary of a parent that is a well-known seasoned issuer pursuant to paragraph (1)(i) of this definition and, as to the subsidiaries' securities that are being or may be offered on that parent's registration statement:

(A) The parent has provided a full and unconditional guarantee, as defined in Rule 3-10 of Regulation S-X, of the payment obligations on the subsidiary's securities and the securities are non-convertible securities, other than common equity;

(B) The securities are guarantees of:

(1) Non-convertible securities, other than common equity, of its parent being registered; or

(2) Non-convertible securities, other than common equity, of another majority-owned subsidiary being registered where there is a full and unconditional guarantee, as defined in Rule 3-10 of Regulation S-X, of such non-convertible securities by the parent; or

(C) The securities of the majority-owned subsidiary meet the conditions of General Instruction I.B.2 of Form S-3 or Form F-3.

(iii) Is not an ineligible issuer as defined in [Rule 405].

(iv) Is not an asset-backed issuer as defined in Item 1101 of Regulation AB.

(v) Is not an investment company registered under the Investment Company Act of 1940 or a business development company as defined in section 2(a)(48) of the Investment Company Act of 1940.

(2) For purposes of this definition, the determination date as to whether an issuer is a well-known seasoned issuer shall be the latest of:

(i) The time of filing of its most recent shelf registration statement; or

(ii) The time of its most recent amendment (by post-effective amendment, incorporated report filed pursuant to section 13 or 15(d) of the Securities Exchange Act of 1934, or form of prospectus) to a shelf registration statement for purposes of complying with section 10(a)(3) of the [Securities] Act (or if such amendment has not been made within the time period required by section 10(a)(3) of the [Securities] Act, the date on which such amendment is required); or

(iii) In the event that the issuer has not filed a shelf registration statement or amended a shelf registration statement for purposes of complying with section 10(a)(3) of the [Securities] Act for sixteen months, the time of filing of the issuer's most recent annual report on Form 10-K or Form 20-F (or if such report has not been filed by its due date, such due date).

Automatic shelf registration provides additional flexibility to WKSIs offering and selling securities and allows WKSIs to tap capital markets even more quickly. The principal features of an automatic shelf registration are as follows. Automatic shelf registration involves filings on Form S-3 or F-3 and is available at the option of eligible WKSIs; a WKSI is not obligated to use the automatic shelf registration process. The automatic shelf registration process permits WKSIs to register unspecified amounts of securities on Form S-3 or F-3 without indicating whether the offering is a primary offering or a secondary offering on behalf of selling security holders. As the SEC explained in the adoption Release, a WKSI that is such because it meets the $700 million public float threshold can use an automatic shelf for any registered offering, other than for business combination transactions. An issuer that is a WKSI because it meets the $1 billion nonconvertible securities issuance threshold can also register any such offering for cash using the automatic shelf process if such issuer is eligible to register a primary offering on Form S-3 or F-3 under General Instruction I.B.1 of such Form. However, a WKSI that only is a WKSI based on satisfying the $1 billion nonconvertible securities threshold but that is ineligible to register a primary offering on Form S-3 or Form F-3 under General Instruction I.B.1 of these Forms may use the automatic shelf procedure to register only securities offerings for cash of nonconvertible securities, other than common equity, whether or not the securities are investment grade. Forms S-3 and F-3 were amended such that automatic shelf issuers are now also allowed, through an expansion of the so-called unallocated shelf procedure, to register classes of securities without allocating the mix of securities registered between the issuer, its eligible subsidiaries, or selling security holders.

Under Rule 462, a registration statement is immediately effective upon filing under automatic shelf registration without any SEC review of the filing; an issuer may not defer effectiveness. Amended Rule 401(g) provides that an automatic shelf registration statement and any posteffective amendment thereto is deemed filed on the proper form unless and until the Commission notifies the issuer that the Commission objects to the issuer's use of such form. Accordingly, as the SEC highlighted in the adoption Release, unless notified by the Commission, an issuer can proceed with its offering with certainty that the issuer has used the proper form for registration. The SEC clarified in the adoption Release that if the SEC notifies an issuer that the issuer is not eligible to use the automatic shelf procedure, securities sold before the SEC notification will not have been sold in violation of §5 of the 1933 Act. Under Rule 413, a WKSI may add additional classes of securities and may add securities of eligible majority-owned subsidiaries to an automatic shelf registration statement already in effect by filing a posteffective amendment to the registration statement. The posteffective amendment will become immediately effective upon filing, as provided under Rule 462.

Along the lines described earlier with respect to certain other shelf registrations, Rule 415(a)(5) requires issuers to file a new automatic shelf registration statement every three years. The new registration statement will effectively restate the issuer's old registration statement and amend it as the issuer determines is needed. The new automatic shelf registration statement will be effective immediately, and any unused fees paid or unsold securities registered may be carried forward to the new registration statement under Rule 415(a)(6). Accordingly, a securities offering begun under the old automatic shelf registration statement can continue without interruption.

WKSIs may pay filing fees in connection with an automatic shelf registration statement at any time prior to a takedown or on a pay-as-you-go basis with filing fees due at the time each takedown off the shelf occurs. Fees paid on a pay-as-you-go basis are calculated in the appropriate amount given the date and the amount of the particular takedown with respect to which fees are being paid.

Although prospectuses are covered in more detail below, some important points should be noted here when it comes to what may be omitted from a prospectus that is part of an automatic shelf registration offering. Under current Rule 409 under the 1933 Act, a WKSI may omit from a base prospectus information that is unknown and not reasonably available. Under Rule 430B, a WKSI may also omit from an automatic shelf registration statement the following information: (i) whether the offering is a primary or secondary offering; (ii) the plan of distribution for the securities; (iii) a description of the securities registered other than an identification of the name or class of the securities (i.e., such identifications of the securities as *debt, common stock, preferred stock,* etc.); and (iv) the names of any selling security holders. This is not to say that investors are forever without this information.

Issuers generally can add information to a prospectus under automatic shelf registration through any of the following means of disclosure: (a) a posteffective amendment to the registration statement; (b) a prospectus filed pursuant to Rule 424(b); or (c) incorporation by reference to 1934 Act reports of the issuer.

***P. 90 n.26, end note.***   As part of the rulemaking resulting in the SEC's 2005 public offering reforms, the Commission requested comment in the proposal Release as to whether it should reevaluate the factors discussed in Rule 176, which would include Rule 176(g) for underwriters. For example, the introduction of the automatic shelf registration presents new concerns regarding the extent of underwriter due diligence requirements under §11. The SEC ultimately decided to make no changes to Rule 176 to address this or any other matter. See generally Coffee, A Section 11 Safe Harbor?, N.Y. L.J., Sept. 15, 2005, at 7.

In WorldCom, Inc. Sec. Litig., 346 F. Supp. 2d 628 (S.D.N.Y. 2004), a high profile case receiving a great deal of attention, Judge Cote addressed the underwriters' due diligence obligations with respect to the financial statements that were incorporated into two WorldCom bond offerings. Judge Cote's opinion included a thoroughgoing analysis of Rule 176 and underwriters' due diligence obligations in the context of shelf offerings.

## 6.  AUCTIONS

***P. 91, after 1st full par.***   The Dutch auction technique for distributing securities, discussed in the context of shelf offerings under Rule 415, began to develop in more recent years as an alternative to more traditional bookbuilding in nonshelf offerings, particularly in initial public offerings of equity securities.

To the extent that the auction method works as predicted in pricing an offering, there should not be a sizable price spike that follows once the security starts trading publicly in the aftermarket. Put differently, the Dutch auction model is said to remedy, or at least ameliorate, any underpricing of the offering that finds the issuer leaving money on the table, so to speak. Indeed, enormous price spikes were part and parcel of the abusive IPO practices that occurred during the technology stock bubble of the latter half of the 1990s. The expectation of a sizable *pop* in the company's stock price after its initial public offering animated favoritism in the allocation process, such as spinning. It should also be noted that underwriting fees tend to be considerably less in a Dutch auction offering than in a traditional underwriting.

In 2004, in the largest and highest-profile Dutch auction public offering to date, Google Inc. filed a particularly notable non-shelf IPO registration statement. A self-styled *Letter from the Founders* included in Google's registration statement explained:

> Informed investors willing to pay the IPO price should be able to buy as many shares as they want, within reason, in the IPO, as on the stock market.
>
> It is important to us to have a fair process for our IPO that is inclusive of both small and large investors. It is also crucial that we achieve a good outcome for Google and its current shareholders. This has led us to pursue an auction-based IPO for our entire offering. Our goal is to have a share price that reflects a fair market valuation of Google and that moves rationally based on changes in our business and the stock market. . . .
>
> Many companies have suffered from unreasonable speculation, small initial share float, and boom-bust cycles that hurt them and their investors in the long run. We believe that an auction-based IPO will minimize these problems.
>
> An auction is an unusual process for an IPO in the United States. Our experience with auction-based advertising systems has been surprisingly helpful in the auction design process for the IPO. As in the stock market, if people try to buy more stock than is available, the price will go up. And of course, the price will go down if there aren't enough buyers. This is a simplification, but it captures the basic issues. Our goal is to have an efficient market price — a rational price set by informed buyers and sellers — for our shares at the IPO and afterward. Our goal is to achieve a relatively stable price in the days following the IPO and that buyers and sellers receive a fair price at the IPO.

Notably, after going public at a price of $85 per share, Google's stock closed the first day of trading at around $100. By early

2006, Google's stock price had skyrocketed to over $450 per share, in large part on the strength of the company's stellar earnings. By the start of the second quarter of 2006, Google was trading at around $400 per share.

To date, Dutch auction offerings remain a rare event compared to more traditional underwritten offerings. It remains to be seen whether this will change and Dutch auction offers will become more common as the Internet continues to play an increasingly significant role in the public offering process and as securities markets become increasingly democratized with the growth of the so-called *investor class* in the United States.

### *P. 91, renumber subsection 6 as subsection 7.*

### 7.   SECURITIES UNDERWRITING IN GENERAL

### *P. 92 n.8, end note.*

Total corporate underwriting in the U.S. reached a second consecutive year of record levels at $2.58 trillion in 2002, edging out the previous year's then record $2.54 trillion, which itself was up an amazing 37% over the $1.85 trillion raised in 2000. Once again total corporate underwriting records were driven by robust fixed income issuance. Last year, a record 94.0% of the dollar volume of corporate underwriting came from debt issuance, just edging out the previous year's then record 93.3%. Twenty years ago, 1983, debt's share of total corporate underwriting matched a previous nadir of only 53.3% of total dollar volume of underwriting.

2003 Securities Industry Fact Book at 6. "On top of the record $2.58 trillion of corporate capital raised publicly, an additional $344 billion was raised through private placements, particularly Rule 144A deals." Ibid. "The ratio of the value of U.S. corporate private placements to public underwriting fell to a new low of 12% in 2002 after six straight years in the 20% range." Ibid.

In recent years there has been a continuing high number and value of U.S. corporate underwritings:

| Year | Number of Issues | Value ($ Billions) |
|------|------------------|--------------------|
| 2002 | 10,572 | 2,581.1 |
| 2003 | 9,648 | 2,889.9 |
| 2004 | 8,913 | 2,859.0 |

2005 Securities Industry Fact Book at 10–11.

## B. THE BASIC PROHIBITIONS OF §5

### 1. THE STATUTORY PATERN

*P. 97, new pars., after 3d par.*   In 2005 the SEC adopted significant reforms that significantly revamped the process by which companies register securities and issue them to the public (referred to hereafter as the *2005 public offering reforms*). Sec. Act Rels. 8501, 83 SEC Dock. 4 (2004) (proposal); 8591, 85 SEC Dock. 2871 (2005) (adoption); 8591A (2006) (technical amendments). These reforms represent one of the most important reformations of the registration and offering process accomplished in one fell swoop in recent decades. The following also provides an overall summary of the reforms impacting the way in which issuers and other offering participants are allowed to communicate with the market during a public offering subject to §5 of the Securities Act.

The SEC's overall objective was to modernize the securities offering and communications processes. Two developments, in particular, argued in favor of updating the regulatory regime that governs how issuers offer their securities to the public. The first development centers on technological advances affecting securities markets. The SEC explained in the adoption Release:

... [S]ignificant technological advances over the last three decades have increased both the market's demand for more timely corporate disclosure and the ability of issuers to capture, process,

29

and disseminate this information. Computers, sophisticated financial software, replaced, to a larger extent, paper, pencils, type-
writers, adding machines, carbon paper, paper mail, travel, and
face-to-face meetings relied on previously. The rules we are adopting today seek to recognize the integral role that technology plays
in timely informing the markets and investors about important
corporate information and developments.

85 SEC Dock. at 2880.

The second development motivating the adoption of the 2005
public offering reforms centers on the important role that a
public company's 1934 Act filings play in keeping the market
up-to-speed and informed about an issuer and its securities. The
SEC again explained in the adoption Release:

> The role that a public issuer's Exchange Act reports play in
> investment decision making is a key component of the rules we
> are adopting today. Congress recognized that the ongoing dis-
> semination of accurate information by issuers about themselves
> and their securities is essential to the effective operation of the
> trading markets. The Exchange Act and underlying rules have
> established a system of continuing disclosure about issuers that
> have offered securities to the public, or that have securities that
> are listed on a national securities exchange or are broadly held by
> the public. The Exchange Act rules require public issuers to make
> periodic disclosures at annual and quarterly intervals, with other
> important information reported on a more current basis. The
> Exchange Act specifically provides for current disclosure to main-
> tain the timeliness and adequacy of information disclosed by
> issuers, and we have significantly expanded our current disclosure
> requirements consistent with the provision in the Sarbanes-Oxley
> Act of 2002 that "[e]ach issuer reporting under Section 13(a) or
> 15(d) ... disclose to the public on a rapid and current basis such
> additional information concerning material changes in the finan-
> cial condition or operations of the issuer ... as the Commission
> determines ... is necessary or useful for the protection of inves-
> tors and in the public interest."

> A public issuer's Exchange Act record provides the basic source
> of information to the market and to potential purchasers regard-
> ing the issuer and its management, business, financial condition,

and prospects. Because an issuer's Exchange Act reports and other publicly available information form the basis for the market's evaluation of the issuer and the pricing of its securities, investors in the secondary market use that information in making their investment decisions. Similarly, during a securities offering in which an issuer uses a short-form registration statement, an issuer's Exchange Act record is very often the most significant part of the information about the issuer in the registration statement.

With the enactment of the Sarbanes-Oxley Act and our recent rulemaking and interpretive actions, we have enhanced significantly the disclosure included in issuers' Exchange Act filings and accelerated the filing deadlines for many issuers. The following are examples of recent regulatory actions that have improved the delivery of timely, high-quality information to the securities markets by issuers under the Exchange Act:

- Requiring the establishment of disclosure controls and procedures;
- Requiring a public issuer's top management to certify the content of periodic reports and highlight their responsibilities for and evaluation of the issuer's disclosure controls and procedures and internal control over financial reporting;
- Modifying the approach to current disclosure by increasing significantly the types of events that must be reported on a current basis and shortening the time for filing current reports;
- Approving listing standard changes intended to improve corporate governance and enhance the role of the audit committee of the issuer's board of directors with regard to financial reporting and auditor independence; and
- Providing further interpretive guidance regarding the content and understandability of Management's Discussion and Analysis of Financial Condition and Results of Operation (MD&A) — a disclosure item we believe is at the core of a reporting issuer's periodic reports.

Many of the recent changes to the Exchange Act reporting framework provide greater rigor to the process that issuers must follow in preparing their financial statements and Exchange Act reports. Senior management now must certify the material adequacy of the content of periodic Exchange Act reports. Moreover, issuers, with the involvement of senior management, now must implement and evaluate disclosure controls and procedures and internal controls over financial reporting. Further, we believe the heightened role of an issuer's board of directors and its audit committee provides a structure that can contribute to improved Exchange Act reports.

... We believe that the enhancements to Exchange Act reporting described above enable us to rely on these reports to a greater degree in adopting our rules to reform the securities offering process.

85 SEC Dock. at 2880–2881.

In short, securities markets are more informed at any given moment about an issuer and its securities as a result of technological advances and enhanced reporting under the Exchange Act, aside from the particular disclosures required by the federal securities laws in connection with a specific registered offering. Such developments, then, allow for the liberalization of the offering process and communications with investors and potential investors during a registered offering without compromising investor protection.

The SEC expressed its belief that the 2005 public offering reforms will:

- Facilitate greater availability of information to investors and the market with regard to all issuers;
- Eliminate barriers to open communications that have been made increasingly outmoded by technological advances;
- Reflect the increased importance of electronic dissemination of information, including the use of the Internet;
- Make the capital formation process more efficient; and
- Define more clearly both the information and the timeliness of the availability of information against which a seller's statements are evaluated for liability purposes.

85 SEC Dock. at 2880.

The SEC provided the following summary of the relaxed communication rules ushered in as part of the 2005 public offering reforms:

Today, we are adopting rules that relate to the following:

- Regularly released factual business information;
- Regularly released forward-looking information;
- Communications made more than 30 days before filing a registration statement;
- Communications by well-known seasoned issuers during the 30 days before filing a registration statement;
- Written communications made in accordance with the safe harbor in Securities Act Rule 134; and
- Written communications (other than a statutory prospectus) by any eligible issuer after filing a registration statement.

The following table provides a brief overview of the operation of the new and amended rules. . . .

| | Could it be an "offer" as defined in Section 2(a)(3)? | Is it a "prospectus" as defined in Section 2(a)(10)? | Is it a prohibited prefiling offer for purposes of Section 5(c)? | Is it a prohibited prospectus for purposes of Section 5(b)(1)? |
|---|---|---|---|---|
| Regularly Released Factual Business Information | Yes | No | Rule defines it as not an offer for Section 5(c) purposes | Section 5(b)(1) relates only to "prospectuses" — it is not applicable |
| Regularly Released Forward-Looking Information | Yes | No | Rule defines it as not an offer for Section 5(c) purposes | Section 5(b)(1) relates only to "prospectuses" — it is not applicable |

continues

| Communications Made More Than 30 Days Before Filing of Registration Statement | Yes | Possibly, based on facts and circumstances | Rule defines it as not an offer for Section 5(c) purposes | Section 5(b)(1) does not apply in the prefiling period—it is not applicable |
|---|---|---|---|---|
| Well-Known Seasoned Issuers— Oral Offers Made Within 30 Days of Filing of Registration Statement | Yes | No | Is exempted from prohibition of Section 5(c) | Section 5(b)(1) does not apply in the prefiling period— it is not applicable |
| Well-Known Seasoned Issuers— Written Offers Made Within 30 Days of Filing of Registration Statement | Yes | Yes. It also is a free-writing prospectus | Is exempted from prohibition of Section 5(c) | Section 5(b)(1) does not apply in the pre-filing period—it is not applicable |
| Well-Known Seasoned Issuers— Free Writing Prospectuses Used Before Filing of Registration Statement | Yes | Yes | Is exempted from prohibition of Section 5(c) | Section 5(b)(1) does not apply in the pre-filing period—it is not applicable |

| | | | | |
|---|---|---|---|---|
| Identifying Statements in Accordance with Rule 134 | Yes | No | Section 5(c) is not applicable, as Rule 134 relates only to the period after the filing of a registration statement | Section 5(b)(1) relates only to "prospectuses"—it is not applicable |
| All Eligible Issuers— Free Writing Prospectuses Used After Filing of Registration Statement | Yes | Yes | Section 5(c) is not applicable, as it does not apply in the post-filing period | Section 5(b)(1) will be satisfied, as the free writing prospectus will be a permitted Section 10(b) prospectus |

. . . .

The new and revised rules we are adopting establish a communications framework that, in some cases, will operate along a spectrum based on the type of issuer, its reporting history, and its equity market capitalization or recent issuances of fixed income securities. Thus, under the rules we are adopting, eligible well-known seasoned issuers will have freedom generally from the gun-jumping provisions to communicate at any time, including by means of a written offer other than a statutory prospectus. Varying levels of restrictions will apply to other categories of issuers. We believe these distinctions are appropriate because the market has more familiarity with large, more seasoned issuers and, as a result of the ongoing market following of their activities, including the role of market participants and the media, these issuers' communications have less potential for conditioning the market for the issuer's securities to be sold in a registered offering. Disclosure obligations and practices outside the offering process, including under the Exchange Act, also determine the scope of communications flexibility the rules give to issuers and other offering participants. The cumulative effect of the rules under the gun-jumping provisions is the following:

- well-known seasoned issuers are permitted to engage at any time in oral and written communications, including use at any time of a free writing prospectus, subject to enumerated conditions (including, in specified cases, filing with us). [Rule 163]
- all reporting issuers are permitted, at any time, to continue to publish regularly released factual business information and forward-looking information. [Rule 168]
- non-reporting issuers are permitted, at any time, to continue to publish regularly released factual business information that is intended for use by persons other than in their capacity as investors or potential investors. [Rule 169]
- communications by issuers more than 30 days before filing a registration statement are not prohibited offers so long as they do not reference a securities offering that is or will be the subject of a registration statement. [Rule 163A]
- all issuers and offering participants are permitted to use free writing prospectuses after the filing of the registration statement, subject to enumerated conditions (including, in specified cases, filing with us). [Rules 164 and 433]
- a broader category of routine communications regarding issuers, offerings, and procedural matters, such as communications about the schedule for an offering or about account-opening procedures, are excluded from the definition of "prospectus." [Rule 134]
- the exemptions for research reports are expanded. [Rules 137, 138, and 139]

. . . [A] number of these rules include conditions of eligibility. Most of the new and amended rules, for example, are not available to blank check companies, penny stock issuers, or shell companies.

The rules we are adopting today ensure that appropriate liability standards are maintained. For example, all free writing prospectuses have liability under the same provisions as apply today to oral offers and statutory prospectuses. Written communications not constituting prospectuses will not be subject to disclosure liability applicable to prospectuses under Securities Act Section 12(a)(2). This result will not affect their status for liability purposes under other provisions of the federal securities laws, including the anti-fraud provisions.

85 SEC Dock. at 2891–2893.

### 3.  THE JURISDICTIONAL BASE OF §5

*P. 101 n.9, end note.*   For other recent examples, see also Geiger v. SEC, 363 F.3d 481, 485 (D.C. Cir. 2004) (in finding a §5(c) violation, court rejected defendant's claim that he did not "offer" to sell securities during prefiling period but "merely accepted outstanding offers" from market makers to buy, and court cited authority to the effect that "price quotations" are commonly understood as inviting an offer); SEC v. Cavanagh, 155 F.3d 129, 134–136 (2d Cir. 1998) (negotiation of final terms for sale of securities previously issued to management was an offer in violation of §5(c)); Goldman, Sachs & Co., Sec. Act Rel. 8434, 83 SEC Dock. 442 (2004) (Goldman Sachs violated §5(c)'s prohibition against prefiling offers when a Goldman Sachs official spoke to the press on behalf of Goldman Sachs to correct a public perception regarding the use of the money to be raised in a yet-to-be-filed public offering).

### 4.  THE PREFILING PERIOD

#### b.  "Beating the Gun"

*P. 106, after 1st full par.*   After amendment in 2005, Rule 135 provides:

(a) *When notice is not an offer*. For purposes of section 5 of the [Securities] Act only, an issuer or a selling security holder (and any person acting on behalf of either of them) that publishes through any medium a notice of a proposed offering to be registered under the [Securities] Act will not be deemed to offer its securities for sale through that notice if:

(1) *Legend*. The notice includes a statement to the effect that it does not constitute an offer of any securities for sale; and

(2) *Limited notice content*. The notice otherwise includes no more than the following information:

(i) The name of the issuer;

(ii) The title, amount and basic terms of the securities offered;

(iii) The amount of the offering, if any, to be made by selling security holders;

(iv) The anticipated timing of the offering;

(v) A brief statement of the manner and the purpose of the offering, without naming the underwriters;

(vi) Whether the issuer is directing its offering to only a particular class of purchasers;

(vii) Any statements or legends required by the laws of any state or foreign country or administrative authority; and

(viii) In the following offerings, the notice may contain additional information, as follows:

(A) *Rights offering*. In a rights offering to existing security holders:

(1) The class of security holders eligible to subscribe;

(2) The subscription ratio and expected subscription price;

(3) The proposed record date;

(4) The anticipated issuance date of the rights; and

(5) The subscription period or expiration date of the rights offering.

(B) *Offering to employees*. In an offering to employees of the issuer or an affiliated company:

(1) The name of the employer;

(2) The class of employees being offered the securities;

(3) The offering price; and

(4) The duration of the offering period.

(C) *Exchange offer*. In an exchange offer:

(1) The basic terms of the exchange offer;

(2) The name of the subject company;

(3) The subject class of securities sought in the exchange offer.

(D) *Rule 145(a) offering*. In a [Rule] 145(a) offering:

(1) The name of the person whose assets are to be sold in exchange for the securities to be offered;

(2) The names of any other parties to the transaction;

(3) A brief description of the business of the parties to the transaction;

(4) The date, time and place of the meeting of security holders to vote on or consent to the transaction; and

(5) A brief description of the transaction and the basic terms of the transaction.

(b) *Correction of misstatements about the offering*. A person that publishes a notice in reliance on this [Rule] may issue a notice that contains no more information than is necessary to correct inaccuracies published about the proposed offering.

Put differently, a notice of proposed offering that contains disclosures in addition to those provided for in Rule 135 will not qualify for the Rule's safe harbor.

***PP. 107–108, 1st full par., substitute:***   2005 Rules 137–139 were amended.

Each of these Rules refers to the publication or distribution of a *research report*, a term that needs to be unpacked before moving on to consider the Rules in chief. *Research report* is defined in each of the Rules as a "written communication ... that includes information, opinions, or recommendations with respect to securities of an issuer or an analysis of a security of an issuer, whether or not it provides information reasonably sufficient upon which to base an investment decision." Rule 405, in turn, defines *written communication* as "any communication that is written, printed, a radio or television broadcast, or a graphic communication." It is worth stressing that, given the definition of *research report*, the research safe harbors under Rules 137–139 do not apply to oral communications. Unpacking the definition of *research report* still further, the term *graphic communication* is defined in Rule 405 to include "all forms of electronic media, including, but not limited to, audiotapes, videotapes, facsimiles, CD-ROM, electronic mail, Internet Web sites, substantially similar messages widely distributed (rather than individually distributed) on telephone answering or voice mail systems, computers, computer networks and other forms of computer data compilation. Graphic communication shall not include a communication that, at the time of the communication, originates live, in real-time to a live audience and does not originate in recorded form or otherwise as a graphic communication, although it is transmitted through graphic means."

Rule 137 presently permits a broker or dealer to publish or distribute "in the regular course of its business" research reports regarding the securities of an issuer which is the subject of an offering pursuant to a registration statement that the issuer proposes to file, has filed, or that is effective. In particular, so long as the Rule's conditions are satisfied, the terms *offers, participates,* or *participation* in the definition of *underwriter* in §2(a)(11) of the Securities Act will not apply to the publication or distribution of the broker-dealer research report. Prior to the 2005 amendments to Rule 137, the Rule only applied to the publication or distribution by brokers or dealers of "information, opinions or recommendations" related to the securities of a registrant required to file reports pursuant to §13 or §15(d) of the 1934 Act which also proposed to file, had filed, or had an effective registration statement under the 1933 Act. In other words, Rule 137 has been expanded to apply to the securities of both reporting and nonreporting issuers, subject to certain specified exceptions. That is, neither the issuer nor any of its predecessors may be or have been during the past three years a blank check company, a shell company (other than a business combination shell company), or a penny stock issuer.

Consistent with the prior version of the Rule, in order to fall within Rule 137, the broker or dealer (and any affiliate) distributing the research report, as well as the person (and any affiliate) that has published the report, (a) must not participate or propose to participate in the distribution of the securities that are or will be the subject of the registered offering, and (b) in connection with the publication or distribution of the research report, must not receive, directly or indirectly, any consideration from, or act under any direct or indirect arrangement or understanding with, (i) the issuer, (ii) a selling security holder, (iii) any participant in the distribution of the securities that are or will be covered by the registration statement, or (iv) any other person interested in such securities. Rule 137 does provide an exception, though, when it comes to certain payments. In particular, Rule 137 generally allows payment of the regular price being paid by the broker or dealer for independent research or the regular subscription or purchase price for the research report.

Rule 138 was substantially amended in 2005. Rule 138 presently provides that, for purposes of §§2(a)(10) and 5(c) of the 1933 Act and so long as certain conditions are met, a broker's or dealer's publication or distribution of research reports about an issuer's securities will not constitute an offer for sale or offer to sell a security which is the subject of an offering pursuant to a registration statement that the issuer proposes to file, has filed, or that is effective, even if the broker or dealer is or will be participating in the registered offering. One notable condition is that (i) the research report relates solely to the issuer's common stock, or debt securities, or preferred stock convertible into its common stock, while the offering involves solely the issuer's nonconvertible debt securities or nonconvertible, nonparticipating preferred stock; or (ii) the research report relates solely to the issuer's nonconvertible debt securities or nonconvertible, nonparticipating preferred stock, while the offering involves solely the issuer's common stock, or debt securities, or preferred stock convertible into its common stock. Another notable condition of Rule 138 is the requirement that the broker or dealer have previously published or distributed research reports on the types of securities in question in the regular course of its business. The requirement that the broker or dealer have published or distributed research on the same types of securities as those securities that are the subject of the research reports is new to the 2005 amendments.

The Rule generally covers research reports on all reporting issuers that are current in filing their periodic reports under the 1934 Act. Before amendment, Rule 138 provided a foreign private issuer must meet the registrant requirements of Form F-3 (other than the reporting history provisions of the Form), meet certain minimum float requirements or investment grade securities provisions of Form F-3, and have had its securities traded for at least 12 months on a designated offshore securities market. The Rule now applies to a foreign private issuer if such issuer has had its equity securities trading on a designated offshore securities market for at least 12 months or has a worldwide market value of outstanding common equity held by nonaffiliates of $700 million or more; meets the requirements of Form F-3 (other than the reporting history provisions of the Form); and either satisfies the public float threshold of Form F-3 or is issuing nonconvertible investment grade securities meeting the applicable provisions of such Form.

Rule 139 is the most significant of this series of rules. So long as certain specified conditions are satisfied, Rule 139 permits a broker or dealer to publish or distribute a research report about an issuer or any of its securities without such report, for purposes of §§2(a)(10) and 5(c) of the 1933 Act, constituting an offer for sale or an offer to sell a security of the issuer that is the subject of an offering pursuant to a registration statement that the issuer proposes to file or has filed, or that is effective, even if the broker or dealer is participating or will participate in the registered offering of such securities.

For issuer-specific research reports to fall within Rule 139, the issuer (i) must be current in filing its required periodic reports under the 1934 Act and (ii) at the later of the time of filing its most recent Form S-3 or Form F-3 or the time of its most recent amendment to such registration statement for purposes of complying with §10(a)(3) of the 1933 Act or, if no Form S-3 or Form F-3 has been filed, at the date of reliance on Rule 139, must meet the requirements of Form S-3 or Form F-3 and either at such date meet the minimum float provisions of such Forms or, at the date of reliance on Rule 139, be, or if a registration statement has not been filed, later be, offering securities meeting the requirements for the offering of investment grade securities pursuant to General Instruction I.B.2. of Form S-3 or Form F-3, or at the date of reliance on Rule 139, must be a well-known seasoned issuer, other than a majority-owned subsidiary that is a well-known seasoned issuer by virtue of paragraph (1)(ii) of the definition of well-known seasoned issuer under Rule 405. The Rule also applies to a foreign private issuer if such issuer (a) meets the requirements of Form F-3 (other than the reporting history provisions), (b) satisfies the public float threshold of Form F-3 or is issuing nonconvertible investment grade securities meeting the provisions of General Instruction I.B.2. of Form F-3, and (c) has had its equity securities trading on a designated offshore securities market for at least 12 months or has a worldwide market value of outstanding common equity held by nonaffiliates of $700 million or more.

Furthermore, in order to fall within Rule 139, the broker or dealer must publish or distribute the research report in the regular course of its business. Additionally, the subject research report must not represent the initiation of publication of research about the issuer or its securities or the reinitiation of coverage by the broker or dealer of such issuer or its securities. The 2005 amendments did away with the earlier requirement that the research also be contained in a publication distributed with *reasonable regularity*. In other words, Rule 139 no longer includes a *reasonable regularity* requirement.

Rule 139 also addresses more general industry reports (i.e., research reports that are not limited to a particular issuer or its securities but that cover an entire industry and mention the issuer). Such industry reports fall within Rule 139 and thus do not constitute an offer of a particular issuer's securities for purposes of §§2(a)(10) and 5(c) of the 1933 Act if, in addition to the issuer satisfying various eligibility requirements, (i) the research report includes similar information for a substantial number of issuers in the issuer's industry or subindustry or contains a comprehensive list of securities currently recommended by the broker or dealer, (ii) the analysis regarding the issuer or its securities is given no materially greater space or prominence in the publication than what is given to other issuers or securities, and (iii) the broker or dealer publishes or distributes research reports in the regular course of its business and, at the time of the publication or distribution of the research report, is including similar information about the issuer or its securities in similar reports. Amended Rule 139 deletes the prior requirement that the brokerdealer research report be no more favorable to the issuer or its securities than the broker-dealer's last report.

The SEC's 2005 public offering reforms ushered in a number of additional regulatory changes that further relaxed communications leading up to and during a securities offering. Many of these developments also helped clarify the types of communications that are permissible without running afoul of §5 of the 1933 Act.

First, Rule 168 creates a nonexclusive safe harbor that permits a reporting issuer, as well as asset backed issuers and certain nonreporting foreign private issuers, to continue to publish or disseminate regularly released factual business and forward-looking information at any time, including leading up to and during a registered offering, without running afoul of the prohibition against gunjumping. Rule 168 provides that, for purposes of §§2(a)(10) and 5(c) of the 1933 Act, the regular release or dissemination by or on behalf of an issuer of communications containing factual business or forward-looking information will not constitute an offer to sell or an offer for sale of a security which is being offered under a registration statement that the issuer proposes to file or has filed, or that is effective if: (i) the issuer is required to file reports under §13 or §15(d) of the 1934 Act; (ii) the issuer is a foreign private issuer that meets the requirements of Form F-3 (other than the reporting history provisions of the Form), either satisfies the public float threshold of Form F-3 or is issuing nonconvertible investment grade securities meeting the applicable provisions of such Form, and either has had its equity securities trading on a designated offshore securities market for at least 12 months or has a worldwide market value of outstanding common equity held by nonaffiliates of $700 million or more; or (iii) the issuer is an asset backed issuer or a depositor, sponsor, or servicer (as Item 1101 of Regulation AB defines such terms) or an affiliated depositor, even if such person is not the issuer. The issuer, however, must not be a registered investment company or a business development company.

Further, in order for the disclosure to be regularly released or disseminated within the meaning of Rule 168, the issuer (or other eligible persons if the issuer is an asset backed issuer) must have previously released or disseminated the same type of information in the ordinary course of its business; and the timing, manner, and form in which the information is released or disseminated must be consistent in material respects with similar past releases or disseminations. These conditions help ensure that the information is not being disclosed to condition the market for the issuer's registered offering.

Rule 168 defines *factual business information* as factual information about the issuer, its business or financial developments, or other aspects of its business; advertisements of, or other information about, the issuer's products or services; and dividend notices.

The Rule defines *forward-looking information* as:

- projections of the issuer's revenues, income (loss), earnings (loss) per share, capital expenditures, dividends, capital structure, or other financial items;
- statements about the issuer management's plans and objectives for future operations, including plans or objectives relating to the products or services of the issuer;
- statements about the issuer's future economic performance, including statements of the type contemplated by the management's discussion and analysis of financial condition and results of operation described in Item 303 of Regulations S-B and S-K or the operating and financial review and prospects described in Item 5 of Form 20-F; and

45

- assumptions underlying or relating to any of the above information.

There is, however, an important exclusion. That is, the Rule 168 safe harbor does not cover communications containing information about the registered offering or that are disclosed as part of the offering activities in the registered offering.

For purposes of Rule 168, a communication is made *by or on behalf of the issuer* if the issuer or its agent or representative, other than an offering participant who is an underwriter or dealer, authorizes or approves the release or dissemination before it is made.

Second, Rule 169 creates a nonexclusive safe harbor from §2(a)(10)'s definition of *prospectus* and §5(c)'s prohibition on prefiling offers for certain communications of regularly released factual business information by reporting and nonreporting issuers, other than registered investment companies and business development companies. In particular, Rule 169 provides that, for purposes of §§2(a)(10) and 5(c) of the 1933 Act, the regular release or dissemination by or on behalf of an issuer of communications containing factual business information will not constitute an offer to sell or an offer for sale of a security by the issuer that is the subject of an offering under a registration statement that the issuer proposes to file or has filed, or that is effective if: (i) the issuer has previously released or disseminated the same type of information in the ordinary course of its business; (ii) the timing, manner, and form in which the information is released or disseminated is consistent in material respects with similar past disclosures; and (iii) the information is disclosed for intended use by persons, such as customers and suppliers (other than in their capacities as investors or potential investors in the issuer's securities), by the issuer's employees or agents who historically have provided such information.

Rule 169 defines *factual business information* falling within its safe harbor as (a) factual information about the issuer, its business or financial developments, or other aspects of its business, and (b) advertisements of, or other information about, the issuers' products or services. Rule 169's safe harbor, however, does not

46

apply to communications containing information about the issuer's registered offering or to communications disclosed as part of the offering activities in the registered offering. It is also worth highlighting that, unlike Rule 168, Rule 169 does not apply to forward-looking information. As with Rule 168, a communication under Rule 169 is *by or on behalf of the issuer* if the issuer or its agent or representative, other than an offering participant who is an underwriter or dealer, authorizes or approves the disclosure before it is made.

Third, Rule 163A creates a nonexclusive bright-line safe harbor for certain communications that are made more than 30 days before an issuer files a registration statement. In particular, except for certain specified communications, in all registered offerings by an issuer, any communication made by or on behalf of an issuer more than 30 days before the registration statement is filed will not constitute an offer to sell, offer for sale, or offer to buy the securities under the registration statement for purposes of §5(c) if (i) the communication does not reference a securities offering that is or will be the subject of a registration statement (other than this restriction, Rule 163A does not regulate the content of communications covered by the Rule) and (ii) the issuer takes reasonable steps within its control to prevent further distribution or publication of such communication during the 30 days immediately before the registration statement is filed. Consistent with Rules 168 and 169, a communication is made "by or on behalf of" an issuer under Rule 163A if the issuer or an agent or representative of the issuer, other than an offering participant who is an underwriter or a dealer, authorizes or approves the communication before it is made. In other words, Rule 163A does not cover communications by offering participants other than the issuer, such as underwriters or dealers. The logic of the Rule is that the 30-day time period allows for a sufficient *cooling off* period if the communication does in fact stimulate the market's interest in the offering. Further, as the SEC explained in the adoption Release, "Because the Rule does not permit information about a securities offering that is or will be the subject of a registration statement, the communications made in reliance on the Rule are less likely to be used to condition the market for the issuer's securities. In addition, the communications are still subject to ... the anti-fraud provisions [of the federal securities laws]."

Fourth, as part of the 2005 public offering reforms, the SEC fashioned the new *free writing prospectus*, a concept that has relevance throughout the offering process, including during the prefiling period, the focus here. Except as otherwise specifically provided or the context otherwise requires, a *free writing prospectus* is defined under Rule 405 as any written communication that constitutes an offer to sell or a solicitation of an offer to buy the securities relating to a registered offering that is used after the registration statement in respect of the offering is filed (or, in the case of a well-known seasoned issuer, whether or not the registration statement is filed) and is made by means other than: (i) a prospectus satisfying the requirements of §10(a) of the 1933 Act, Rule 430, Rule 430A, Rule 430B, Rule 430C, or Rule 431; (ii) a written communication used in reliance on Rule 167 and Rule 426; or (iii) a written communication that constitutes an offer to sell or solicitation of an offer to buy such securities that falls within the exception from the definition of prospectus in clause (a) of §2(a)(10) of the 1933 Act.

Rule 163 establishes a nonexclusive safe harbor that in effect permits offers to be made by or on behalf of a WKSI (but not other issuers) during the prefiling period without violating §5(c). In particular, Rule 163 provides that in a securities offering by or on behalf of a WKSI that will be or is at the time intended to be registered, an offer by or on behalf of such WKSI is exempt from §5(c)'s prohibition against offers to sell, offers for sale, or offers to buy its securities before a registration statement has been filed so long as certain conditions are satisfied as summarized below. A communication is made *by or on behalf of an issuer* if the issuer or its agent or representative, other than an offering participant who is an underwriter or dealer, authorizes or approves the communication before it is made. In other words, underwriters and dealers cannot avail themselves of Rule 163. Rule 163(a)(1) provides that any written communication that is an offer made in reliance on Rule 163's exemption will be a free writing prospectus and a prospectus under §2(a)(10) relating to a public offering of the securities to be covered by the registration statement.

Under Rule 163(b), any such free writing prospectus that is an offer made in reliance on the Rule must contain a specified legend that notifies potential investors that the issuer may file a registration statement (including a prospectus) with the Commission for the offering to which the communication relates and that instructs potential investors to read the relevant prospectus before investing, as well as any other SEC filings the issuer has made. The legend must also indicate how potential investors can obtain a prospectus. Notably, the Rule provides a limited opportunity to cure a failure to meet the legend requirement. An immaterial or unintentional failure to include the required legend in a free writing prospectus will not result in a §5(c) violation or the inability to rely on Rule 163's exemption if: (i) a good faith and reasonable effort was made to comply with the legend requirement; (ii) the free writing prospectus is amended to include the required legend as soon as practicable after the omitted or incorrect legend is discovered; and (iii) if the free writing prospectus has been transmitted without the required legend, the free writing prospectus is subsequently retransmitted with the legend by substantially the same means as, and directed to substantially the same potential investors to whom, the free writing prospectus was originally transmitted.

In addition, for Rule 163 to apply, the issuer generally must file the free writing prospectus with the SEC promptly upon filing the registration statement or an amendment thereto covering the securities that have been offered in reliance on the Rule's exemption. If no such registration statement or amendment is filed, then the free writing prospectus does not have to be filed with the Commission. There is limited opportunity to cure any failure to satisfy this filing condition. An immaterial or unintentional failure to file or delay in filing the free writing prospectus will not result in a §5(c) violation or the inability to rely on Rule 163's exemption if a good faith and reasonable effort was made to comply with the filing requirement and the free writing prospectus is filed as soon as practicable after the failure to file is discovered.

Rule 163's exemption from §5(c) does not apply to communications relating to business combination transactions subject to Rule 165 or 166, communications by a registered investment

49

company, or communications by a business development company.

***P. 108, new par. after 2d par.***   In 2004, as part of the Commission's Regulation AB adopted Release, Sec. Act Rel. 8518, 84 SEC Dock. 1624, 1698–1700 (2004) (adoption), the Commission also adopted a new Rule 139a safe harbor provision which provides in part:

> The publication or distribution by a broker or dealer of information, an opinion or a recommendation with respect to asset-backed securities meeting the criteria of General Instruction I.B.5 of Form S-3 shall not be deemed to constitute an offer for sale or offer to sell S-3 ABS registered or proposed to be registered for purposes of sections 2(a)(10) and 5(c) of the Act, even if such broker or dealer is or will be a participant in the distribution of the registered securities [if specified conditions are met similar to those required under Rule 139 and if registered securities are proposed to be offered, offered, or part of an unsold allotment or subscription, the information, opinion or recommendation, does not contain any *ABS informational or computation material* as defined in Reg. S-K Item 1101].

A new Rule 167 lists securities conditions under which ABS informational and computation material may be used after the effective date of an ABS security registration statement and before sending a §10(a) final prospectus without violating §5(b)(1). New Rule 426 requires filings of Rule 167 prospectuses on Form 8-K.

Rule 139a was amended in 2005 in light of the SEC's changes to Rule 139 deleting the prior Rule 139 requirement that a research report regarding an issuer or its securities can only be included in an industry report if the broker-dealer's last publication contained a recommendation as or more favorable to the issuer or any class of its securities. The comparable requirement included in Rule 139a(c) for asset backed securities was deleted, and paragraphs (d) and (e) of Rule 139a were redesignated as paragraphs (c) and (d). However, although the *reasonable regularity* requirement was also deleted from Rule 139, a comparable requirement in paragraph (a) of Rule 139a was not deleted as part of the 2005 public offering reforms.

## 5.  THE WAITING PERIOD

### c.  The *Tombstone Ad* [§2(a)(10)(b), Rule 134]

***P. 112, 1st full par., substitute:***    After a registration statement has been filed with the Commission, Rule 134 permits a communication limited to some or all of the following categories of information without such communication constituting a *prospectus* or *free writing prospectus*:

- The names of selling security holders, if then disclosed in the prospectus that is part of the filed registration statement;
- The names of securities exchanges or other securities markets where any class of the issuer's securities are, or will be, listed;
- The ticker symbols, or proposed ticker symbols, of the issuer's securities;
- The CUSIP number as defined in Rule 17Ad-19(a)(5) of the Securities Exchange Act of 1934 assigned to the securities being offered; and
- Information disclosed in order to correct inaccuracies previously contained in a communication permissibly made pursuant to Rule 134.

Rule 134 was amended in 2005 as part of the SEC's public offering reforms to expand the amount of information that Rule 134 allows to be communicated during the waiting period.

A communication used pursuant to Rule 134 must contain the following: (a) if the registration statement has not yet become effective, a specified statement to the effect that a registration statement has been filed with the SEC but has not yet become effective and that the securities covered by the registration statement may not be sold nor may offers to buy be accepted before the registration statement becomes effective; and (b) the name and address of one or more persons from whom a written §10 prospectus (other than a free writing prospectus), including, when required, a price range, may be obtained. There is a limited exception to this requirement, however. That is, it is not necessary to include the information described in the immediately preceding (a) and (b) if the communication that contains the information permitted by Rule 134(x) does no more than state from whom and include the uniform resource locator (URL) where a written prospectus that meets the requirements of §10 of the 1933 Act (other than a free writing prospectus) may be obtained, identify the security, state its price, and state by whom orders will be executed, or (y) is accompanied or preceded by a prospectus or a summary prospectus (other than a free writing prospectus) which satisfies §10's requirements, including a price range where required, at the date of such communication. In other words, the one item of information that must be included in every tombstone ad, whether the old fashioned or the expanded variety, is the identity of at least one person from whom a §10 prospectus may be obtained—the one exception being the case where the prospectus actually accompanies or precedes the ad.

Rule 134(d) allows a communication sent or delivered to any person in reliance on the Rule if such communication is accompanied or preceded by a prospectus that satisfies §10's requirements (other than a free writing prospectus), including a price range where required, to solicit from the recipient of the communication an offer to buy or an indication of interest if the communication contains a statement to the effect that no offer to buy can be accepted and no part of the purchase price can be received until the effective date and any such offer can be withdrawn or revoked, without any obligation or commitment of any kind, at any time prior to notice of its acceptance after the effective date. Otherwise, Rule 134 does not permit a sender of the communication to solicit an offer to buy or an indication of interest.

Under Rule 134(f), for purposes of Rule 134, an active hyperlink to a §10 prospectus in an electronic Rule 134 notice satisfies the requirement that the prospectus accompany or precede that notice in cases when such requirement must be met. It should be noted, though, that a hyperlink or URL may not be to an address with information other than the types of information that Rule 134 allows. Rule 134(e) also provides that a §10 prospectus that is included in any Rule 134 communication remains a prospectus for all purposes of the 1933 Act.

Rule 134(g) provides that the Rule does not apply to a registered investment company or a business development company.

### d.   The Preliminary Prospectus [§10(a), Rule 430]

***P. 113, text after 1st full par., substitute:***

The information in this prospectus is not complete and may be changed. We may not sell these securities until the registration statement filed with the Securities and Exchange Commission is effective. This prospectus is not an offer to sell these securities and it is not soliciting an offer to buy these securities in any state where the offer or sale is not permitted.

The legend must be prominent and in a print type that is easy to read.

### e.   The Summary Prospectus [§10(b), Rule 431]

(ii) *Investment Companies*

***P. 115, add at end of par.***   In 2003 the Commission eliminated the Rule 134 provisions that applied specifically to investment companies and enhanced investment company disclosure under Rule 482 and amended several Investment Company Act forms. The SEC emphasized in the adoption Release that with the elimination of the *substance of which* requirement from Rule 482, mutual funds would no longer need to rely on Rule 134. Indeed, presently Rule 134(e) expressly states that the Rule does not apply to registered investment companies.

### f.   Free Writing Prospectus and Electronic Road Shows [Rules 164 and 433]

***P. 115, add new pars. after 3d full par.***   Before addressing the substantive rules that govern the use of free writing prospectuses and electronic road shows, it is worth first explaining two

53

important definitions, adopted by the SEC in 2005 as part of the Commission's public offering reforms. The definitions of *written communication* and *graphic communication* more precisely distinguish between written and oral communications. These definitions provide some needed clarity and certainty in light of recent technological developments that often make it difficult to distinguish between written and oral communications. The ability to so distinguish has important implications for gunjumping under §5 of the 1933 Act.

Rule 405 defines *written communication* as "any communication that is written, printed, a radio or television broadcast, or a graphic communication as defined in [Rule 405.]" The term *graphic communication*, in turn, is defined in Rule 405 to include "all forms of electronic media, including, but not limited to, audiotapes, videotapes, facsimiles, CD-ROM, electronic mail, Internet Web sites, substantially similar messages widely distributed (rather than individually distributed) on telephone answering or voice mail systems, computers, computer networks and other forms of computer data compilation. Graphic communication shall not include a communication that, at the time of the communication, originates live, in real-time to a live audience and does not originate in recorded form or otherwise as a graphic communication, although it is transmitted through graphic means."

It should be made clear that any communication that is not a *written communication* is an oral communication.

Regarding voicemails, the SEC added that an individual voicemail from a live telephone call will not constitute a written communication, but that broadly disseminated or blast voicemail messages will constitute a written communication.

The concept of a free writing prospectus, which originated as part of the SEC's public offering reforms adopted in 2005, was introduced earlier insofar as a free writing prospectus can be used by a WKSI under certain circumstances during the prefiling period. A free writing prospectus can also be used after the registration statement has been filed as provided under Rules 164 and 433, the focus here. The free writing prospectus allows greater flexibility when it comes to making written offers.

Rule 164 provides that so long as certain conditions set forth in Rule 433 are satisfied, after the filing of the registration statement, a free writing prospectus of an eligible issuer or any underwriter, dealer, or other offering participant will constitute a §10(b) prospectus for purposes of §5(b)(1) of the 1933 Act. Put differently, a free writing prospectus may be used during the waiting period without violating §5(b)(1)'s prohibition on the use of a prospectus that is not a statutory prospectus once the registration statement has been filed.

Rule 433(a) provides that a free writing prospectus, which can contain information the substance of which is not included in the registration statement, that satisfies the conditions of Rule 433 is a prospectus permitted under §10(b) of the 1933 Act for purposes of §§2(a)(10), 5(b)(1), and 5(b)(2) of the 1933 Act. The rest of Rule 433 sets forth the key conditions that must be satisfied for a free writing prospectus to be used after the filing of the registration statement. These conditions relate to the delivery or availability of the statutory prospectus when the free writing prospectus is used; the information that the free writing prospectus contains; legend requirements; filing requirements; and record retention requirements.

First, in terms of prospectus delivery and availability requirements, in offerings of securities of a seasoned issuer or a well-known seasoned issuer (WKSI), the issuer or other offering participant in the offering may use a free writing prospectus in registered securities offerings once a registration statement regarding the offering has been filed containing a §10 statutory prospectus, other than a prospectus that satisfies §10 as a summary prospectus permitted under Rule 431 or as a permitted free writing prospectus. There is no requirement that the statutory prospectus actually be delivered in order to use the free writing prospectus. However, as described further below, there is a legend requirement designed to notify recipients of a free writing prospectus that a registration statement has been filed and how the statutory prospectus can be obtained.

The prospectus delivery and availability requirements are more demanding for nonreporting issuers and unseasoned issuers. In short, the statutory prospectus must actually be delivered prior to or with the free writing prospectus. For non-reporting issuers and unseasoned issuers, if (a) the free writing prospectus is or was prepared by or on behalf of or used or referred to by an issuer or other offering participant, (b) the issuer or other offering participant has or will give consideration for the dissemination (in any format) of the free writing prospectus, including any published article, publication, or advertisement, or (c) §17(b) of the 1933 Act requires disclosure that consideration has been or will be given by the issuer or other offering participant for any activity described in §17(b) in connection with the free writing prospectus, then a free writing prospectus may be used in an offering if (x) the registration statement has been filed for the offering and it includes a §10 statutory prospectus, including a price range where required by rule, other than a prospectus that satisfies §10 as a summary prospectus permitted under Rule 431 or as a permitted free writing prospectus, and (y) the free writing prospectus is preceded or accompanied by the most recent such statutory prospectus. Put simply, in these cases, anyone receiving a free writing prospectus must actually be provided the most recent statutory prospectus; simply indicating the availability of the statutory prospectus is not enough. Consequently, it might be infeasible to disseminate the free writing prospectus broadly other than in an electronic form. The prospectus delivery requirement will be satisfied if an electronic free writing prospectus includes an active hyperlink to the §10 prospectus. There is no need to get any advance consent of recipients for such electronic delivery.

The second set of conditions on the use of a free writing prospectus after the filing of the registration statement relates to the information contained in a free writing prospectus. Other than as provided below, there are no content conditions under Rules 164 and 433 for a free writing prospectus used after the filing of a registration statement. Under Rule 433(c), a free writing prospectus can contain information the substance of which is not contained in the registration statement if the information does not conflict with information contained in the registration statement, including any prospectus or prospectus supplement that is part of the registration statement and not superseded or modified, or any of the issuer's reports filed with or furnished to the SEC under §13 or §15(d) of the 1934 Act that the registration statement incorporates by reference and that are not superseded or modified.

Further, the free writing prospectus must contain substantially the following legend:

> The issuer has filed a registration statement (including a prospectus) with the SEC for the offering to which this communication relates. Before you invest, you should read the prospectus in that registration statement and other documents the issuer has filed with the SEC for more complete information about the issuer and this offering. You may get these documents for free by visiting EDGAR on the SEC Web site at www.sec.gov. Alternatively, the issuer, any underwriter or any dealer participating in the offering will arrange to send you the prospectus if you request it by calling toll-free 1-8-[xx-xxx-xxxx].

The legend may also provide an e-mail address to request the documents and may indicate that the documents also are available on the issuer's Web site and include the Internet address and the particular location of the documents on the Web site.

Under Rule 164(c), an immaterial or unintentional failure to include the specified legend in a free writing prospectus as required under Rule 433 will not result in a violation of §5(b)(1) of the 1933 Act or the inability to rely on Rule 164(i) if a good faith and reasonable effort was made to comply with the legend condition; (ii) if the free writing prospectus is amended to include the specified legend as soon as practicable after discovery of the omitted or incorrect legend; and (iii) if transmitted without the legend, if the free writing prospectus is retransmitted with the legend by substantially the same means as, and directed to substantially the same prospective purchasers to whom, the free writing prospectus was originally transmitted.

Third, Rule 433(d) sets forth certain filing conditions for use of a free writing prospectus. In order to use a free writing prospectus, except in certain cases, such prospectus or the information contained in it must be filed with the SEC no later than the date the free writing prospectus is first used. More particularly, subject to certain specified exceptions, the issuer must file with the SEC any *issuer free writing prospectus*; any *issuer information* contained in a free writing prospectus prepared by or on behalf of or used by any other offering participant (but not information prepared by or on behalf of a person other than the issuer on the basis of or derived from such issuer information); and a description of the final terms of the issuer's securities in the offering or of the offering contained in a free writing prospectus or portion thereof prepared by or on behalf of the issuer or any offering participant, after such terms have been established for all classes in the offering. Also subject to certain specified exceptions, any offering participant other than the issuer must file with the SEC any free writing prospectus that is used or referred to by such offering participant and distributed by or on behalf of such participant in a manner reasonably designed to lead to its broad unrestricted dissemination.

Any filing with the Commission that Rule 433 requires generally must be made no later than the date the free writing prospectus is first used. However, under Rule 433(d)(5)(ii), a free writing prospectus or portion thereof that contains only a description of the final terms of the issuer's securities in the offering or of the offerings must be filed by the issuer within two days of the later of the date the final terms have been established for all classes of the offering and the date first used.

Rule 433(d)(1) makes clear that the free writing prospectus that is filed under the Rule will not be filed as part of the registration statement subject to §11 liability, although the free writing prospectus might still be a basis of liability under §12(a)(2) of the 1933 Act and the antifraud provisions of the federal securities laws.

Under Rule 164(b), any immaterial or unintentional failure to file or delay in filing a free writing prospectus as required under Rule 433 will not result in a violation of §5(b)(1) of the 1933 Act or the inability to rely on Rule 164 if a good faith and reasonable effort was made to comply with the filing requirement and the free writing prospectus is filed as soon as practicable after discovery of the failure to file.

Rule 433 also addresses road shows specifically, including electronic road shows. Rule 433(d)(8) concerns filing conditions as they apply to *road shows* conducted by issuers and underwriters to market securities offerings. First, two terms need to be defined. Rule 433(h) defines a *road show* as:

> [A]n offer (other than a statutory prospectus or a portion of a statutory prospectus filed as part of a registration statement) that contains a presentation regarding an offering by one or more members of the issuer's management (and in the case of an offering of asset-backed securities, management involved in the securitization or servicing function of one or more of the depositors, sponsors, or servicers (as such terms are defined in Item 1101 of Regulation AB) or an affiliated depositor) and includes discussion of one or more of the issuer, such management, and the securities being offered.

In turn, a *bona fide electronic road show,* such as might be conducted or Web cast over the Internet to investors, is defined as:

> [A] road show that is a written communication transmitted by graphic means that contains a presentation by one or more officers of an issuer or other persons in an issuer's management (and in the case of an offering of asset-backed securities, management involved in the securitization or servicing function of one or more of the depositors, sponsors, or servicers (as such terms are defined in Item 1101 of Regulation AB) or an affiliated depositor) and, if more than one road show that is a written communication is being used, includes discussion of the same general areas of information regarding the issuer, such management, and the securities being offered as such other road show or shows for the same offering that are written communications.

Under Rule 433(d)(8), a road show that is a written communication is a free writing prospectus, except that a written communication that is a road show generally does not have to be filed. In the case of a road show that is a written communication for an offering of common equity or convertible equity securities by a nonreporting issuer that is not required to file reports under §13 or §15(d) of the 1934 Act when the registration statement for the offering is filed, such a road show must be filed unless the issuer makes at least one version of a *bona fide electronic road show* available without restriction by means of graphic communication to any person, including any potential investor in the securities (and if there is more than one version of a road show for the offering that is a written communication, the version available without restriction is made available no later than the other versions).

Technology impacts the offering process through more ways than just electronic road shows. Issuers can post information on their Web sites or can link to others' Web sites that post information about the issuer or the issuer's offering. Rule 433(e) addresses these possibilities. Under Rule 433(e), an offer of an issuer's securities that is contained on the issuer's Web site or that is hyperlinked by the issuer to a third party's Web site is a written offer by the issuer. Accordingly, the filing conditions of Rule 433 generally apply to such an offer. That having been said, under Rule 433(e)(2), historical issuer information will not be considered a current offer of the issuer's securities and thus will not be a free writing prospectus, meaning that, among other things, the information will not have to be filed with the SEC, if the historical information is identified as such, is located in a separate section of the issuer's Web site containing historical information, has not been incorporated by reference into or otherwise included in a prospectus for the offering, and has not otherwise been used or referred to in connection with the offering.

The final condition for the use of a free writing prospectus after filing the registration statement concerns record retention. Rule 433(g) requires that issuers and other offering participants retain all free writing prospectuses they have used and that have not been filed with the SEC for three years after the initial bona fide offering of the securities in question. Under Rule 164(d), an immaterial or unintentional failure to retain a free writing prospectus will not result in a violation of §5(b)(1) of the 1933 Act or the inability to rely on Rule 164 if a good faith and reasonable effort was made to comply with the record retention condition.

Rule 433(f) separately addresses free writing prospectuses that are published or distributed by the media, which in recent years have played an increasingly important role in disseminating information about issuers and their offerings.

Under Rule 433(f), any written offer that includes information provided, authorized, or approved by or on behalf of the issuer or another offering participant and that is prepared and published or disseminated by a person unaffiliated with the issuer or other offering participant that is in the business of publishing, radio or television broadcasting, or otherwise disseminating written communications would be a free writing prospectus prepared by or on behalf of the issuer or such other offering participant. However, the Rule 433 conditions are modified for any such free writing prospectus. Namely, the prospectus delivery requirements for non-reporting and unseasoned issuers under Rule 433(b)(2)(i) will not apply and the legend and filing conditions under Rules 433(c)(2) and 433(d), respectively, will be deemed satisfied if (i) no payment is made and no consideration is given by or on behalf of the issuer or any other offering participant for the written communication or its dissemination, and (ii) the issuer or other offering participant in question files the written communication with the SEC, and includes in the filing the legend required by Rule 433(c)(2), within four business days after the issuer or other offering participant becomes aware of the publication, radio or television broadcast, or other dissemination of the written communication. The free writing prospectus, however, does not have to be filed if its substance has previously been filed with the SEC. Additionally, any filing that is made may include information that the issuer or other offering participant reasonably believes is necessary or appropriate to correct information included in the written communication; and in lieu of filing the actual written communication as published or disseminated, the issuer or other offering participant may file a copy of the materials provided to the media, including transcripts of interviews or similar materials, so long as the copy or transcripts contain all the information given to the media.

*P. 115, re-letter subsection f, State Blue Sky Laws, as subsection g.*

### 6. THE POSTEFFECTIVE PERIOD

#### f. The Dealer's Exemption

*P. 120 n.38, end note.* As part of the 2005 public offering reforms, the SEC amended Rule 153 to account for the reality that many transactions occur other than on a stock exchange and for the fact that electronic filings of final prospectuses on EDGAR and other technological developments had, as the SEC put it, largely rendered the paper-based system upon which Rule 153 has been based "outmoded and unnecessary." As amended in 2005, Rule 153 provides that brokers or dealers who are effecting transactions on or through a registered national securities exchange or facility thereof, trading facility of a national securities association, or an alternative trading system will satisfy §5(b)(2)'s requirement to deliver a prospectus to the broker or dealer on the other side of the transaction if: (1) securities of the same class as the securities that are the subject of the transaction are trading on such exchange or facility thereof, trading facility of a national securities association, or alternative trading system; (2) the registration statement for the offering is effective and is not the subject of any pending proceeding or examination under §8(d) or §8(e) of the 1933 Act; (3) neither the issuer nor any underwriter or participating dealer is the subject of a pending proceeding under §8A of the 1933 Act in connection with the offering; and (4) the issuer has filed or will file with the SEC a final §10(a) prospectus.

*P. 121, after 1st full par.*    Rule 174 was amended in 2005 as part of the SEC's 2005 public offering reforms to add new Rule 174(h) to the effect that, except for filings with regard to offerings by blank check companies under Rule 174(g), any obligation of a dealer under §4(3) and Rule 174 to deliver a prospectus may be satisfied by compliance with Rule 172, which implements the *access equals delivery* model adopted as part of the 2005 public offering reforms.

h.   Electronic Delivery of Prospectus

*P. 124, after 1st full par.*    In April 2000 the Securities and Exchange Commission published another Interpretive Release on Use of Electronic Media. Sec. Act Rel. 7856, 72 SEC Dock. 753 (2000). This Release stated in part:

## I. Introduction

By facilitating rapid and widespread information dissemination, the Internet has had a significant impact on capital-raising techniques and, more broadly, on the structure of the securities industry.... [M]any publicly traded companies are incorporating Internet-based technology into their routine business operations, including setting up their own web sites to furnish company and industry information. Some provide information about their securities and the markets in which their securities trade. Investment companies use the Internet to provide investors with fund-related information, as well as shareholder services and educational materials. Issuers of municipal securities also are beginning to use the Internet to provide information about themselves and their outstanding bonds, as well as new offerings of their securities. The increased availability of information through the Internet has helped to promote transparency, liquidity, and efficiency in our capital markets....

## II. Interpretive Guidance

### A. Electronic Delivery

We first published our views on the use of electronic media to deliver information to investors in 1995. [Sec. Act Rel. 7233, 60 SEC Dock. 1091 (1995).] The 1995 Release focused on electronic delivery of prospectuses, annual reports to security holders and proxy solicitation materials under the Securities Act of 1933, the Securities Exchange Act of 1934 and the Investment Company Act of 1940. Our 1996 electronic media release [Sec. Act Rel. 7288, 61 SEC Dock. 2167 (1996)] focused on electronic delivery of required information by broker-dealers (including municipal securities dealers) and transfer agents under the Exchange Act and investment advisers under the Investment Advisers Act of 1940.

We believe that the framework for electronic delivery established in these releases continues to work well in today's technological environment. Issuers and market intermediaries therefore must continue to assess their compliance with legal requirements in terms of the three areas identified in the releases — notice, access and evidence of delivery. Although we believe that this framework continues to be appropriate, we provide below guidance that will clarify some regulatory issues relating to electronic delivery.

### 1. Telephone Consent

... [O]ne of the three elements of satisfactory electronic delivery is obtaining evidence of delivery. The 1995 Release provided that one method for satisfying the evidence-of-delivery element is to obtain an informed consent from an investor to receive information through a particular electronic medium. The 1996 Release stated that informed consent should be made by written or electronic means. Some securities lawyers have concluded that, based on the 1996 Release, telephonic consent generally is not permitted. Others have opined that telephonic consent may be permissible if an issuer or intermediary retains a record of consent.

... We are of the view ... that an issuer or market intermediary may obtain an informed consent telephonically, as long as a record of that consent is retained. As with written or electronic consent, telephonic consent must be obtained in a manner that assures its authenticity.

### 2. Global Consent

The 1995 Release stated that consent to electronic delivery could relate to *all* documents to be delivered by or on behalf of a single issuer. . . .

We believe that an investor may give a global consent to electronic delivery — relating to all documents of any issuer — so long as the consent is informed. Given the broad scope of a global consent and its effect on an investor's ability to receive important documents, we believe intermediaries should take particular care to ensure that the investor understands that he or she is providing a global consent to electronic delivery. For example, a global consent that is merely a provision of an agreement that an investor is required to execute to receive other services may not fully inform the investor. To best inform investors, broker-dealers could obtain consent from a new customer through an account-opening agreement that contains a separate section with a separate electronic delivery authorization, or through a separate document altogether. We believe that a global consent to electronic delivery would not be an informed consent if the opening of a brokerage account were conditioned upon providing the consent.

Therefore, absent other evidence of delivery, we believe that if the opening of an account were conditioned upon providing a global consent, evidence of delivery would not be established.

Similarly, because of the broad scope of a global consent, an investor should be advised of his or her right to revoke the consent at any time and receive all covered documents in paper format....

Although a global consent must identify the various types of electronic media that may be used to constitute an informed consent, it need not specify the medium to be used by any particular issuer. Additionally, the consent need not identify the issuers covered by the consent. If the consent does identify the covered issuers, it also may provide that additional issuers can be added at a later time without further consent. Investors cannot be required to accept delivery via additional media at a later time without further informed consent.

### 3. Use of Portable Document Format

The 1995 Release stated that "the use of a particular medium should not be so burdensome that intended recipients cannot effectively access the information provided."... We believe that issuers and market intermediaries delivering documents electronically may use PDF if it is not so burdensome as effectively to prevent access. For example, PDF could be used if issuers and intermediaries:

- inform investors of the requirements necessary to download PDF when obtaining consent to electronic delivery; and
- provide investors with any necessary software and technical assistance at no cost.

### 4. Clarification of the "Envelope Theory"

The 1995 Release provided a number of examples designed to assist issuers and market intermediaries in meeting their delivery obligations through electronic media. One example provided that documents in close proximity on the same web site menu are considered delivered together. Other examples confirmed the proposition that documents hyperlinked to each other are considered delivered together as if they were in the same paper envelope. The premise underlying these examples has come to be called the "envelope theory."...

Nevertheless, some issuers and intermediaries believe that the envelope theory has created ambiguities as to appropriate web site content when an issuer is in registration. Some securities lawyers have expressed concern that if a Section 10 prospectus is posted on a web site, the operation of the envelope theory causes everything on the web site to become part of that prospectus. They also have raised concerns that information on a web site that is outside of the four corners of the Section 10 prospectus, but in close proximity to it, would be considered free writing.

Information on a web site would be part of a Section 10 prospectus only if an issuer (or person acting on behalf of the issuer, including an intermediary with delivery obligations) acts to make it part of the prospectus. For example, if an issuer includes a hyperlink within a Section 10 prospectus, the hyperlinked information would become a part of that prospectus. When embedded hyperlinks are used, the hyperlinked information must be filed as part of the prospectus in the effective registration statement and will be subject to liability under Section 11 of the Securities Act. In contrast, a hyperlink from an external document to a Section 10 prospectus would result in both documents being delivered together, but would not result in the non-prospectus document being deemed part of the prospectus. Issuers nevertheless may be subject to liability under Section 12 of the Securities Act for the external document depending on whether the external document is itself a prospectus or part of one.

With respect to the free writing concern, the focus on the location of the posted prospectus is misplaced. Regardless of whether or where the Section 10 prospectus is posted, the web site content must be reviewed in its entirety to determine whether it contains impermissible free writing. . . .

## B. Web Site Content

. . .

### 1. Issuer Responsibility for Hyperlinked Information

. . . Whether third-party information is attributable to an issuer depends upon whether the issuer has involved itself in the preparation of the information or explicitly or implicitly endorsed or approved of the information. In the case of issuer liability for statements by third parties such as analysts, the courts and we have referred to the first line of inquiry as the "entanglement" theory and the second as the "adoption" theory.

In the case of hyperlinked information, liability under the "entanglement" theory would depend upon an issuer's level of prepublication involvement in the preparation of the information. In contrast, liability under the "adoption" theory would depend upon whether, after its publication, an issuer, explicitly or implicitly, endorses or approves the hyperlinked information. . . .

### a. Context of the Hyperlink

Whether third-party information to which an issuer has established a hyperlink is attributable to the issuer is likely to be influenced by what the issuer says about the hyperlink or what is implied by the context in which the issuer places the hyperlink. An issuer might explicitly endorse the hyperlinked information. For example, a hyperlink might be incorporated in or accompany a statement such as "XYZ's web site contains the best description of our business that is currently available". . . .

In the context of a document required to be filed or delivered under the federal securities laws, we believe that when an issuer embeds a hyperlink to a web site within the document, the issuer should always be deemed to be adopting the hyperlinked information. In addition, when an issuer is in registration, if the issuer establishes a hyperlink (that is not embedded within a disclosure document) from its web site to information that meets the definition of an "offer to sell," "offer for sale," or "offer" under Section 2(a)(3) of the Securities Act, a strong inference arises that the issuer has adopted that information for purposes of Section 10(b) of the Exchange Act and Rule 10b-5. . . .

### 2. Issuer Communications During a Registered Offering

. . .

An issuer that is in registration should maintain communications with the public as long as the subject matter of the communications is limited to ordinary course business and financial information, which may include the following:

- Advertisements concerning the issuer's products and services;

67

- Exchange Act reports required to be filed with the Commission;
- Proxy statements, annual reports to security holders and dividend notices;
- Press announcements concerning business and financial developments;
- Answers to unsolicited telephone inquiries concerning business matters from securities analysts, financial analysts, security holders and participants in the communications field who have a legitimate interest in the issuer's affairs; and
- Security holders' meetings and responses to security holder inquiries relating to these matters.

Statements containing information falling within any of the foregoing categories, or an available Securities Act safe harbor, may be posted on an issuer's web site when in registration, either directly or indirectly through a hyperlink to a third-party web site, including the web site of a broker-dealer that is participating in the registered offering.

Although our original guidance was directed at communications by reporting issuers when in registration, it also should be observed by non-reporting issuers preparing to offer securities to the public for the first time. A non-reporting issuer that has established a history of ordinary course business communications through its web site should be able to continue to provide business and financial information on its site consistent with our original guidance. A non-reporting issuer preparing for its first registered public offering that contemporaneously establishes a web site, however, may need to apply this guidance more strictly when evaluating its web site content because it may not have established a history of ordinary-course business communications with the marketplace. Thus, its web site content may condition the market for the offering and, due to the unfamiliarity of the marketplace with the issuer or its business, investors may be unable to view the issuer's communications in an appropriate context while the issuer is in registration. In other words, investors may be less able to distinguish offers to sell an issuer's securities in a registered offering from product or service promotional activities or other business or financial information.

## C. Online Offerings

### 1. Online Public Offerings

Increasingly, issuers and broker-dealers are conducting public securities offerings online, using the Internet, electronic mail and other electronic media to solicit prospective investors. Examples of these electronic communications include investor questionnaires on investment qualifications, broker-dealer account-opening procedures and directives on how to submit indications of interest or offers to buy in the context of a specific public offering. These developments present both potential benefits and dangers to investors. On the positive side, numerous "online brokers" appear to have begun to give individual investors more access to public offerings, including initial public offerings, or IPO's. Still, dangers accompany these expanded online investment opportunities. Retail investors often are unfamiliar with the public offering process generally, and, in particular, with new marketing practices that have evolved in connection with online public offerings. We are concerned that there may be insufficient information available to investors to enable them to understand fully the online public offering process. We also are concerned that investors are being solicited to make hasty, and perhaps uninformed investment decisions.

Two fundamental legal principles should guide issuers, underwriters, and other offering participants in online public offerings. First, offering participants can neither sell, nor make contracts to sell, a security before effectiveness of the related Securities Act registration statement. A corollary to this principle dictates that "[n]o offer to buy . . . can be accepted and no part of the purchase price can be received until the registration statement has become effective."

Second, until delivery of the final prospectus has been completed, written offers and offers transmitted by radio and television cannot be made outside of a Section 10 prospectus except in connection with business combinations. After filing the registration statement, two limited exceptions provide some flexibility to offering participants to publish notices of the offering. Following effectiveness, offering participants may disseminate sales literature and other writings so long as these materials are accompanied or preceded by a final prospectus. Oral offers, in contrast, are permissible as soon as the registration statement has been filed. Offering participants may use any combination of electronic and more traditional media, such as paper or the telephone, to communicate with prospective investors, provided that use of these media is in compliance with the Securities Act....

The SEC's 2005 public offering reforms also addressed the growing use of technology in securities offerings. Most notably for present purposes, the SEC adopted the *access equals delivery* model of delivering a final prospectus. Sec. Act Rels. 8501, 83 SEC Dock. 4 (2004) (proposal); 8591, 85 SEC Dock. 2871 (2005) (adoption). Rule 172(b), adopted in 2005 as part of the SEC's public offering reforms, provides that any obligation under §5(b)(2) of the 1933 Act for a final §10(a) prospectus to precede or accompany the carrying or delivery of a security is treated as satisfied if the issuer has filed with the SEC a prospectus for the offering that satisfies §10(a) of the 1933 Act or the issuer will make a good faith and reasonable effort to file such a final prospectus within the time required by Rule 424. If the issuer fails to file timely such a prospectus, the issuer must file the prospectus as soon as practicable.

Undoubtedly, the regulation of securities markets will continue to evolve in response to technological developments. There is every reason to be confident that the offering and periodic disclosure processes will become increasingly efficient, promoting the goal of capital formation, as the SEC continues to account for the pervasiveness of the Internet and other technological advances.

### i.  Registration of Underlying Securities in Assest Backed Securities Transactions

***P. 124 new par. after 1st full par.***    In 2004, the Commission adopted Rule 190 as part of (1) Regulation AB Release. Sec. Act Rel. 8518, 84 SEC Dock. 1624 (2004) (adoption). Rule 190(a) requires registration of the relevant underlying securities in an offering of asset backed securities where the asset pool includes securities of another issuer, unless the underlying securities are exempt under §3 or all of the following conditions are established:

(1) Neither the issuer of the underlying securities nor any of its affiliates has a direct or indirect agreement, arrangement, relationship or understanding, written or otherwise, relating to the underlying securities and asset-backed securities transaction;

(2) Neither the issuer of the underlying securities nor any of its affiliates is an affiliate of the sponsor, depositor, issuing entity or underwriter of the asset-backed securities transaction; and

(3) The depositor would be free to publicly resell the underlying securities without registration under the Act. For example:

(i) If the underlying securities are restricted securities, as defined in [Rule]144(a)(3), the underlying securities must meet the conditions set forth in [Rule]144(k) for the sale of restricted securities; and

(ii) The offering of the asset-backed security does not constitute part of a distribution of the underlying securities. An offering of asset-backed securities with an asset pool containing underlying securities that at the time of the purchase for the asset pool are part of a subscription or unsold allotment would be a distribution of the underlying securities. For purposes of this section, in an offering of asset-backed securities involving a sponsor, depositor or underwriter that was an underwriter or an affiliate of an underwriter in a registered offering of the underlying securities, the distribution of the asset-backed securities will not constitute part of a distribution of the underlying securities if the underlying securities were purchased at arm's length in the secondary market at least three months after the last sale of any unsold allotment or subscription by the affiliated underwriter that participated in the registered offering of the underlying securities.

## C.   THE REGISTRATION PROCEDURE: A STUDY IN ADMINISTRATIVE TECHNIQUE

### 1.   THE STATUTORY PATTERN

***P. 125, last par., substitute:***   In the Investor and Capital Markets Fee Relief Act of 2002, fees under §6(b) of the Securities Act were reduced to $92 per $1 million of the maximum aggregate price at which securities are proposed to be offered, with annual adjustments scheduled for 2003 to 2011 so that the rate required "is reasonably likely to produce aggregate fee collections ... equal to the target offsetting collection amount for such fiscal year." P.L. 107-123, 115 Stat. 2390 (2002).

## 2.   THE PREEFFECTIVE PERIOD

### b.   The Price Amendment or Rule 430A

*P. 131, after 1st full par.*   The 2005 public offering reforms amended Rule 424(b)(2), which now currently provides that a "prospectus that is used in connection with a primary offering of securities pursuant to Rule 415(a)(1)(x) or a primary offering of securities registered for issuance on a delayed basis pursuant to Rule 415(a)(1)(vii) or (viii) and that, in the case of Rule 415(a)(1)(viii) discloses the public offering price, description of securities or similar matters, and in the case of Rule 415(a)(1)(vii) and (x) discloses information previously omitted from the prospectus filed as part of an effective registration statement in reliance on Rule 430B, shall be filed with the Commission no later than the second business day following the earlier of the date of the determination of the offering price or the date it is first used after effectiveness in connection with a public offering or sales, or transmitted by a means reasonably calculated to result in filing with the Commission by that date."

As part of the 2005 public offering reforms, the SEC eliminated Rule 434 and made corresponding amendments to other rules, such as Rule 497, that referred to Rule 434.

### c.   Acceleration

*P. 134, 1st full par., before last sentence.*  ; or (5) in the case of a significant secondary offering at the market, the registrant, selling security holders and underwriters have not taken sufficient measures to assure compliance with Regulation M.

*P. 135, new text after carryover par.*

### d.  The Base Prospectus and Rule 430B

Rule 430B was adopted as part of the 2005 public offering reforms. Rule 430B is the corollary to Rule 430A for shelf offerings insofar as Rule 430B allows certain information to be excluded from the base prospectus in certain Rule 415 shelf offerings. Rule 430B is understood largely to codify existing practice.

Rule 430B(a) provides that a prospectus filed as part of a registration statement for a shelf offering under Rule 415(a)(1)(vii) or (a)(1)(x) may omit information that is "unknown or not reasonably available" to the issuer pursuant to Rule 409. Rule 430B(a) further provides that a prospectus filed as part of an automatic shelf registration statement for offerings under Rule 415(a) (other than Rule 415(a)(1)(vii) or (viii)) also may omit information as to whether the offering is a primary offering or an offering on behalf of persons other than the issuer (or a combination thereof), the plan of distribution for the securities, a description of the securities registered other than an identification of the name or class of securities, and the identification of other issuers. Each such prospectus will be deemed to have been filed as part of the registration statement for purposes of §7 of the 1933 Act.

Under Rule 430B(b), a prospectus filed as part of a registration statement for shelf offerings under Rule 415(a)(1)(i) by an issuer that is eligible to use Form S-3 or F-3 for primary offerings pursuant to General Instruction I.B.1 (a) may omit the information described in Rule 430B(a) and (b) may also omit the identities of selling security holders and amounts of securities to be registered on their behalf if: (1) the registration statement is an automatic shelf registration statement; or (2) numerous conditions specified in Rule 430B(b)(2) are all satisfied.

Rule 430B(c) provides that a prospectus that omits information in reliance on Rule 430B meets the requirements of §10 of the 1933 Act for purposes of §5(b)(1), but such a prospectus that omits information does not meet the requirements of §10(a) of the 1933 Act for purposes of §5(b)(2), or §2(a)(10)(a) (i.e., the traditional free writing prospectus after the effective date).

Rule 430B(d) allows flexibility in how information omitted from a prospectus that is part of an effective registration statement may be included later in the prospectus. In particular, such omitted information may be included subsequently in the prospectus that is part of the registration statement by: (1) a post-effective amendment to the registration statement; (2) a prospectus supplement filed under Rule 424(b); or (3) subject to Rule 430B(h), if the applicable form permits, including the information in the issuer's reports filed under §13 or §15(d) of the 1934 Act that are incorporated or deemed incorporated by reference into the prospectus.

Rule 430B(e)–(g) concerns liability under §11 of the Securities Act. Most notably, these provisions, included below, provide that a prospectus supplement filed under Rule 424 will be deemed part of and included in the registration statement containing the base prospectus that the supplement relates to and reset the effective date of registration statements for purposes of §11 liability in certain instances.

## 6. ELECTRONIC FILING

*P. 148, after 2d full par.*    On October 25, 2001, the SEC approved the first completely paperless securities offering for a variable annuity with the offering to be conducted solely through the issuer's Web site. Am. Separate Account 5 of Am. Life Ins. Co. of N.Y., Sec. Act Rel. 8027, 76 SEC Dock. 181 (2001). The Commission order was limited to the facts and circumstances of this offering but marked the first tentative step toward a paper-less offering process. See Berenson & Menconi, To Boldly Go Where No Security Offering Has Gone Before: Paperless, 35 Rev. Sec. & Commodities Reg. 137 (2002).

In 2005 the Commission also adopted new Rule 313 under Regulation S-T and amended various other rules, the effect of which was to expand the information that the SEC requires certain investment companies to submit to the Commission electronically through the EDGAR system and to make it easier for investors to search open-end management company and insurance company separate account filings on EDGAR by requiring that certain open-end management investment companies and insurance company separate accounts identify in their EDGAR filings information regarding their series and classes (or contracts, in the case of separate accounts). The rule changes also made certain technical changes to the EDGAR system. See Sec. Act Rels. 8401, 82 SEC Dock. 1532 (2004) (proposal); 8590, 85 SEC Dock. 2849 (2005) (adoption).

In Sec. Act Rel. 8529, 84 SEC Dock. 2615 (2005) (adoption), the Commission adopted rule and form amendments to permit registrants to submit voluntarily supplemental "tagged" financial information using the eXtensible Business Reporting Language (XBRL). See also SEC Press Rel. 2005-64 (Apr. 26, 2005). This voluntary program would enable the Commission to evaluate the usefulness of data tagging to registrants, investors, the SEC, and the marketplace.


## D.  CONTENTS OF THE REGISTRATION STATEMENT AND PROSPECTUS (HEREIN OF THE SEC'S ACCOUNTING ROLE)


### 2.  REGULATION S-K (NONFINANCIAL DATA)


a.  Commission Policy on Forward Looking Statements
[Item 10(b); Sec. Act §27A; Sec. Ex. Act §21E]

*P. 165, new text end of page.*   In Asher v. Baxter Int'l, Inc., 377 F.3d 727 (7th Cir. 2004), the court declined to dismiss a complaint whose projections the defendant urged were shielded from liability by the PSLRA safe harbors. Judge Easterbrook wrote in part:

Whether or not Baxter could have made the cautions more helpful by disclosing assumptions, methods, or confidence intervals, none of these is required. The PSLRA does not require the *most* helpful caution; it is enough to "identify[ ] important factors that could cause actual results to differ materially from those in the forward-looking statement." This means that it is enough to point to the principal contingencies that could cause actual results to depart from the projection. The statute calls for issuers to reveal the "important factors" but not to attach probabilities to each potential bad outcome, or to reveal in detail what could go wrong; as we have said, that level of detail might hurt investors (by helping rivals) even as it improved the accuracy of stock prices.... Moreover, "if enterprises cannot make predictions about themselves, then securities analysts, newspaper columnists, and charlatans have protected turf. There will be predictions by persons whose access to information is not as good as the issuer's. When the issuer adds its information and analysis to that assembled by outsiders, the *collective* assessment will be more accurate even though a given projection will be off the mark." *Wielgos*, 892 F.2d at 514 (emphasis in original).

Yet Baxter's chosen language may fall short. There is no reason to think — at least, no reason that a court can accept at the pleading stage, before plaintiffs have access to discovery — that the items mentioned in Baxter's cautionary language were those thought at the time to be the (or any of the) "important" sources of variance. The problem is not that what actually happened went unmentioned; issuers need not anticipate all sources of deviations from expectations. Rather, the problem is that there is no reason (on this record) to conclude that Baxter mentioned those sources of variance that (at the time of the projection) were the principal or important risks. For all we can tell, the major risks Baxter knew that it faced when it made its forecasts were exactly those that, according to the complaint, came to pass, yet the cautionary statement mentioned none of them.

Moreover, the cautionary language remained fixed even as the risks changed. When the sterility failure occurred in spring 2002, Baxter left both its forecasts and cautions as is. When Baxter closed the plants that (according to the complaint) were its least-cost sources of production, the forecasts and cautions continued without amendment. This raises the possibility — no greater confidence is possible before discovery — that Baxter knew of important variables that would affect its forecasts, but omitted them from the cautionary language in order to depict the projections as more certain than internal estimates at the time made them. Thus this complaint could not be dismissed under the safe harbor, though we cannot exclude the possibility that if after discovery Baxter establishes that the cautions did reveal what were, *ex ante*, the major risks, the safe harbor may yet carry the day.

In Baron v. Smith, 380 F.3d 49, 53–54 (1st Cir. 2004), the court concluded that a press release announcing the filing of a voluntary reorganization was protected by the statutory safe harbor to the extent it contained forward-looking statements.

## f.  Item 402: Executive Compensation

***P. 182 n.73 end note.***   In July 2003, Microsoft announced that it would stop issuing options and instead begin giving its 50,000 employees restricted stock. Guth & Lublin, Tarnished Gold: Microsoft Ushers Out Era of Options, Wall St. J., July 9, 2003, at A1.

New questions regarding executive compensation arose in the wake of NYSE Chairman Richard Grasso's resignation in September 2003 after revelations that he had received a retirement and deferred pay compensation package of at least $139.5 million and annual compensation as high as $30.6 million in 2001, sharply higher than the $2.2 million he received in 1995, his first year as Chairman. Morgenson & Thomas, Chairman Quits Stock Exchange in Furor over Pay, N.Y. Times, Sept. 18, 2003, at A1; Craig & Kelly, Weakened NYSE Must Face Challenges, Wall St. J., Sept. 18, 2003, at C1; Grasso Declines Additional $48 M; Details of Compensation Package Provided, 35 Sec. Reg. & L. Rep. (BNA) 1480 (2003).

In 2004, New York State Attorney General Eliot Spitzer filed a complaint under the New York Not-for-Profit Corporation Law challenging compensations and benefits paid to Richard Grasso on grounds that the amounts were not "reasonable" and "commensurate with the services rendered," that the compensation provider was beset with conflicts of interest and dominated by

Grasso, and that there had been a lack of full disclosure. See New York AG Spitzer Sues Ex-NYSE Chairman Grasso Over Pay, 36 Sec. Reg. & L. Rep. (BNA) 997 (2004). A federal district court subsequently declined to remove the action from the New York courts. New York v. Grasso, 350 F. Supp. 2d 498 (S.D.N.Y. 2004); In Setback for Grasso, NYSE Suit Over Pay Package Returned to N.Y. Court, 36 Sec. Reg. & L. Rep. (BNA) at 2237.

In 2004, the IASB adopted a standard that requires covered companies to expense stock options. IASB Issues Standard Requiring Expensing of Stock Options; U.K. Board to Follow Suit, 36 Sec. Reg. & L. Rep. (BNA) 365 (2004).

Shortly later the FASB also proposed that companies be required to report stock options as an expense. Norris, Accounting Board Wants Options to be Reported as an Expense, N.Y. Times, Apr. 1, 2004, at C1; FASB Formally Proposes Requirement to Expense Employee Stock Compensation, 36 Sec. Reg. & L. Rep. (BNA) 642 (2004).

In December 2004, the FASB adopted revisions to Statement of FAS Standard No. 123 and required public entities to expense stock options at specified dates in 2005. See also FASB, Statement of Financial Accounting Standards No. 123 (revised 2004), Share-Based Payment: Frequently Asked Questions (Dec. 16, 2004).

Appendix B, Basis for Conclusions, explained why the FASB reconsidered FAS Statement No. 123, in ¶¶83, 84–85:

> B2. Statement 123 was issued in 1995. Its requirements for share-based employee compensation transactions were effective for financial statements for fiscal years beginning after December 15, 1995. As originally issued, Statement 123 established the fair-value-based method of accounting as preferable for share-based compensation awarded to employees and encouraged, but did not require, entities to adopt it. The Board's decision at that time was based on practical rather than conceptual considerations. Paragraphs 60 and 61 of Statement 123 stated:
> The debate on accounting for stock-based compensation unfortunately became so divisive that it threatened the Board's future working relationship with some of its constituents. Eventually, the nature of the debate threatened the future of accounting standards setting in the private sector.

The Board continues to believe that financial statements would be more relevant and representationally faithful if the estimated fair value of employee stock options was included in determining an entity's net income, just as all other forms of compensation are included....

B4. Before 2002, virtually all entities chose to continue to apply the provisions of Opinion 25 rather than to adopt the fair-value-based method to account for share-based compensation arrangements with employees. The serious financial reporting failures that came to light beginning in 2001 led to a keen interest in accounting and financial reporting issues on the part of investors, regulators, members of the U.S. Congress, and the media. Many of the Board's constituents who use financial information said that the failure to recognize compensation cost for most employee share options had obscured important aspects of reported performance and impaired the transparency of financial statements.

B5. The increased focus on high-quality, transparent financial reporting stemming from the financial reporting failures in the early years of the 21st century created a growing demand for entities to recognize compensation cost for employee share options and similar instruments—a demand to which entities began to respond. As of March 2003, when the Board added this project to its agenda, 179 public companies had adopted or announced their intention to adopt the fair-value-based accounting method in Statement 123. By May 2003, that number had grown to 276 public companies, of which 93 were companies included in the Standard & Poor's (S&P) 500 Index; those companies represented 36 percent of the index based on market capitalization. By February 2004, the number had increased to 483 public companies, 113 of which represented 41 percent of the S&P 500 Index based on market capitalization, and by July 2004, the number had increased to 753 public companies.

Revised FAS Statement No. 123 requires in ¶¶1 and 16:

that the cost resulting from all share-based payment transactions be recognized in the financial statements. This Statement establishes fair value as the measurement objective in accounting for share-based payment arrangements and requires all entities to apply a fair-value-based measurement method in accounting for share-based payment transactions with employees except for equity instruments held by employee share ownership plans....

The measurement objective for equity instruments awarded to employees is to estimate the fair value at the grant date of the equity instruments that the entity is obligated to issue when employees have rendered the requisite service and satisfied any other conditions necessary to earn the right to benefit from the instruments (for example, to exercise share options). That estimate is based on the share price and other pertinent factors, such as expected volatility, at the grant date.

A variety of valuation techniques satisfy the criteria of Revised Statement No. 123 including the Black-Scholes-Merton formula, a lattice model, or a Monte Carlo simulation technique. Id. at ¶A13 n.48.

Paragraph 4 defined the scope of Revised Statement No. 123:

This Statement applies to all share-based payment transactions in which an entity acquires goods or services by issuing (or offering to issue) its shares, share options, or other equity instruments (except for equity instruments held by an employee share ownership plan) or by incurring liabilities to an employee or other supplier (a) in amounts based, at least in part, on the price of the entity's shares or other equity instruments or (b) that require or may require settlement by issuing the entity's equity shares or other equity instruments.

Revised Statement No. 123 includes specified disclosure requirements in ¶64:

An entity with one or more share-based payment arrangements shall disclose information that enables users of the financial statements to understand:

a. The nature and terms of such arrangements that existed during the period and the potential effects of those arrangements on shareholders
b. The effect of compensation cost arising from share-based payment arrangements on the income statement

    c. The method of estimating the fair value of the goods or services received, or the fair value of the equity instruments granted (or offered to grant), during the period

    d. The cash flow effects resulting from share-based payment arrangements.

In 2003, the Commission approved the NYSE and NASD equity compensation plan amendments. Sec. Ex. Act Rel. 48,108, 80 SEC Dock. 1596 (2003) (adoption). The NYSE proposal adopts §303A(8) of the NYSE's Listed Company Manual to require shareholder approval of all equity compensation plans and material revisions to the plans with limited exemptions. The new Rule replaces a NYSE pilot program relating to broadly based stock options, found in §§312.01, 312.03, and 312.04 of the NYSE Listed Company Manual.

In Walt Disney Co. Deriv. Litig., 2005 Del. Ch. LEXIS 113 (Del. Ch. 2005), after a 37 day trial Chancellor Chandler concluded that the Walt Disney directors did not breach their fiduciary duties or commit waste with respect to Michael Ovitz's compensation. The court was critical of CEO Michael Eisner but did not conclude that Eisner's actions should lead to liability for a violation of the duty of care by either Eisner or the board.

In 2006, in the first major Rule initiated by the Cox Chairmanship, the Commission proposed amendments to the disclosure requirements for executive and director compensation, related party transactions, director independence, and securing ownership of officers and directors. Sec. Act Rel. 8655, _____ SEC Dock. _____ (2006) (proposal).

Proposed Regulation S-K Item 402(b) would add a new Compensation Discussion and Analysis section. In making this proposal the Commission expressly cited Gordon, Executive Compensation: If There's a Problem, What's the Remedy? The Case for "Compensation Discussion and Analysis," 30 J. Corp. L. 675 (2006).

Proposed Rule 402(b)(1) was intended to be an overview that put into context compensation disclosure data provided elsewhere. Id. at _____ [n.54]. The proposed Rule 402(b)(1) specifically requires:

    (i) The objectives of the registrant's compensation programs;

(ii) What the compensation program is designed to reward and not reward;

(iii) Each element of compensation;

(iv) Why the registrant chooses to pay each element;

(v) How the registrant determines the amount (and, where applicable, the formula) for each element to pay; and

(vi) How each compensation element and the registrant's decisions regarding that element fit into the registrant's overall compensation objectives and affect decisions regarding other elements.

Rule 402(b)(2) limited disclosure to material information, observed that the required disclosure "will vary depending upon facts and circumstances," then offered several possible examples of what may be disclosed:

(i) The policies for allocating between long-term and currently paid out compensation;

(ii) The policies for allocating between cash and non-cash compensation, and among different forms of non-cash compensation;

(iii) For long-term compensation, the basis for allocating compensation to each different form of award (such as relationship of the award to the achievement of the registrant's long-term goals, management's exposure to downside equity performance risk, correlation between cost to registrant and expected benefits to the registrant);

(iv) For equity-based compensation, how the determination is made as to when awards are granted;

(v) What specific items of corporate performance are taken into account in setting compensation policies and making compensation decisions;

(vi) How specific forms of compensation are structured to reflect the named executive officer's individual performance and/or individual contribution to these items of the registrant's performance, describing the elements of individual performance and/or contribution that are taken into account;

(vii) How specific forms of compensation are structured to reflect these items of the registrant's performance, including whether discretion can be exercised (either to award compensation absent attainment of the relevant performance goal(s) or to reduce or increase the size of an award);

(viii) The factors considered in decisions to increase or decrease compensation materially;

(ix) How compensation or amounts realizable from prior compensation (*e.g.*, gains from prior option or stock awards) are considered in setting other elements of compensation (*e.g.*, how gains from prior option or stock awards are considered in setting retirement benefits);

(x) The impact of the accounting and tax treatments of the particular form of compensation;

(xi) The registrant's equity or other security ownership requirements or guidelines (specifying applicable amounts and forms of ownership), and any registrant policies regarding hedging the economic risk of such ownership;

(xii) Whether the registrant engaged in any benchmarking of total compensation, or any material element of compensation, identifying the benchmark and, if applicable, its components (including component companies); and

(xiii) The role of executive officers in determining executive compensation.

The proposal Release advocated this theme:

The proposed Compensation Discussion and Analysis requirement would be principles-based, in that it identifies the disclosure concept and provides several illustrative examples. The application of a particular example must be tailored to the company. However, the scope of the Compensation Discussion and Analysis is intended to be comprehensive, so that it would call for discussion of post-termination as well as in-service compensation arrangements. Boilerplate disclosure would not comply with the proposed item. . . .

The Compensation Discussion and Analysis should be sufficiently precise to identify material differences in compensation policies and decisions for individual named executive officers where appropriate. Where policies or decisions are materially similar, officers could be grouped together. Where, however, the policy for an executive officer is materially different, for example in the case of a principal executive officer, his or her compensation would be discussed separately.

Id. at _____ [n.55].

The Compensation Discussion and Analysis will be considered filed as part of the proxy statement and subject to liability under §18 of the 1934 Act as well as certification requirements of Rule 13A–M. Id. at _____ [nn.57–58].

Simultaneously the Commission proposed to eliminate the Performance Graph and Compensation Committee Report currently required by Regulation S-K Items 402(k)–(l). Id. at _____ [nn.60–61].

The proposal Release emphasized "that much about the tabular approach to eliciting compensation disclosure is sound," id. at _____ [n.62], but proposed a reorganization and streamlining of compensation tables into three broad categories:

1. compensation with respect to the last fiscal year (and the two preceding fiscal years), as reflected in a revised Summary Compensation Table that presents compensation paid currently or deferred (including options, restricted stock and similar grants) and compensation consisting of current earnings or awards that are part of a plan, and as supplemented by two tables providing back-up information for certain data in the Summary Compensation Table;

2. holdings of equity-based interests that relate to compensation or are potential sources of future compensation, focusing on compensation-related equity-based interests that were awarded in prior years and are "at risk," as well as recent realization on these interests, such as through vesting of restricted stock or the exercise of options and similar instruments; and

3. retirement and other post-employment compensation, including retirement and deferred compensation plans, other retirement benefits and other post-employment benefits, such as those payable in the event of a change in control.

Reorganizing the tables along these themes should help investors understand how compensation components relate to each other. At the same time we would retain the ability for investors to use the tables to compare compensation from year to year and from company to company.

We note that in more clearly organizing the compensation tables to explain how the elements relate to each other, we may in some situations be requiring disclosure of both amounts earned (or potentially earned) and amounts subsequently paid out. This approach raises the risk of "double counting" some elements of compensation. However, we believe the risk inherent in such double disclosure is outweighed by the clearer and more complete picture it would provide to investors. We would encourage companies to use the narrative following the tables (and where appropriate the Compensation Discussion and Analysis) to explain how disclosures relate to each other in their particular circumstances.

Id. at _____–_____ [nn.63–66].

Under the proposed approach the Summary Compensation Table "would continue to serve as the principal disclosure vehicle regarding executive compensation." Id. at _____ [n.67]. As streamlined, the proposed Table would require:

## Summary Compensation Table

| Name and Principal Position | Year | Total ($) | Salary ($) | Bonus ($) | Stock Awards ($) | Option Awards ($) | Non-Stock Incentive Plan Compensation ($) | All Other Compensation ($) |
|---|---|---|---|---|---|---|---|---|
| (a) | (b) | (c) | (d) | (e) | (f) | (g) | (h) | (i) |
| PEO | ___ ___ ___ | | | | | | | |
| PFO | ___ ___ | | | | | | | |
| A | ___ ___ ___ | | | | | | | |
| B | ___ ___ ___ | | | | | | | |
| C | ___ ___ ___ | | | | | | | |

The proposed new approach to compensation eliminates the distinction between "annual" and "long term" compensation to avoid confusion. The proposal Release explained:

> ... In eliminating this distinction, we also propose to revise the definition of "long term incentive plan" to eliminate any distinction between a "long term" plan and one that may provide for periods shorter than one year, because, like the captions, the current approach creates distinctions that may be confusing to users and preparers. The proposals would thus define an "incentive plan" as any plan providing compensation intended to serve as incentive for performance to occur over a specified period. Consistent with this change ... we propose to merge the current Other Annual Compensation column into the proposed All Other Compensation column, and include current information regarding incentive plan compensation in the appropriate column for the relevant form of award.

Id. at _____ [n.123].

Item 402(k) requires narrative disclosure of potential payments upon termination or change in control, specifically including:

- the specific circumstances that would trigger payment(s) under the termination or change-in-control arrangements or the provision of other benefits (references to benefits include perquisites);
- the estimated payments and benefits that would be provided in each termination circumstance, and whether they would or could be lump-sum or annual, disclosing the duration and by whom they would be provided;
- the specific factors used to determine the appropriate payment and benefit levels under the various circumstances that would trigger payments or provision of benefits;
- any material conditions or obligations applicable to the receipt of payments or benefits, including but not limited to non-compete, non-solicitation, non-disparagement or confidentiality covenants; and

- any other material features necessary for an understanding of the provisions.

The item contemplates disclosure of the duration of non-compete and similar agreements, and provisions regarding waiver of breach of these agreements, and disclosure of tax gross-up payments.

As proposed, a company would be required to provide quantitative disclosure under these requirements even where uncertainties exist as to amounts payable under these plans and arrangements. In the event that uncertainties exist as to the provision of payments or benefits or the amounts involved, the company would be required to make reasonable estimates and disclose material assumptions underlying such estimates in its disclosure. In such event, the disclosure would be considered forward-looking information as appropriate that falls within the safe harbor for disclosure of such information.

Id. at _____–_____ [nn.158–160].

Under the proposed Item 402, rather than the covered officers including the chief executive officer and four other most highly compensated officers, the Commission proposed the principal executive officer, the principal financial officer, and three other most highly compensated executive officers. Cf. similar nomenclature for principal executive and financial officers in Form 8-K Item 5.02. "In addition, as is currently the case, up to two additional individuals for whom disclosure would have been required but for the fact that they were no longer serving as executive officers at the end of the last completed fiscal year would be included." Id. at _____ [n.162].

The Commission also proposed revising the total threshold for disclosure of named executive officers other than the principal executive and financial officers to $100,000 of total compensation for the last fiscal year, rather than the current $100,000 of total annual salary and bonus. See id. at _____–_____ [nn.166–170].

The proposal Release eliminated the exclusion under Item 402 of transactions between the company and a third party that are reported under Item 404.

We also propose instructions to Item 404 that would clarify what compensation does not need to be reported under Item 404. In some cases the result may nevertheless be that compensation information is disclosed under Item 402 while a related person transaction giving rise to that compensation is disclosed under Item 404. We believe the possibility of additional disclosure in the context of each of the respective items is preferable to the possibility that compensation is not properly and fully disclosed under Item 402.

Id. at _____ [nn.172–173].

The Commission also proposed to eliminate the current exclusion from Item 402 of relocation plans, including those generally available to all salaried employees. Id. at ___ [nn.174–177].

Director compensation has evolved from simple cash compensation packages to more complex packages involving share based compensation, incentive plans, and other forms of compensation. Proposed Item 402(1) would require a disclosure of a Director Compensation Table:

## Director Compensation Table

| Name | Total ($) | Fees earned or paid in cash ($) | Stock Awards ($) | Option Awards ($) | Non-Stock Incentive Plan Compensation ($) | All Other Compensation ($) |
|---|---|---|---|---|---|---|
| (a) | (b) | (c) | (d) | (e) | (f) | (g) |
| A | | | | | | |
| B | | | | | | |
| C | | | | | | |
| D | | | | | | |
| E | | | | | | |

The Commission further proposed significant revisions to Item 404, which addresses Certain Relationships and Related

Transactions Disclosure. The intent was to move toward a streamlined, more principle based approach. Id. at _____ [n.231].

Item 404(a) would contain a general disclosure requirement for related person transactions, but be clearer and easier to follow:

> The proposals would retain the principles for disclosure of related person transactions that are specified in current Item 404(a), but would no longer include all of the instructions that serve to delineate what transactions are reportable or excludable from disclosure based on bright lines that can depart from a more appropriate materiality analysis. Instead, proposed Item 404(a) would consist of a general statement of the principle for disclosure, followed by specific disclosure requirements and instructions. The instructions would explain the related persons covered by the Item, the scope of transactions covered by the Item, the method for computation of the amounts involved in the relationship or transaction, the interaction with Item 402, special requirements for indebtedness with banks, and the materiality of certain ownership interests.
>
> The proposed Item would extend to disclosure of indebtedness. Currently, Item 404(a) requires disclosure regarding transactions involving the company and certain related persons, and Item 404(c) requires disclosure regarding indebtedness. We propose to consolidate these two provisions in order to eliminate confusion regarding the circumstances in which each item applies and streamline duplicative portions of current paragraphs (a) and (c) of Item 404.

Id. at _____ [nn.236–237].

Proposed Item 404(a) would begin by broadly requiring a company to disclose:

- any transaction since the beginning of the company's last fiscal year, or any currently proposed transaction;
- in which the company was or is to be a participant;
- in which the amount involved exceeds $120,000; and
- in which any related person had, or will have, a direct or indirect material interest.

Id. at _____ [n.238].

Proposed Item 404(a) would require disclosure of:

- the person's relationship to the company;
- the person's interest in the transaction with the company, including the related person's position or relationship with, or ownership in, a firm, corporation, or other entity that is a party to or has an interest in the transaction; and
- the dollar value of the amount involved in the transaction and of the related person's interest in the transaction.

Registrants would also be required to disclose any other information regarding the transaction or the related person in the context of the transaction that is material to investors in light of the circumstances of the particular transaction. . . .

Currently, disclosure must be provided regarding amounts possibly owed to the company under Section 16(b) of the Exchange Act. The purpose of related person transaction disclosure differs from the purpose of Section 16(b). Accordingly, the rule proposals eliminate this Section 16(b)-related disclosure requirement.

Id. at ___ [nn.258–259].

Item 404 would except disclosure of compensation to any executive officer if:

- the compensation is reported pursuant to Item 402 of Regulation S-K; or
- the executive officer is not an immediate family member of a related person and such compensation would have been reported under Item 402 as compensation earned for services to the company if the executive officer was a named executive officer, and such compensation had been approved as such by the compensation committee of the board of directors (or group of independent directors performing a similar function) of the company.

Disclosure of compensation to a director (or nominee for director) would be required if:

- the compensation is reported pursuant to proposed Item 402(l).

Id. at _____ [nn.260–261].

Other categories of transactions also would be excepted:

First, in the case of transactions involving indebtedness, the following items of indebtedness would be excluded from the calculation of the amount of indebtedness and need not be disclosed because they do not have the potential to impact the parties as the transactions for which disclosure is required: amounts due from the related person for purchases of goods and services subject to usual trade terms, for ordinary business travel and expense payments and for other transactions in the ordinary course of business.

Second, also in the case of a transaction involving indebtedness, if the lender is a bank, savings and loan association, or broker-dealer extending credit under Federal Reserve Regulation T and the loans are not disclosed as nonaccrual, past due, restructured or potential problems, disclosure under proposed paragraph (a) of Item 404 may consist of a statement, if correct, that the loans to such persons satisfied the following conditions:

- they were made in the ordinary course of business;
- they were made on substantially the same terms, including interest rates and collateral, as those prevailing at the time for comparable loans with persons not related to the bank; and
- they did not involve more than the normal risk of collectibility or present other unfavorable features.

This proposed exception is based on a current instruction to Item 404(c), and is modified to be more consistent with the prohibition of the Sarbanes-Oxley Act on personal loans to officers and directors.

Finally, we propose an instruction that indicates that a person who has a position or relationship with a firm, corporation, or other entity that engages in a transaction with the company shall not be deemed to have an indirect "material" interest within the meaning of paragraph (a) of Item 404 if:

- the interest arises only: (i) from the person's position as a director of another corporation or organization which is a party to the transaction; or (ii) from the direct or indirect ownership by such person and all other related persons, in the aggregate, of less than a ten percent equity interest in another person (other than a partnership) which is a party to the transaction; or (iii) from both such position and ownership; or

- the interest arises only from the person's position as a limited partner in a partnership in which the person and all other related persons, have an interest of less than ten percent, and the person is not a general partner of and does not have another position in the partnership.

Id. at_____–_____ [nn.263–269].

Proposed Item 404(b) would require disclosure of the company's policies and procedures for the review, approval, or notification of related party transactions that would be reportable under Item 404(a):

The description would include the material features of these policies and procedures that are necessary to understand them. While the material features of such policies and procedures would vary depending on the particular circumstances, examples of such features may include, in given cases, among other things:

- the types of transactions that are covered by such policies and procedures, and the standards to be applied pursuant to such policies and procedures;
- the persons or groups of persons on the board of directors or otherwise who are responsible for applying such policies and procedures; and
- whether such policies and procedures are in writing and, if not, how such policies and procedures are evidenced.

The proposal would also require identification of any transactions required to be reported under paragraph (a) of Item 404 where the company's policies and procedures did not require review, approval or ratification or where such policies and procedures were not followed.

Id. at _____ [n.270].

Proposed Item 404(c) would require disclosure of the identity of promoters if the company had one during the last five fiscal years; the name and amount if anything received by each promoter from the company and the nature and amount of any consideration received from the company; and additional information regarding any assets acquired by the company from a promoter.

Proposed Item 407 would consolidate existing Regulation S-K Items 306, 401(h), (i), and (j), 402(i), and 404(b) and Schedule 14A Item 7, which address director independence and related corporate governance requirements. In the proposal single Item format:

> ... if the company is an issuer with securities listed, or for which it has applied for listing, on a national securities exchange or in an automated inter-dealer quotation system of a national securities association which has requirements that a majority of the board of directors be independent, the proposal would require disclosure of those directors and director nominees that the company identifies as independent (and committee members not identified as independent), using a definition for independence for directors (and for committee members) that is in compliance with the applicable listing standards. If the company is not a listed issuer, the proposals would require disclosure of those directors and director nominees that the company identifies as independent (and committee members not identified as independent) using the definition for independence for directors (and for committee members) of a national securities exchange or a national securities association, specified by the company. The company would be required to apply the same definition consistently to all directors and also to use the independence standards of the same national securities exchange or national securities association for purposes of determining the independence of members of the compensation, nominating and audit committees.
>
> The proposals would require an issuer that has adopted definitions of independence for directors and committee members to disclose whether those definitions are posted on the company's Web site, or include the definitions as an appendix to the company's proxy materials at least once every three years or if the policies have been materially amended since the beginning of the company's last fiscal year. Further, if the policies are not on the company's Web site, or included as an appendix to the company's proxy statement, the company would have to disclose

in which of the prior fiscal years the policies were included in the company's proxy statement.

In addition, the proposals would require, for each director or director nominee identified as independent, a description of any transactions, relationships or arrangements not disclosed pursuant to paragraph (a) of Item 404 that were considered by the board of directors of the company in determining that the applicable independence standards were met.

This independence disclosure would be required for any person who served as a director of the company during any part of the year for which disclosure must be provided, even if the person no longer serves as director at the time of filing the registration statement or report or, if the information is in a proxy statement, if the director's term of office as a director will not continue after the meeting. In this regard, we believe that the independence status of a director is material while the person is serving as director, and not just as a matter of reelection.

The proposals also would revise the current disclosure required regarding the audit committee and nominating committee to eliminate duplicative committee member independence disclosure and to update the required audit committee charter disclosure requirement for consistency with the more recently adopted nominating committee charter disclosure requirements. As a result, the audit committee charter would no longer be required to be delivered to security holders if it is posted on the company's Web site. We also propose moving the disclosure required by Section 407 of the Sarbanes-Oxley Act regarding audit committee financial experts to Item 407, although we are not proposing any substantive changes to that requirement.

In addition to the disclosures currently required regarding audit and nominating committees of the board of directors, we propose requiring similar disclosure regarding compensation committees. The company would also be required to describe its processes and procedures for the consideration and determination of executive and director compensation including:

- the scope of authority of the compensation committee (or persons performing the equivalent functions);
- the extent to which the compensation committee (or persons performing the equivalent functions) may delegate

any authority to other persons, specifying what authority may be so delegated and to whom;

- whether the compensation committee's authority is set forth in a charter or other document, and if so, the company's Web site address at which a current copy is available if it is so posted, and if not so posted, attaching the charter to the proxy statement once every three years;
- any role of executive officers in determining or recommending the amount or form of executive and director compensation; and
- any role of compensation consultants in determining or recommending the amount or form of executive and director compensation, identifying such consultants, stating whether such consultants are engaged directly by the compensation committee (or persons performing the equivalent functions) or any other person, describing the nature and scope of their assignment, the material elements of the instructions or directions given to the consultants with respect to the performance of their duties under the engagement and identifying any executive officer within the company the consultants contacted in carrying out their assignment.

In addition, as noted above, disclosure would be required regarding each member of the compensation committee that the registrant has identified as not independent.

Further, the rule proposals would consolidate into this compensation committee disclosure requirement the disclosure currently required in Item 402 regarding compensation committee interlocks and insider participation in compensation decisions.

Finally, for registrants other than registered investment companies, the rule proposals would eliminate an existing proxy disclosure requirement regarding directors that have resigned or declined to stand for re-election which is no longer necessary since it has been superseded by a disclosure requirement in Form 8-K. For registered investment companies, which do not file Form 8-K, the requirement would be moved to Item 22(b) of Schedule 14A. Also, the rule proposals would combine various proxy disclosure requirements regarding board meetings and committees into one location. In addition, we propose two instructions to Item 407 to combine repetitive provisions, one relating to

independence disclosure, and the other relating to board committee charters.

Id. at _____–_____ [nn.277–293].

The proposed executive compensation disclosure rules were
adopted substantially as proposed in August 2006.


### 3.   FINANCIAL STATEMENTS—THE SEC AND ACCOUNTING (HEREIN OF REGULATION S-X)


#### c.   The Commission and Auditing

***P. 194 n.109, end note.***   In Ernst & Young, Init. Dec. Rel. 249,
82 SEC Dock. 2472 (2004), quoting the text, Chief Administrative Law Judge Murray found serious violations of independence
Rule 2-01(b); see also Codification of Financial Reporting Policies §602.02.g, and Rule of Practice 102(e)(1)(iv)(B)(2). Judge
Murray wrote in part:

> The overwhelming evidence is that during the relevant period,
> EY's day-to-day operations were profit-driven and ignored con-
> siderations of auditor independence in business relationships with
> PeopleSoft. EY's partners shared in the pooled revenues of the
> firm's three practice areas, and each EY partner was evaluated
> annually on his or her achievement toward five preset goals, one
> of which was sales. . . .
>
> EY had no procedures in place that could reasonably be
> expected to deter violations and assure compliance with the
> rules on auditor independence with respect to business dealings
> with audit clients. As an expert in audits, EY knew or should have
> known that a worldwide firm with thousands of employees could
> not rely on voluntary compliance. The fact that EY relied on self-
> interested people to voluntarily raise independence issues and to
> file forms where positive responses would cause a loss of income
> are strong indications that EY was negligent.

Id. at 2477–2508.

Four sanctions were entered: (1) A cease and desist order; (2) disgorgement of $1,686,500 received by Ernst & Young for auditing between 1994 and 1999 and prejudgment interest of $729,302; (3) a requirement that an independent consultant be hired by Ernst & Young acceptable to the Division of Enforcement; and (4) a six month suspension of Ernst & Young from accepting new audit clients. Ernst & Young chose not to appeal this decision.

See also Royal Dutch Petroleum and the "Shell" Transport & Trading Co., p.l.c., Sec. Ex. Act Rel. 50,233, 83 SEC Dock. 1881 (2004) (related consent settlement).

### d.   The Sarbanes–Oxley Act

***P. 200 n.127, end note.***   In 2003 a court appointed examiner in the Enron bankruptcy proceeding amplified the Powers Report's conclusions with respect to Arthur Andersen. Appendix B (Role of Andersen), Final Report of Neal Batson, Court-Appointed examiner, Enron Corp., Ch. 11, Case No. 01-16034 (AJG) (Bankr. S.D.N.Y. 2003). The Report concluded in part:

[T]he evidence reviewed by the Examiner is sufficient for a factfinder to conclude that Andersen breached its duty of care and was negligent as to certain portions of work it performed for Enron. In public statements and testimony, Andersen has acknowledged that it made material errors. The Examiner has reviewed evidence that suggests additional acts of negligence beyond those previously acknowledged. This includes evidence indicating Andersen's failure to discharge its duties in communicating with Enron's Audit Committee, as well as evidence indicating a failure to perform appropriate audit procedures to learn of facts that were critical to Andersen's understanding of the SPE transactions.

Beyond instances of negligence, the Examiner has also determined that a factfinder could conclude that, in connection with certain transactions, Andersen aided and abetted Enron officers in breaches of fiduciary duty. The evidence suggests that, on multiple occasions, Andersen accountants had actual knowledge of the wrongful conduct giving rise to breaches of fiduciary duty by

Enron officers with respect to those transactions, and gave substantial assistance to those officers by: (i) approving accounting that made Enron's financial statements materially misleading; and (ii) not communicating to the Audit Committee in accordance with applicable standards.

In July 2004, the Justice Department filed a criminal complaint against Kenneth L. Lay and the SEC filed a separate civil complaint against him. United States v. Caviey et al., Cr. No. H-04-25 (S-2) (superseding indictment) (S.D. Tex. 2004); SEC v. Lay, Civil Action No. H-04-0284 (Harmon)(Second Amended Complaint) (S.D. Tex. 2004).

The criminal complaint alleged a conspiracy involving Lay, Jeffrey K. Skilling, Richard Causey and others. The complaint alleged that Lay, Skilling and Causey spearheaded an effort to conceal the true state of Enron. With respect to Lay, the complaint largely, but not exclusively, focused on the August to November 2001 time period. Counts 38 to 41 of the complaint also alleged that Lay had engaged in bank fraud over a period from 1999 to 2001.

The SEC Complaint emphasized false and misleading forms 10-K (FY 1999, 2000), 10-Q (3d Quarter 1999, 1st-3rd Quarters 2000, 1st-3rd Quarters 2001), registration statements (2000–2001) and Form 8-K (Nov. 9, 2001) and $90 million of stock sales by Lay in 2001. Lay and Skilling were convicted of most counts in 2006. Jury Finds Lay, Skilling Guilty of Fraud, Conspiracy in Enron Collapse, 38 Sec. Reg. & L. Rep. (BNA) 935 (2006).

See also with $2B J.P. Morgan Settlement, Recovery in WorldCom Suit Could Top $6B, 37 id. 507 (2005).

After filing two interim reports (dated November 4, 2002 and June 9, 2003), the Bankruptcy Court Examiner Dick Thornburgh published a 450 page Third and Final Report in WorldCom, Inc., Case No. 02-13533 (AJG) (Jan. 26, 2004). The Report explained in part:

The Examiner believes that WorldCom has causes of action against a number of persons and entities that bear responsibility for WorldCom's injuries. The potential claims identified by the Examiner are briefly summarized as follows:

- Claims for malpractice and negligence against KPMG to recover any interest and/or penalties paid by the Company to any state taxing authorities based upon the flawed advice KPMG provided to WorldCom in connection with the state tax minimization program. The Company may also have claims to require KPMG to return the millions of dollars in fees paid to KPMG for its flawed advice.
- Claims for breaches of the fiduciary duties of loyalty and good faith against Mr. Ebbers for awarding investment banking business to Salomon and SSB in return for lucrative financial favors, including extraordinary allocations of shares in initial public offerings ("IPO's") from 1996 until August 2000 and extraordinary loan assistance in 2000–2002. The Examiner also believes that the Company has claims against Salomon and SSB for aiding and abetting Mr. Ebbers' breaches of his fiduciary duties.
- Claims for breaches of the fiduciary duties of loyalty and good faith against Mr. Ebbers for accepting more than $400 million in loans from WorldCom at non-commercial interest rates and for accepting loans without disclosing his inability to repay them. The Examiner also believes that WorldCom has claims against the remaining former Directors for their breaches of their duties of care and loyalty in connection with such loans. WorldCom also has a claim against Mr. Ebbers for breach of his April 30, 2002 Severance Agreement.
- Claims for fraud and breaches of fiduciary duties of loyalty and good faith against former Chief Financial Officer ("CFO") Scott Sullivan and those other former WorldCom employees who have pled guilty to crimes related to the Company's accounting irregularities. In addition, claims related to the accounting irregularities may exist against other former WorldCom personnel, including Mr. Ebbers.
- Claims for accounting malpractice or negligence and breach of contract against Arthur Andersen and certain of its former personnel based upon their failure to satisfy professional standards in their audits of WorldCom's financial statements for audit years 1999 through 2001.
- Claims for breaches of the fiduciary duties of loyalty and good faith against Messrs. Ebbers and Sullivan for causing WorldCom to proceed with the Intermedia merger

> amendment in February 2001 without proper authoriza-
> tion by the Company's Board of Directors. The Examiner
> also believes that WorldCom has claims against all other
> former Directors who later voted in favor of the Intermedia
> transaction for breaches of their fiduciary duty of care,
> based upon their failure to investigate whether to proceed
> with the Intermedia merger amendment and their failure
> to confront Messrs. Ebbers and Sullivan for authorizing the
> Intermedia merger amendment without Board approval.

Id. at 4–5.

In March 2005, a jury convicted Bernard Ebbers of nine counts of criminal culpability for WorldCom's $11 billion accounting fraud. Jury Convicts WorldCom's Ebbers of Directing $11 Billion Fraud Scheme, 37 id. 534.

In August 2004, a Special Committee of the Board of Directors of Hollinger Int'l, Inc. filed a 521 page report detailing allegations that Hollinger's former CEO Conrad M. Black and its former COO F. David Radler took more than $400 million in cash over a seven year period or 95.2 percent of Hollinger's adjusted net income during 1997 to 2003. Id. at 1. The Committee at the time of the report had already commenced a civil action in Illinois against Black, Radler and others seeking $1.25 billion in damages, see id. at 3. Separately the Delaware Chancery Court ruled that Conrad Black repeatedly breached the duty of loyalty he owed to Hollinger. Hollinger Int'l, Inc. v. Black, 844 A.2d 1022, 1028–1029 (Del. Ch. 2004).

***P. 208 n.141, end note.*** In June 2003 the House Committee on Financial Services published Sarbanes–Oxley Act: The First Year. The Report explained in part:

> Sarbanes–Oxley has resulted in positive change in corporate
> auditing control and compliance procedures. Writing in the May
> 2003 edition of Chief Executive magazine, Edward Nusbaum
> (CEO of Grant Thornton, the fifth largest accounting firm in the
> U.S.) wrote that a "hidden benefit in Sarbanes–Oxley is that CEOs
> may find that the new requirements provide them with useful tools

for running their companies more confidently." A survey released in March 2003 by PricewaterhouseCoopers of senior executives at large U.S. multinationals found that Sarbanes–Oxley had resulted in changes in auditing controls and compliance procedures at 84 percent of the companies. Of the executives interviewed, 82 percent expressed confidence their companies are in full compliance with the law. . . .

Although some critics have considered the compliance costs of Sarbanes–Oxley to be substantial, a Congressional Research Service (CRS) review conducted for the Committee found evidence to the contrary in a survey done by PricewaterhouseCoopers. "A significant number of corporate executives characterize the startup costs of implementing Sarbanes–Oxley as unsubstantial. Sixty-one percent of the senior executives who responded to the Management Barometer survey characterized the initial expense of implementing Sarbanes–Oxley as either not at all costly (15 percent) or not particularly costly (46 percent)." The survey also found that 70 percent of the executives who indicated that Sarbanes–Oxley would not have any future cost impact gave a positive assessment about Sarbanes–Oxley. CRS also reported, "some academics observed that: 'Because of companies' initial uncertainty about how to comply with the Act, we expect the effects of Sarbanes–Oxley to be somewhat negative in the short run with compliance costs declining over time."

According to survey results by the American Society of Corporate Secretaries, which has over 4,000 members representing approximately 2,800 companies, compliance costs appear to parallel the size of the company. Forty percent of the respondent companies have under $1 billion in revenues, and 45 percent of the respondents estimated their costs at under $1 million, another 34 percent have revenues between $1–5 billion and 31 percent estimated costs at between $1–5 million.

Given the substantial loss of investor wealth, estimated at over $7 trillion, the benefits of preventing future losses and restoring investor confidence greatly outweigh the costs of compliance. . . .

Corporate boards are changing in advance of the listing requirements of the exchanges. Many have already adopted the NYSE guidelines and changed board and audit committee structure accordingly. But the new requirements do not appear to be stifling innovation or creativity among corporate management. . . .

In June, the Business Roundtable, an association of CEOs of 150 leading U.S. corporations, surveyed corporate governance practices among its members. John J. Castellani, president of the Business Roundtable, commented that, "America's corporations are demonstrating their dedication to shareholder and investor confidence." The important findings from the survey are as follows:

- 80 percent of Roundtable companies report that their boards are at least 75 percent independent, and 90 percent report that at least two-thirds of their boards are independent;
- 55 percent of Roundtable companies have (or will have by the end of 2003) an independent chairman, independent lead director or presiding outside director;
- Outside directors at 97 percent of Roundtable companies are meeting in executive session at least once each year, and 55 percent expect to do so at least five times this year; and
- 90 percent of Roundtable companies now encourage, require, or conduct education programs for new (54 percent), and in some cases all (36 percent), directors.

The American Society of Corporate Secretaries conducted a survey in July to gauge the changes underway in the past year in corporate governance, even before the listing rules are finalized. According to survey results, respondent companies have already made significant changes in director independence and involvement, without excessive compliance costs, as follows:

- One year ago, only 26 percent of respondent corporate secretaries had an independent chairman, an independent lead director, or a presiding outside director. Today, 62 percent of the respondents reportoneof those three as a corporate leader.
- During 2002, the outside directors of 156 companies, or just over 56 percent of respondents, met in executive session more than twice per year. During 2003, the number will rise to 257 companies, almost 82 percent of the respondents.
- 75 percent of the respondent secretaries said they have seen more involvement by directors in board meetings in

the past year, while 89 percent said the number or length of audit committee meetings has increased.

The law firm of Shearman and Sterling examined the corporate governance policies of the Fortune 500 companies, based on annual reports and corporate information available as of May 2003. Of these 100 companies, 96 were listed on the NYSE, and four on the NASDAQ. The survey found early and growing compliance with the proposed guidelines, as follows:

- 56 companies have publicly available governance guidelines;
- 53 companies require at least a majority of independent directors;
- 38 companies have defined director independence;
- 58 companies have already adopted new audit committee charters that generally comply with the proposed NYSE rules, and 37 of these held more than 6 audit committee meetings in 2002;
- 65 companies have reported stock ownership guidelines for directors, executives or both; and
- 82 companies have publicly disclosed how board compensation is determined. At 45 companies, compensation is recommended by the corporate governance and/or the nominating committee and approved by the board, and at 26 companies, compensation is recommended by the compensation committee and approved by the board.

In April, the American Corporate Counsel Association (ACCA) and the National Association of Corporate Directors (NACD) joined forces to interview their respective members on corporate governance trends. According to a joint survey, corporate counsels and directors have placed the highest degrees of responsibility for the corporate scandals on CEOs and senior management (over 93 percent), followed by accounting firms. The survey also found that directors appear satisfied with the independence standard set for them in Sarbanes–Oxley; 74 percent of the directors described themselves as comfortable with the definition.

It appears that directors are already reviewing financial reporting matters in more detail. The Investor Responsibility Research Center reviewed SEC filings for 1,250 companies in the S&P 500,

MidCap, and SmallCap Indexes and found that the number of audit committee meetings in 2003 has increased, on average, 39 percent from 2002 among the companies. . . .

As awareness of the legal necessity for good governance spreads, an increasing number of companies and stakeholders are turning to various compliance vehicles and independent ratings of corporate governance practices. For instance, major financial institutions formed Regulatory DataCorp, Int'l LLC (RDC), to aggregate public information and to enable companies to comply with Sarbanes–Oxley and other legal requirements. RDC searches publicly available data sources such as government lists, regulators' announcements, and sector-specific media for names of individuals and organizations of interest to corporate financial managers and public accountants. RDC is building a real-time capability to share its data with clients as they consider transactions and prepare SEC and PCAOB filings.

Groups issuing corporate governance ratings include Institutional Shareholder Services (ISS), GovernanceMetrics International (GMI), The Corporate Library (TCL), Moody's Investors Service, and Standard & Poors (S&P). As an example, ISS, which provides research and advice to institutional investors, launched its Corporate Governance Quotient (CGQ) in 2002 as a subscription service. ISS now expects to issue two percentile scores for 9,500 publicly traded companies during the 2003 proxy season. The first score shows how the company's corporate governance practices compare against all other companies in relevant stock market index. The second score compares each company to its peers in S&P's 23 industry groups.

ISS ratings are based on eight core topics, with 61 sub-topics. The core topics are: auditor independence; board structure and composition; anti-takeover charter and bylaw provisions; laws in the company's state of incorporation; executive and director compensation; qualitative factors, including financial performance; directors' and officers' stock ownership; and director education. ISS conducts its own research, but also invites input by the companies through the ISS Web site. . . .

Another major corporate governance development is the trend among the Delaware state judiciary, considered among the most experienced state judiciary in corporate law in the country.

"From mid-2002 to [February of 2003], the Delaware Supreme Court has issued a series of opinions in cases involving the performance by directors of their fiduciary duties. In every one of these recent cases, the Supreme Court held for the shareholders and against the directors.... The recent decisions and comments by noted Delaware jurists indicate that if corporations do not themselves fix these problems, the courts may hold defendants, including directors, lawyers and accountants accountable for corporate greed out of control," said Ira Millstein.

On July 9, 2002, President Bush established the Corporate Fraud Task Force, which is chaired by the deputy attorney general and includes the SEC, Treasury Department, and numerous agencies involved in labor, energy, and commodities regulation and enforcement. The efforts so far have led to prosecutions of Enron, WorldCom, Adelphia, Arthur Andersen, and others. As of May 31, 2003, the task force had

- Obtained over 250 corporate fraud convictions or guilty pleas, including at least 25 former chief executive officers;
- Charged 354 defendants with some type of corporate fraud crime in connection with 169 filed cases;
- Investigated over 320 potential corporate fraud matters, involving more than 500 individuals and companies; and
- Obtained restitution, fines, and forfeitures in excess of $85 million since inception of the task force, in connection with cases involving securities fraud, commodities fraud, investment fraud, and advanced fee schemes, conduct which is often part of corporate wrongdoing....

Accordingly, the number of SEC actions has drifted lower in the past year, although they remain high when viewed long-term.

- The SEC's enforcement actions increased from 484 in 2001 to 598 in 2002. In 2003, the SEC filed 443 enforcement actions, 137 of which involved financial fraud or reporting.
- The number of temporary restraining orders filed increased 54 percent from 2001 to 2002, followed by a 41 percent decrease from 2002 to 2003.
- There was a 47 percent increase in the number of asset freezes from 2001 to 2002, followed by a 52 percent decrease in 2003.

The SEC's tough oversight has not decreased, as proven by the number of administrative actions:

- The number of officer and director bars sought in 2002 was 147 percent higher than in 2001. This vigorous SEC approach has continued on into 2003, with 124 bars being sought thus far.
- The SEC continues to seek justice from those responsible for any infractions. The number of individuals from whom disgorgement of compensation was sought has increased by 88 percent in the past three years.
- The number of trading suspension ordered by the SEC was 450 percent greater in 2002 than 2001, and in 2003 to date, the number is currently equal to that of the total number in 2002.

Id. at 6, 8, 10–15. See also Donaldson Tells Forum Sarbanes–Oxley Has Led to Board's Recapturing Influence, 35 Sec. Reg. & L. Rep. (BNA) 1492 (2003).

In 2005 one out of 12 U.S. listed companies, a total of 1,295 companies, including 100 foreign companies, filed restatements. The number soared in part because of implementation of §404. Glass, Lewis Reports New Record of Nearly 1,300 Restatements in 2005, 38 Sec. Reg. & L. Rep. (BNA) 403 (2006).

In Free Enter. Fund v. PCAOB, Case No. 1:06CV00217 (D.D.C. 2006), a conservative public interest organization and a small public accounting firm challenged the constitutionality of the creation of the PCAOB by the Sarbanes–Oxley Act of 2002. The Complaint stated in part:

> This is an action challenging the formation and operation of the Public Company Accounting Oversight Board (the "Board"), an entity created by the Sarbanes–Oxley Act of 2002 (the "Act") to "oversee the audit of public companies that are subject to the securities laws." In carrying out this mandate, the Board is authorized to and does exercise broad governmental power, including the power to "enforce compliance" with the Act and the securities laws, to regulate the conduct of auditors through rulemaking and

adjudication, and to set its own budget and to fund its own operations by fixing and levying a tax on the nation's public companies. As a result, and notwithstanding the Act's effort to characterize the Board as a private corporation, the Board is a government entity subject to the limits of the United States Constitution, including the Constitution's separation of powers principles and the requirements of the Appointments Clause. The Board's structure and operation, including its freedom from Presidential oversight and control and the method by which its members are appointed, contravene these principles and requirements. For this reason, the Board and all power and authority exercised by it violate the Constitution.

Id. at ¶1.

See also Lawsuit Challenges Constitutionality of Audit Board's Creation under SOX, 38 Sec. Reg. & L. Rep. (BNA) 268 (2006).

## E.   INTERNATIONAL OFFERINGS

### 2.   OFFERINGS FROM A FOREIGN COUNTRY INTO THE UNITED STATES

#### a.   The Foreign Integrated Disclosure System

*P. 211 n.4, end note.*   In 2005, the Commission adopted amendments to Form 20-F by adding a new Instruction G to allow an eligible foreign private issuer to omit from SEC filings for its first year of reporting under the International Financial Reporting Standards the earliest of three years of financial statements. Sec. Act Rel. 8567, 85 SEC Dock. 406 (2005) (adoption).

### 3.   OFFERINGS FROM THE UNITED STATES INTO A FOREIGN COUNTRY [REGULATION S]

*P. 227 n.30, end note.*   In SEC v. Autocorp Equities, Inc., 292 F. Supp. 2d 1310, 1327–1328 (D. Utah 2003), the court concluded:

Although securities issued under Regulation S are exempt from the registration requirement, once the SEC has established a prima facie case for a Section 5 violation, the burden of proof shifts back to the defendant to establish that he has satisfied the requirements of the exemption. Furthermore, Regulation S does not exempt securities that are issued as "part of a plan to evade the registration provisions of the Securities Act."

In recent years, the SEC has frequently successfully litigated fraud cases against defendants who inappropriately relied on Regulation S when there has been a prima facie violation of the Securities Acts and the securities involved are "part of a plan to evade the registration provisions of the Securities Act." See, e.g., Geiger v. SEC, 363 F.3d 481, 488 (D.C. Cir. 2004) (transaction amounted to a design to evade registration when there was "[resort] to fraud"); SEC v. Autocorp Equities, Inc., 292 F. Supp. 2d 1310, 1327–1328 (D. Utah 2003); Charles F. Kirby, Init. Dec. No. 177, 2000 SEC LEXIS 2681 ("Regulation S is not available with respect to any transaction or series of transactions that, although in technical compliance with these rules, is part of a plan or scheme to evade the registration provisions of the [Securities Act]"); SEC v. Corporation Relations Group, Inc., Case No. 6:99-cv-1222-Orl.-28KRS (M.D. Fla. 2003) ("The evidence shows no confusion or misapprehension on the part of the defendants, but rather a calculated albeit failed attempt to evade a regulation that they well understood"). "Regulation S shelters only bona fide overseas transactions." SEC v. Softpoint, 958 F. Supp. 846, 860 (S.D.N.Y. 1997). Regulation S is not available for "bogus" transactions. SEC v. Schiffer, 1998 U.S. Dist. 8579 at 18–21 (S.D.N.Y. 1998).

# CHAPTER 3

# COVERAGE OF THE SECURITIES ACT OF 1933: DEFINITIONS AND EXEMPTIONS

## A. DEFINITIONS

### 1. *SECURITY* [§2(a)(1)]

#### a. Introduction

***P. 231 n.1, end note.*** In states where the definition of the term *security* has been taken from the federal securities laws, state courts have looked to federal law to define it. See, e.g., Poyser v. Flora, 780 N.E.2d 1191 (Ind. 2003); Caldwell v. Texas, 95 S.W.3d 563 (Tex. Ct. App. 2003); but see King v. Pope, 91 S.W.3d 314 (Tenn. 2003) (following risk capital rather than *Howey* test).

#### c. Oil, Gas, or Other Mineral Rights

***P. 243 n.35, end note.*** In SEC v. Shoreline Dev. Co., 2005 Fed. Sec. L. Rep. (CCH) ¶93,356 (9th Cir. 2005), the court found that the defendants created fractional interests when they sold fractions of their interests in wells to the public.

### d.    Investment Contracts

***P. 248 new n.38.1, 1st full par., end 1st sentence.***    In SEC v. Edwards, 540 U.S. 389, 394–395 (2004), the U.S. Supreme Court quoted this language from *Howey*, then added, quoting the text:

> Those laws were the precursors to federal securities regulation and were so named, it seems, because they were "aimed at promoters who 'would sell building lots in the blue sky in fee simple.'" 1 L. Loss & J. Seligman, Securities Regulation 36, 31–43 (3d ed. 1998) (quoting Mulvey, Blue Sky Law, 36 Can. L. Times 37 (1916)). The state courts had defined an investment contract as "a contract or scheme for 'the placing of capital or laying out of money in a way intended to secure income or profit from its employment,' " and had "uniformly applied" that definition to "a variety of situations where individuals were led to invest money in a common enterprise with the expectation that they would earn a profit solely through the efforts of the promoter or [a third party]."

(i)    *Elements of the* Howey *Investment Contract Test*

***P. 251 n.47, end note.***    In SEC v. Edwards, 540 U.S. 389 (2004), the United States Supreme Court reversed a lower court holding that return on investment was not "derived solely from the efforts of others" when the purchaser had a contractual entitlement to the return. The Court's analysis of this issue described vertical relationships where the investing public was "attracted by representations of investment income" and the defendants were "unscrupulous marketers," id. at 394, and where the "investors have bargained for a return on their investment." Id. at 397.

***P. 256, new text after carryover par.***    In SEC v. Edwards, 540 U.S. 389 (2004), quoting the text, the Supreme Court held that the term *profits* would include a scheme that offered a contractual entitlement to a fixed, rather than a variable, return, writing in part:

Thus, when we held that "profits" must "come solely from the efforts of others," we were speaking of the profits that investors seek on their investment, not the profits of the scheme in which they invest. We used "profits" in the sense of income or return, to include, for example, dividends, other periodic payments, or the increased value of the investment.

There is no reason to distinguish between promises of fixed returns and promises of variable returns for purposes of the test, so understood. In both cases, the investing public is attracted by representations of investment income, as purchasers were in this case by ETS' invitation to "'watch the profits add up.'" [Citation deleted.] Moreover, investments pitched as low-risk (such as those offering a "guaranteed" fixed return) are particularly attractive to individuals more vulnerable to investment fraud, including older and less sophisticated investors. See S. Rep. No. 102–261, Vol. 2, App., p. 326 (1992) (Staff Summary of Federal Trade Commission Activities Affecting Older Consumers). Under the reading respondent advances, unscrupulous marketers of investments could evade the securities laws by picking a rate of return to promise. We will not read into the securities laws a limitation not compelled by the language that would so undermine the laws' purposes.

Respondent protests that including investment schemes promising a fixed return among investment contracts conflicts with our precedent. We disagree. No distinction between fixed and variable returns was drawn in the blue sky law cases that the *Howey* Court used, in formulating the test, as its evidence of Congress' understanding of the term. *Howey*, [328 U.S. 293 (1946), at 298, and n.4]. Indeed, two of those cases involved an investment contract in which a fixed return was promised. [Citing cases.]

None of our post-*Howey* decisions is to the contrary. In *United Housing Foundation, Inc. v. Forman*, 421 U.S. 837 (1975), we considered whether "shares" in a nonprofit housing cooperative were investment contracts under the securities laws. We identified the "touchstone" of an investment contract as "the presence of an investment in a common venture premised on a reasonable expectation of profits to be derived from the entrepreneurial or managerial efforts of others," and then laid out two examples of investor interests that we had previously found to be "profits." *Id.* at 852. Those were "capital appreciation resulting from the development of the initial investment" and "participation in earnings resulting from the use of investors' funds." *Ibid.* We contrasted those examples, in which "the investor is 'attracted solely by the prospects of a return'" on the investment, with housing cooperative shares, regarding which the purchaser "is motivated by a desire to use or consume the item purchased." *Id.*, at 852–853 (quoting *Howey, supra,* at 300). Thus, *Forman* supports the commonsense understanding of "profits" in the *Howey* test as simply "financial returns on ... investments." 421 U.S., at 853.

Concededly, *Forman*'s illustrative description of prior decisions on "profits" appears to have been mistaken for an exclusive list in a case considering the scope of a different term in the definition of a security, "note." See *Reves*, 494 U.S., at 68, n.4. But that was a misreading of *Forman*, and we will not bind ourselves unnecessarily to passing dictum that would frustrate Congress' intent to regulate all of the "countless and variable schemes devised by those who seek the use of the money of others on the promise of profits." *Howey*, 328 U.S., at 299. . . .

The Eleventh Circuit's perfunctory alternative holding, that respondent's scheme falls outside the definition because purchasers had a contractual entitlement to a return, is incorrect and inconsistent with our precedent. We are considering investment *contracts*. The fact that investors have bargained for a return on their investment does not mean that the return is not also expected to come solely from the efforts of others. Any other conclusion would conflict with our holding that an investment contract was offered in *Howey* itself. 328 U.S., at 295–296 (service contract entitled investors to allocation of net profits).

We hold that an investment scheme promising a fixed rate of return can be an "investment contract" and thus a "security" subject to the federal securities laws.

Id. at 394–397.


(iii) *Partnerships*


**P. 259 n.73, end note.**    In Robinson v. Glynn, 349 F.3d 166 (4th Cir. 2003) an interest in a two person limited liability company was held not to be an investment contract when the plaintiff "was not a passive investor relying on the efforts of others, but a knowledgeable executive actively protecting his interest and position in the company." Id. at 172. The court also rejected the notion that the LLC membership interest was *stock* under Land-reth Timber Co. v. Landreth, 471 U.S. 681 (1985), because: (1) the LLC membership interests did not share in profits in propor-tion to their interests; (2) the interests were not freely negotiable; (3) the interest could be pledged, but the pledgee would not acquire control rights; and (4) the interests were not called stock. Id. at 172–174.

### j.   Equipment Trust Certificates

**P. 297, end carryover par.**   In 2004, the Commission defined *issuer* in §2(a)(4), in relation to asset backed securities in its Regulation AB Release. See Sec. Act Rel. 8518, 84 SEC Dock. 1624, 1654 (2004) (adoption). Rule 191(a)–(b) provide in rele-vant part:

> (a) The depositor for the asset-backed securities acting solely in its capacity as depositor to the issuing entity is the *issuer* for purposes of the asset-backed securities of that issuing entity.
>
> (b) The person acting in the capacity as the depositor specified in paragraph (a) of this section is a different issuer from that same person acting as a depositor for another issuing entity or for purposes of that person's own securities.

An identical definition was also adopted in Rule 3b-19 of the 1934 Act.

## B.   EXEMPTED SECURITIES

### 1.   EXEMPTED SECURITIES VERSUS EXEMPTED TRANSACTIONS

### b.   Fraud Provisions

**P. 343, new n.4.1, 1st full par. at 6th line.**   As later amended, exemption extends to §3(a)(14) as well as to §3(a)(2). Securities within §§3(a)(2) or (14) are exempt from §12(a)(2) liability. Lieberman v. Cambridge Partners, LLC, 2003–2004 Fed. Sec. L. Rep. (CCH) ¶92,650 (C.D. Pa. 2003).

## D.   RESALES OF CONTROL AND RESTRICTED SECURITIES

### 3.   RULE 144A

***P. 438 n.52, end note.***     Several authorities support the proposition that a §11 case cannot be brought against those who participate in a legitimate Rule 144A transaction. See also Safety-Kleen Bondholders Litig., NO C/A 3:00-1145-17, 2002 WL 32,349,819 (D.S.C. 2002); Hayes Lemmerz Int'l Inc. Equity Sec. Litig. v. Cucuz, 271 F. Supp. 2d 1007 (E.D. Mich. 2003); American High-Income Trust v. AlliedSignal, 329 F. Supp. 2d 534, 540–542 (S.D.N.Y. 2004). *Safety-Kleen*, in turn, relied on an amicus curiae letter from SEC General Counsel David M. Becker (Aug. 9, 2001).

Presumably these authorities do not address §11 or §12 liability when the Rule 144A transaction was not valid. *Livent*, see 151 F. Supp. 2d at 430–432, *Safety-Kleen Corp.*, 2002 WL 32,349,819 at 2, and *Hayes Lemmerz*, 271 F. Supp. 2d at 1026–1029, did not question the propriety of the initial Rule 144A offerings. Similarly SEC General Counsel Becker's conclusion in his amicus curiae letter in *Safety-Kleen* is that "the concept of integration for Section 5 purposes is not relevant in this case" was expressly contingent upon the premise that: "plaintiffs, however, explicitly disclaim any assertion that the Rule 144A offering should have been registered."

Whether a Rule 144A transaction is valid itself may present a fact question for the trier of fact. Cf. *SEC v. Parnes*, 2001–2002 Fed. Sec. L. Rep. (CCH) ¶91,678 (S.D.N.Y. 2001) ("whether the proof is sufficient to establish a scheme to evade registration requirements and preclude application of the exemption is a question for trial"); Enron Corp. Sec., Derivatives & ERISA Litig., 310 F. Supp. 2d 819, 859–866 (S.D. Tex. 2004).

# CHAPTER 4

# PROTECTIVE COMMITTEE REFORM: THE TRUST INDENTURE ACT OF 1939 AND SEC FUNCTIONS UNDER THE BANKRUPTCY CODE

## B. THE SEC'S FUNCTIONS IN BANKRUPTCY PROCEEDINGS

### 2. THE COMMISSION'S PRESENT ROLE UNDER CHAPTER 11

#### b. SEC Participation

*P. 449 n.4, end note.* When the Commission retains a pecuniary interest on part of the debt sought to be discharged resulting from orders against the defendant in an SEC enforcement action, the Commission has standing to seek dismissal of a Chapter 7 motion for bankruptcy. Sherman v. SEC, 441 F.3d 794 (7th Cir. 2006).

# CHAPTER 6

# REGISTRATION AND POSTREGISTRATION PROVISIONS OF THE 1934 ACT

## A. REGISTRATION

### 5. NONSTATUTORY REQUIREMENTS OF THE EXCHANGES AND THE NASD

#### b. Voting Rights Standards

*P. 508, end text.* In 2003, after amendments, the Commission approved new NYSE and NASD corporate governance standards. Sec. Ex. Act Rels. 47,672, 79 SEC Dock. 3074 (2003) (NYSE proposal); 47,516, 79 SEC Dock. 2407 (2003) (NASD proposal); 48,745, 81 SEC Dock. 1586 (2003) (adoption of both NYSE and NASD proposals). See also NYSE Listed Company Manual §303A Corporate Governance Listing Standards Frequently Asked Questions (Jan. 19, 2004), www.nyse.com.

As approved, after three amendments, the revised NYSE Manual of Listing Standards §303A(1) requires the board of each listed company to consist of a majority of independent directors.

Under §303A(2) no director would qualify as independent unless the board of directors determines that the director has no material relationship with the company. Specifically the NYSE tightened its definition of *independent director* in §303A(2)(b), as the adoption Release explained:

> First, a director who is an employee, or whose immediate family member is an executive officer, of the company would not be independent until three years after the end of such employment relationship ("NYSE Employee Provision"). Employment as an interim Chairman or CEO would not disqualify a director from being considered independent following that employment.
>
> Second, a director who receives, or whose immediate family member receives, more than $100,000 per year in direct compensation from the listed company, except for certain permitted payments, would not be independent until three years after he or she ceases to receive more than $100,000 per year in such compensation ("NYSE Direct Compensation Provision").
>
> Third, a director who is affiliated with or employed by, or whose immediate family member is affiliated with or employed in a professional capacity by a present or former internal or external auditor of the company would not be independent until three years after the end of the affiliation or the employment or auditing relationship.
>
> Fourth, a director who is employed, or whose immediate family member is employed, as an executive officer of another company where any of the listed company's present executives serve on that company's compensation committee would not be independent until three years after the end of such service or the employment relationship ("NYSE Interlocking Directorate Provision").
>
> Fifth, a director who is an executive officer or an employee, or whose immediate family member is an executive officer, of a company that makes payments to, or receives payments from, the listed company for property or services in an amount which, in any single fiscal year, exceed the greater of $1 million, or 2% of such other company's consolidated gross revenues, would not be independent until three years after falling below such threshold. . . .
>
> The NYSE [defines] "immediate family member" to include a person's spouse, parents, children, siblings, mothers- and fathers-in-law, sons- and daughters-in-law, brothers- and sisters-in-law, and anyone (other than domestic employees) who shares such

person's home. The NYSE [intended] references to "company" include any parent or subsidiary in a consolidated group with the company.

Sec. Ex. Act Rel. 48,745, 81 SEC Dock. at 1590–1591.

Nonmanagement directors, under §303A(3), would be required to meet at regular intervals without management.

Each listed company, under §303A(4)(a), would be required to have a nomination/corporate governance committee composed entirely of independent directors. The nominating/corporate governance committee, under §303A(4)(b), would be required to have a written charter that addresses the committee's purpose and responsibilities, and an annual performance evaluation of the nominating/corporate governance committee.

Each listed company would be required under §303A(5) further to have a compensation committee composed entirely of independent directors. The compensation committee similarly would be required to have a written charter that addressed the committee's purpose and responsibilities and to prepare an annual performance evaluation of the compensation committee. "The Compensation Committee also would be required to produce a compensation committee report on executive compensation, as required by Commission rules to be included in the company's annual proxy statement or annual report on Form 10-K filed with the Commission." Id. at 1591.

Revised §§303A(6) and (7) requires each NYSE-listed company to have a minimum three person audit committee that meets the independence standards of *both* §303A(2) and SEC Rule 10A-3. NYSE §303A(7) also requires each member of the audit committee to be *financially literate* as that term is interpreted by the full board or to become financially literate within a reasonable period of time after being appointed to the audit committee. In addition at least one member of the audit committee would be required to have accounting or related financial marketing expertise. Any person who satisfies the definition of *audit committee financial expert* in Item 401(e) of Regulation S-K is presumed to satisfy §303A(7)(a).

If a person serves on the audit committee of more than three public companies, each public company board would be required under §303A(7)(a) to determine that such simultaneous service would not impair the ability of the person to effectively serve on that company's audit committee. This determination must be disclosed.

Each audit committee, under §303A(7)(c), is required to have a written charter that addresses "(i) the committee's purpose; (ii) an annual performance evaluation of the audit committee; and (iii) the duties and responsibilities of the audit committee." Id. at 1592. The NYSE version of the charter at a minimum must include the substance of Rule 10A-3(b)(2)–(5):

> as well as the responsibility to annually obtain and review a report by the independent auditor; discuss the company's annual audited financial statement and quarterly financial statements with management and the independent auditor; discuss the company's earnings press releases, as well as financial information and earnings guidance provided to analysts and rating agencies; discuss policies with respect to risk assessment and risk management; meet separately, periodically, with management, with internal auditors (or other personnel responsible for the internal audit function), and with independent auditors; review with the independent auditors any audit problems or difficulties and management's response; set clear hiring policies for employees or former employees of the independent auditors; and report regularly to the board.

Ibid.

Section 303A(9) requires each listed company to adopt and disclose corporate governance guidelines that must include "director qualification standards; director responsibilities, director access to management and, as necessary and appropriate, independent advisors; director compensation; director orientation and continuing education; management succession; and annual performance evaluation of the board." Ibid.

In addition, §303A(10) requires each listed company to adopt and disclose a Code of Business Conduct and Ethics for directors, officers, and employees. Any waiver of this Code must be promptly disclosed. Commentary to §303A(10) discusses the most important topics to be addressed in the Code, which include "conflicts of interest; corporate opportunities; confidentiality of information; fair dealing; protection and proper use of company assets; compliance with laws, rules and regulations (including insider trading laws); and encouraging the reporting of any illegal or unethical behavior." Id. at 1593.

Under §303A(12)(a), the CEO of each listed company must certify that he or she is not aware of any violation of the NYSE's corporate governance listing standards. Under §303A(12)(b) the CEO must promptly notify the NYSE when any executive officer of the listed company becomes aware of *any* material noncompliance with any applicable provision of the new standards.

Section 303A(13) permits the NYSE to issue a public reprimand to any listed company that violates an NYSE listing standard.

There are exceptions to the requirement that a company have a majority of independent directors and nominating/corporate governance and compensation committee comprised entirely of independent directors for (1) any listed company of which more than 50 percent of its voting stock is held by an individual, group, or another company; (2) limited partnerships; and (3) companies in bankruptcy proceedings. Id. at 1593. The NYSE generally excepts from §303A management investment companies registered under the Investment Company Act. Ibid. A more limited series of exceptions is available for business development companies that are *not* registered under the Investment Company Act. Id. at 1594.

Except as otherwise required by Rule 10A-3, the new requirements would not apply to trusts, derivatives, special purpose securities, or listed companies listing only preferred or debt securities on the NYSE. Ibid.

Foreign private issuers would be permitted to follow home country practice except that these companies would be required to "(1) have an audit committee that satisfies the requirements of Rule 10A-3; (2) notify the NYSE in writing after any executive officer becomes aware of any non-compliance with any applicable provision; and (3) provide a brief, general summary of the significant ways in which its governance differs from those followed by domestic companies under NYSE listing standards." Ibid.

Nasdaq adopted somewhat similar, but less demanding, standards.

In 2004, the Commission approved rule changes to §303A of the NYSE Listed Company Manual. Sec. Ex. Act Rel. 50,625, 84 SEC Dock. 179 (2004) (adoption). The amendments, among other matters, addressed the definition of independent directors in §303A.02(b), added a new definition of executive officer in §303A-02(b)(i), and added a requirement that a nonmanaging director preside over each executive session.

## B. REPORTING REQUIREMENTS

### 1. IN CONNECTION WITH EXCHANGE ACT REGISTRATION

#### a. Annual Reports

*P. 511, end page.* In 2005 the Commission adopted amendments to its accelerated filer deadlines for large accelerated filers. Sec. Act Rels. 8617, 86 SEC Dock. 660 (2005) (proposal); 8644, 86 SEC Dock. 2355 (2005) (adoption). The new Commission standard provides that large accelerated filers (those with a market value of outstanding voting and nonvoting common equity held by nonaffiliates of $700 million or more) will become subject to the accelerated filing transition schedule that will require Form 10-K annual reports to be filed within 60 days after the end of a fiscal year on or after October 15, 2006. Large accelerated filers would also remain subject to the current 40 day deadline for Form 10-Q reports rather than the further adopted 35 day deadline, and other accelerated filers would similarly continue under current deadlines (75 days after fiscal year end for Form 10-K annual reports and 40 days for Form 10-Q quarterly reports).

The proposal also would revise the definition of *accelerated filer* to permit an accelerated filer with less than a $50 million float to exit accelerated filer status and begin filing its annual and quarterly reports on a nonaccelerated filer basis. The proposals similarly would permit a *large accelerated filer* that has less than a $500 million float to promptly exit large accelerated filer status.

The adoption Release included the following chart depicting three tiers of filing deadlines that will take effect for fiscal years ending after December 15, 2005, as a result of the amendment:

| Category of Filer | Revised Deadlines for Filing Periodic Reports | |
|---|---|---|
| | Form 10-K Deadline | Form 10-Q Deadline |
| Large Accelerated Filer ($700MM or more) | 75 days for fiscal years ending before December 15, 2006 and 60 days for fiscal years ending on or after December 15, 2006 | 40 days |
| Accelerated Filer ($75MM or more and less than $700MM) | 75 days | 40 days |
| Non-accelerated Filer (less than $75MM) | 90 days | 45 days |

Sec. Ex. Act Rel. 8644, 86 SEC Dock. at 2363–2364.

Conforming amendments were made to Regulation S-X Rules 3-01, 3-09, and 3-12 and the 1994 Act Rule 12b-2 definitions of *accelerated filer* and *large accelerated filer*.

### b.   Quarterly and Current Reports

***P. 512 n.14, end note.***   Early in 2004 the Commission added eight new items to Form 8-K, expanded specified existing disclosures under that Form, and reorganized the required Form 8-K disclosure items into topical categories. Simultaneously the Commission shortened the Form 8-K filing deadline to two business days after the occurrence of a triggering event to better provide the "real time issuer disclosure" required by §409 of the Sarbanes–Oxley Act. Under Rule 12b-25 there is provision for an automatic two day business extension.

In the new topical reorganization, there are eight operative Form 8-K sections of disclosure items:

Section 1 — Registrant's Business and Operations

   Item 1.01 Entry into a Material Definitive Agreement
   Item 1.02 Termination of a Material Definitive Agreement
   Item 1.03 Bankruptcy or Receivership

Section 2 — Financial Information

Item 2.01 Completion of Acquisition or Disposition of Assets
Item 2.02 Results of Operations and Financial Condition
Item 2.03 Creation of a Direct Financial Obligation or an Obligation under an Off-Balance Sheet Arrangement of a Registrant
Item 2.04 Triggering Events That Accelerate or Increase a Direct Financial Obligation or an Obligation under an Off-Balance Sheet Arrangement
Item 2.05 Costs Associated with Exit of Disposal Activities
Item 2.06 Material Impairments

Section 3 — Securities and Trading Markets

Item 3.01 Notice of Delisting or Failure to Satisfy a Continued Listing Rule or Standard; Transfer of Listing
Item 3.02 Unregistered Sales of Equity Securities
Item 3.03 Material Modifications to Rights of Security Holders

Section 4 — Matters Related to Accountants and Financial Statements

Item 4.01 Changes in Registrant's Certifying Accountant
Item 4.02 Non-Reliance on Previously Issued Financial Statements or a Related Audit Report or Completed Interim Review

Section 5 — Corporate Governance and Management

Item 5.01 Changes in Control of Registrant
Item 5.02 Departure of Directors or Principal Officers; Election of Directors; Appointment of Principal Officers
Item 5.03 Amendments to Articles of Incorporation or By laws; Change in Fiscal Year
Item 5.04 Temporary Suspension of Trading under Registrant's Employee Benefit Plans
Item 5.05 Amendments to the Registrant's Code of Ethics, or Waiver of a Provision of the Code of Ethics

Section 6 — [Reserved]

Section 7 — Regulation FD

Item 7.01 Regulation FD Disclosure

Section 8 — Other Events

Item 8.01 Other Events

Section 9 — Financial Statements and Exhibits

Item 9.01 Financial Statements and Exhibits

The eight new Form 8-K disclosure Items are: Item 1.01, Entry into a Material Definitive Agreement; Item 1.02, Termination of a Material Definitive Agreement; Item 2.03, Creation of a Direct Financial Obligation or an Obligation under an Off-Balance Sheet Arrangement of a Registrant; Item 2.04, Triggering Events that Accelerate or Increase a Direct Financial Obligation or an Obligation under an Off-Balance Sheet Arrangement; Item 2.05, Costs Associated with Exit or Disposal Activities; Item 2.06, Material Impairments; Item 3.01, Notice of Delivery or Failure to Satisfy a Continued Listing Rule or Standard; Transfer of Listing; Item 4.02, Non-Reliance on Previously Issued Financial Statements or a Related Audit Report or Completed Interim Review.

The two items that were modified from existing disclosure requirements in periodic reports are Item 3.02, Unregistered Sales of Equity Securities, and Item 3.03, Material Modifications to Rights of Security Holders.

Many of the Form 8-K Items retain the substance of former Form 8-K Items: Item 1.03 retains the substance of former Item 3; Item 2.01 (former Item 2); Item 2.02 (former Item 12); Item 4.01 (former Item 4); Item 5.01 (former Item 1); Item 5.02 (former Item 6); Item 5.03 (former Item 5); Item 5.04 (former Item 11); Item 5.05 (former Item 10); Item 7.01 (former Item 9); Item 8.01 (former Item 5); and Item 9.01 (former Item 7).

The Commission also adopted a new limited safe harbor from public and private claims under §10(b) and Rule 10b-5 for a failure to file a Form 8-K regarding Items 1.01, 1.02, 2.03, 2.04, 2.05, 2.06, and 402(a). See also Sec. Ex. Act Rel. 49,424A,

83 SEC Dock. 1427 (2004) (technical amendments); Sec. Act Rel. 8518, 84 SEC Dock. 1624, 1723 (2004) (amendments for use of Form 8-K by asset backed issuers). See also Horwich, New Form 8-K and Real-Time Disclosure, 37 Rev. Sec. & Commodities Reg. 109 (2004).

*P. 517, new text after 2d full par.*

### d. Management Report and Internal Controls

In June 2003 the Commission adopted new or amended provisions to Regulations S-B, S-K, and S-X; 1934 Act Rules 12b-15, 13a-14, 13a-15, 15d-14, and 15d-15; Forms 10-Q, 10-QSB, 10-K, 10-KSB, 20-F, 40-F; Investment Company Act Rules 8b-15, 30a-2, and 30a-3; and Forms N-CSR and N-SAR to implement the Sarbanes-Oxley Act §404 requirement that companies reporting under the 1934 Act include in their annual report a management report on the company's internal control over financial reporting. Sec. Ex. Act Rels. 46,701, 78 SEC Dock. 1907 (2002) (proposal); 47,986, 80 SEC Dock. 1014 (2003) (adoption). The Commission also amended 1934 Act Rules 13a-14 and 15d-14 and Investment Company Act Rule 30a-2 to require companies to file certifications mandated by §§302 and 906 of the Sarbanes-Oxley Act as exhibits to annual, semiannual, and quarterly reports. Id. at 1017. See also Sec. Ex. Act Rel. 47,551, 79 SEC Dock. 2558 (2003) (proposal).

To address confusion over the exact meaning of the phrase *internal control over financial reporting*, it was defined in 1934 Act Rules 13a-15(f), 15d-15(f), and similarly in Investment Company Act Rule 30a-2(d) to mean

> a process designed by, or under the supervision of, the issuer's principal executive and principal financial officers, or persons performing similar functions, and effected by the issuer's board of directors, management and other personnel, to provide reasonable assurance regarding the reliability of financial reporting and the preparation of financial statements for external purposes in accordance with generally accepted accounting principles and includes those policies and procedures that:

(1) Pertain to the maintenance of records that in reasonable detail accurately and fairly reflect the transactions and dispositions of the assets of the issuer;

(2) Provide reasonable assurance that transactions are recorded as necessary to permit preparation of financial statements in accordance with generally accepted accounting principles, and that receipts and expenditures of the issuer are being made only in accordance with authorizations of management and directors of the issuer; and

(3) Provide reasonable assurance regarding prevention or timely detection of unauthorized acquisition, use or disposition of the issuer's assets that could have a material effect on the financial statements.

The adoption Release emphasized: "From the outset, it was recognized that internal control is a broad concept that extends beyond the accounting functions of a company." Sec. Ex. Act Rel. 47,986, 80 SEC Dock. at 1018. The new term was intended to be distinguishable from other uses of the term *internal* control. Id. at 1017–1019.

As amended, Regulations S-B and S-K Item 308 and Forms 20-F and 40-F require the company's annual report to include management's *"internal control over financial reporting"* report, specifically including:

(1) A statement of management's responsibility for establishing and maintaining adequate internal control over financial reporting for the registrant;

(2) A statement identifying the framework used by management to evaluate the effectiveness of the registrant's internal control over financial reporting as required by para-graph (c) of §240.13a-15 or 240.15d-15 of this chapter;

(3) Management's assessment of the effectiveness of the registrant's internal control over financial reporting as of the end of the registrant's most recent fiscal year, including a statement as to whether or not internal control over financial reporting is effective. This discussion must include disclosure of any material weakness in the registrant's internal control over financial reporting identified by management. Management is not permitted to conclude that the registrant's internal control over financial

127

reporting is effective if there are one or more material weaknesses in the registrant's internal control over financial reporting; and

(4) A statement that the registered public accounting firm that audited the financial statements included in the annual report containing the disclosure required by this Item has issued an attestation report on management's assessment of the registrant's internal control over financial reporting.

As adopted, the Commission modified the final requirements to specify that management must base its evaluation of the effectiveness of the company's internal control over financial reporting on a suitable, recognized control framework that is established by a body or group that has followed due-process procedures, including the broad distribution of the framework for public comment.

The COSO Framework satisifies our criteria and may be used as an evaluation framework for purposes of management's annual internal control evaluation and disclosure requirements.... The final rules require management's report to identify the evaluation framework used by management to assess the effectiveness of the company's internal control over financial reporting.

Sec. Ex. Act Rel. 47,986, 80 SEC Dock. at 1024.

The term *material weakness* has the same meaning in the adopted rules as in the definition under GAAS and attestation standards. Id. at 1025 and n.73.

Quarterly evaluations of internal controls over financial reporting can be less extensive than annual evaluations. Id. at 1026–1027. See also id. at 1028–1030. See Regulations S-B and S-K Item 308(c).

The Commission separately defined *disclosure controls and procedures* in 1934 Act Rules 13a-15(e) and 15d-15(e) and similarly in Investment Company Act Rule 30a-2(c), to mean

controls and other procedures of an issuer that are designed to ensure that information required to be disclosed by the issuer in the reports that it files or submits under the Act is recorded, processed, summarized and reported, within the time periods specified in the Commission's rules and forms. Disclosure controls and procedures include, without limitation, controls and procedures designed to ensure that information required to be disclosed by an issuer in the reports that it files or submits under the Act is accumulated and communicated to the issuer's management, including its principal executive and principal financial officers, or persons performing similar decisions regarding required disclosure.

With respect to potential confusion between *internal control over financial reporting* and *disclosure controls and procedure*, the Commission explained:

> While there is substantial overlap between a company's disclosure controls and procedures and its internal control over financial reporting, there are both some elements of disclosure controls and procedures that are not subsumed by internal control over financial reporting and some elements of internal control that are not subsumed by the definition of disclosure controls and procedures.
>
> With respect to the latter point, clearly, the broad COSO description of internal control, which includes the efficiency and effectiveness of a company's operations and the company's compliance with laws and regulations (not restricted to the federal securities laws), would not be wholly subsumed within the definition of disclosure controls and procedures. . . .
>
> We agree that some components of internal control over financial reporting will be included in disclosure controls and procedures for all companies. In particular, disclosure controls and procedures will include those components of internal control over financial reporting that provide reasonable assurances that transactions are recorded as necessary to permit preparation of financial statements in accordance with generally accepted accounting principles.

Id. at 1027–1028.

Section 404 of the Sarbanes–Oxley Act exempts registered investment companies. See id. at 1034–1036. In its adoption Release, the SEC delayed the compliance date for foreign private issuers, id. at 1031; excluded asset backed issuers from its new requirements, id. at 1031–1032; provided extended compliance periods for small business issuers, id. at 1032; and afforded bank and thrift holding companies the option either to comply with the Commission's new rules implementing §404 or provisions in 12 C.F.R. part 363 [the FDIC Regulations], id. at 1032–1034.

For many boards of directors and outside auditors §404 has emerged as one of the key new responsibilities of the board. Under most state corporate law statutes, the board is "fully protected" when it relies on the report of an outside accountant or management. See Del. Gen. Corp. L. §141(e). Section 404 and the new SEC rules, in contrast, place responsibility on the management "to [establish] and [maintain] an adequate internal control structure and procedures for financial reporting" and to annually assess its effectiveness. The registered public accounting firm is required to attest to this assessment. §404(b).

To better harmonize §§302 and 906 of the Sarbanes–Oxley Act, the Commission also amended

> the exhibit requirements of Forms 20-F and 40-F and Item 601 of Regulations S-B and S-K to add the Section 302 certifications to the list of required exhibits. In the final rules, the specific form and content of the required certifications is set forth in the applicable exhibit filing requirement. To coordinate the rules requiring an evaluation of *disclosure controls and procedures and internal control over financial reporting*, we are moving the definition of the term *disclosure controls and procedures* from Exchange Act Rules 13a-14(c) and 15d-14(c) and Investment Company Act Rule 30a-2(c) to new Exchange Act Rules 13a-15(c) and 15d-15(c) and Investment Company Act Rule 30a-3(c), respectively.
>
> [Amended] Exchange Act Rules 13a-14 and 15d-14 and Investment Company Act Rule 30a-2 ... require the Section 906 certifications to accompany periodic reports containing financial statements as exhibits. We also are amending the exhibit requirements in Forms 20-F, 40-F and Item 601 of Regulations S-B and S-K to add the Section 906 certifications to the list of required exhibits to be included in reports filed with the Commission. In addition, we are amending Item 10 of Form N-CSR to add the Section 906 certifications as a required exhibit. Because the Section 906 certification requirement applies to periodic reports containing financial statements that are filed by an issuer pursuant to Section 13(a) or 15(d) of the Exchange Act, the exhibit

requirement will only apply to reports on Form N-CSR filed under these sections and not to reports on Form N-CSR that are filed under the Investment Company Act only. A failure to furnish the Section 906 certifications would cause the periodic report to which they relate to be incomplete, thereby violating Section 13(a) of the Exchange Act. In addition, referencing the Section 906 certifications in Exchange Act Rules 13a-14 and 15d-14 and Investment Company Act Rule 30a-2 subjects these certifications to the signature requirements of Rule 302 of Regulation S-T.

Id. at 1038.

Subsequently the PCAOB adopted Audit Standard No. 2, An Audit of Internal Controls over Financial Reporting Performed in Conjunction with an Audit of Financial Statements. PCAOB Rel. No. 2004-001, 2003–2004 Fed. Sec. L. Rep. (CCH) ¶87,151 (Mar. 9, 2004). If approved by the SEC the new standard was estimated to increase audit costs by as much as 30-100 percent. Experts Split on Costs and Benefits of PCAOB's Proposed Audit Standard, 36 Sec. Reg. & L. Rep. (BNA) 163 (2004); Ernst & Young, Emerging Trends in Internal Controls: Initial Survey (Jan. 2004) (survey of 100 major companies found initial budgets of 10,000 to 200,000 new hours for §404 compliance).

Within weeks of the SEC approval of PCAOB Audit Standard No. 2, the PCAOB Staff published Staff Questions and Answers: Audit Internal Control over Financial Reporting (June 23, 2004). The SEC Office of the Chief Accountant & Division of Corporate Finance published a briefer Management Report on Internal Control over Financial Reporting and Disclosure in Exchange Act Periodic Reports: Frequently Asked Questions, 2004–2005 Fed. Sec. L. Rep. (CCH) ¶87,262 (Oct. 6, 2004), which focused on the impact of §404 on material acquisitions expected to close near the end of a fiscal year.

Subsequently, the Commission issued a Statement on Implementation of Internal Control Reporting Requirements (Press Rel. 2005-74 May 16, 2005). The Statement explained in part:

From the Commission's April 13th Roundtable on Implementation of Internal Control Reporting Provisions — as well as from the extensive materials submitted in response to our request for feedback—we believe two messages came through clearly: First, compliance with Section 404 is producing benefits, including a heightened focus on internal controls at the top levels of public companies.... Second, implementation in the first year also resulted in significant costs. While a portion of the costs likely reflect start-up expenses from this new requirement, it also appears that some non-trivial costs may have been unnecessary, due to excessive, duplicative or misfocused efforts.

The accompanying Staff Statement on Management's Report on Internal Control over Financial Reporting explained in part:

## THE PURPOSE OF INTERNAL CONTROL OVER FINANCIAL REPORTING

An overall purpose of internal control over financial reporting is to foster the preparation of reliable financial statements that must be materially accurate. Therefore, a central purpose of the assessment of internal control over financial reporting is to identify material weaknesses that have, as indicated by their very definition, more than a remote likelihood of leading to a material misstatement in the financial statements. While identifying control deficiencies and significant deficiencies represents an important component of management's assessment, the overall focus of internal control reporting should be on those items that could result in material errors in the financial statements....

In adopting its rules implementing Section 404, the Commission expressly declined to prescribe the scope of assessment (including testing) that should be supported by a reasonable level of evidential matter. Each company should also use informed judgment in documenting and testing its controls to fit its own operations, risks and procedures. Management should use its own experience and informed judgment in designing an assessment process that fits the needs of that company. Management should not allow the goal and purpose of the internal control over financial reporting provisions—the production of reliable financial statements—to be overshadowed by the process....

## The Concept of Reasonable Assurance

Management is required to assess whether the company's internal control over financial reporting is effective in providing reasonable assurance regarding the reliability of financial reporting. Management is not required by Section 404 of the Act to assess other internal controls. Further, while "reasonable assurance" referred to in the Commission's implementing rules relates back to similar language in the FCPA. Exchange Act Section 13(b)(7) defines "reasonable assurance" and "reasonable detail" as "such level of detail and degree of assurance as would satisfy prudent officials in the conduct of their own affairs."

In addition, the staff recognizes that while "reasonableness" is an objective standard, there is a range of judgments that an issuer might make as to what is "reasonable" in implementing Section 404 and the Commission's rules. Thus, the terms "reasonable," "reasonably" and "reasonableness" in the context of Section 404 implementation do not imply a single conclusion or methodology, but encompass the full range of potential conduct, conclusions or methodologies upon which an issuer may reasonably base its decisions. Different conduct, conclusions and methodologies by different issuers in a given situation do not by themselves mean that implementation by any of those issuers is unreasonable. This also suggests that registered public accounting firms should recognize that there is zone of reasonable conduct by issuers that should be recognized as acceptable in the implementation of Section 404....

## Top-Down/Risk-Based Assessments

The feedback indicated that one reason why too many controls and processes were identified, documented and tested was that in many cases neither a top-down nor a risk-based approach was effectively used. Rather, the assessment became a mechanistic, check-the-box exercise. This was not the goal of the Section 404 rules, and a better way to view the exercise emphasizes the particular risks of individual companies. Indeed, an assessment of internal control that is too formulaic and/or so detailed as to not allow for a focus on risk may not fulfill the underlying purpose of the requirements. The desired approach should devote resources to the areas of greater risk and avoid giving all significant accounts and related controls equal attention without regard to risk....

## Scope of Assessment

An issue frequently cited in the comments concerned the determination of the appropriate scope of management's assessment. Many felt that overly conservative interpretations of the applicable requirements and a hesitancy by the independent auditor to use professional judgment in evaluating management's assessment resulted in many cases in too many controls being identified, documented and tested. . . .

# EVALUATING INTERNAL CONTROL DEFICIENCIES

If control deficiencies are identified, an important part of the assessment of internal control over financial reporting is the consideration of the significance of those deficiencies and whether the risk is mitigated by compensating controls. As with determining the scope of the assessment, management must exercise judgment in a reasonable manner in the evaluation of deficiencies in internal control over financial reporting, and such evaluations may appropriately consider both qualitative and quantitative analyses. Among other things, the qualitative analysis should factor in the nature of the deficiency, its cause, the relevant financial statement assertion the control was designed to support, its effect on the broader control environment and whether other compensating controls are effective.

One particular area brought to the staff's attention involved financial statement restatements due to errors. Neither Section 404 nor the Commission's implementing rules require that a material weakness in internal control over financial reporting must be found to exist in every case of restatement resulting from an error. Rather, both management and the external auditor should use their judgment in assessing the reasons why a restatement was necessary and whether the need for restatement resulted from a material weakness in controls. Such an evaluation should be based on all the facts and circumstances, including the probability of occurrence in light of the assessed effectiveness of the company's internal control, keeping in mind that internal control over financial reporting is defined as operating at the level of "reasonable assurance."

## DISCLOSURES ABOUT MATERIAL WEAKNESSES

A number of companies have reported material weaknesses in their internal control over financial reporting in this first year of implementation. When a company identifies a material weakness, and such material weakness has not been remediated prior to its fiscal year-end, it must conclude that its internal control over financial reporting is ineffective. The Commission's rule implementing Section 404 was thus intended to bring information about material weaknesses in internal control over financial reporting into public view. The staff believes that, as a result, companies should consider including in their disclosures:

- nature of any material weakness,
- its impact on financial reporting and the control environment, and
- management's current plans, if any, for remediating the weakness.

Disclosure of the existence of a material weakness is important, but there is other information that also may be material and necessary for an overall picture that is not misleading. There are many different types of material weaknesses and many different factors that may be important to the assessment of the potential effect of any particular material weakness. We received feedback suggesting that some companies believe that they are not permitted to distinguish among reported material weaknesses. While management is required to conclude and state in its report that internal control over financial reporting is ineffective when there is one or more material weakness, companies may, and are strongly encouraged to, provide disclosure that allows investors to assess the potential impact of each particular material weakness. The disclosure will likely be more useful to investors if management differentiates the potential impact and importance to the financial statements of the identified material weaknesses, including distinguishing those material weaknesses that may have a pervasive impact on internal control over financial reporting from those material weaknesses that do not. The goal underlying all disclosure in this area is to provide increased investor information so that an investor who chooses to do so can treat the disclosure of the existence of a material weakness as the starting point for analysis rather than the only point available. . . .

## COMMUNICATIONS WITH AUDITORS

Feedback from both auditors and registrants revealed that one potential unintended consequence of implementing Section 404 and Auditing Standard No. 2, An Audit of Internal Control Over Financial Reporting Performed in Conjunction with An Audit of Financial Statements, has been a chilling effect in the level and extent of communications between auditors and management regarding accounting and financial reporting issues. Historically, the external auditor may have provided management with advice, based on the auditor's knowledge, experience and judgment in accounting, auditing, and financial reporting matters. Since introduction of the Act and the new auditing requirements, the staff understands that management at times has hesitated to ask auditors technical accounting, auditing, and financial reporting questions or to provide auditors with early drafts of the financial statements (which, due to their draft nature, may contain errors), because of a concern that these actions could result in the unwarranted identification of internal control deficiencies by the auditors. Additionally, the staff understands that auditors also have a heightened concern that providing management with advice might impair the auditor's independence. . . .

The staff recognizes that questions arise in certain circumstances as to the proper application of accounting standards. Investors benefit when auditors and management engage in dialogue, including regarding new accounting standards and the appropriate accounting treatment for complex or unusual transactions. The staff believes that as long as management, and not the auditor, makes the final determination as to the accounting used, including determination of estimates and assumptions, and the auditor does not design or implement accounting policies, such auditor involvement is appropriate and is not of itself indicative of a deficiency in the registrant's internal control over financial reporting. Further, timely dialogue between management and the auditor may positively impact audit quality and the quality of financial reporting.

In October 2005 SEC Chief Accountant Donald Nicolaisen and Corporation Finance Division Director Alan Beller issued a Statement Regarding New Guidance on Section 404 Compliance (Rel. 2005-153), which commended the Committee of Sponsoring Organizations of the Treadway Commission (COSO) for publishing proposed new Guidance for Smaller Public Companies Reporting on Internal Control over Financial Reporting, www.coso.org.

The SEC Advisory Committee on Smaller Public Companies proposed in February 2006 to fully exempt from §404 (1) microcap companies (with equity capital below approximately $128 million and annual revenue less than $125 million) as well as (2) small cap companies (with equity capital between approximately $128 million and $787 million and less than $10 million in annual revenue). Former SEC Chair Arthur Levitt and former Federal Reserve Chair Paul Volcker sharply criticized this proposal for potentially removing an estimated 80 percent of all public companies subject to §404 38 Sec. Reg. & L. Rep. (BNA) 341 (2006).

In April 2006 the Advisory Committee published its Final Report, with 33 recommendations. The Report itself was skeptical that all 33 recommendations would be addressed at once, see id. at 3, but emphasized two tier prioritization of its recommendations, stating in part:

> The first tier—the recommendations to which we assign the highest priority—we refer to as our "primary recommendations." ...
>
> Our first primary recommendation concerns establishment of a new system of scaled or proportional securities regulation for smaller public companies based on a stratification of smaller public companies into two groups, microcap companies and smallcap companies. The recommendation reads as follows:
>
> - Establish a new system of scaled or proportional securities regulation for smaller public companies using the following six determinants to define a "smaller public company";
>
> - The total market capitalization of the company;

137

- A measurement metric that facilitates scaling of regulation;
- A measurement metric that is self-calibrating;
- A standardized measurement and methodology for computing market capitalization;
- A date for determining total market capitalization; and
- Clear and firm transition rules, i.e., small to large and large to small.

Develop a specific scaled or proportional regulation for companies under the system if they qualify as "microcap companies" because their equity market capitalization places them in the lowest 1% to 5% of total U.S. equity market capitalization, with the result that all companies comprising the lowest 6% would be considered for scaled or proportional regulation.

Several studies noted declining implementation costs of §404. See CRA Int'l, Sarbanes–Oxley Section 404 Costs and Implementation Issues: Survey Update (declines of 39 percent in recent years for smaller companies; 42 percent for larger companies); FEI Survey on Sarbanes–Oxley Section 404 Implementation (Mar. 2006) (declines ranging from 11.8 percent to 22.7 percent).

In May 2006 the Commission announced several steps it intends to take to improve §404 implementation. Press Rel. 2006-75 (May 17, 2006). These steps include:

- **Guidance for Companies.** The Commission has received many requests for additional guidance for management on how to complete its assessment of internal control over financial reporting, as required by Section 404(a) of the Sarbanes-Oxley Act. To prepare for the issuance of management guidance, the Commission intends to take the following steps:

  - **Concept Release and Opportunity for Public Comment.** The Commission expects to issue a Concept Release covering a variety of issues that might be the subject of Commission guidance for management. With the Concept Release, the Commission will solicit views on the management assessment process to ensure that the guidance the Commission ultimately proposes addresses the needs and concerns of all public companies. We will also seek input on the appropriate role of outside auditors in connection with the management assessment required by Section 404(a) of Sarbanes-Oxley, and on the manner in which outside auditors provide the attestation required by Section 404(b), to assist in our consideration of possible alternatives to the current approach.

- **Consideration of Additional Guidance from COSO.** The Commission has long been supportive of the Committee of Sponsoring Organizations of the Treadway Commission (COSO) as it works to provide guidance on COSO's 1992 Internal Control—Integrated Framework to address the needs of smaller companies. The Commission anticipates that this forthcoming guidance will help organizations of all sizes to better understand and apply the control framework as it relates to internal control over financial reporting. As the SEC develops guidance for management on how to assess its internal control over financial reporing, we will consider the extent to which the additional guidance that COSO provides is useful to smaller public companies in completing their Section 404(a) assessments.

- **Issuance of Guidance.** Commentary submitted to the Commission has suggested that management assessments under Section 404 have not fully reflected the top-down, risk-based approach the Commission intended. Building from the information gathered in response to the Concept Release, and from the anticipated COSO guidance, the Commission currently anticipates that it will issue guidance to management to assist in its performance of a top-down, risk-based assessment of internal control over financial reporting. To ensure that this guidance is of help to non-accelerated filers and smaller public companies, the Commission intends that this future guidance will be scalable and responsive to their individual circumstances. The guidance will also be sensitive to the fact that many companies have already invested substantial resources to establish and document programs and procedures to perform their assessments over the last few years. The form of the guidance has yet to be determined.

139

- **Revisions to Auditing Standard No. 2.** The PCAOB announced today that it intends to propose revisions to its Auditing Standard No. 2, An Audit of Internal Control over Financial Reporting Performed in Conjunction with an Audit of Financial Statements. Any final revision of AS No. 2 would be subject to SEC approval. The proposed revisions would:

  - Seek to ensure that auditors focus during integrated audits on areas that pose higher risk of fraud or material error;
  - Incorporate key concepts contained in the guidance issued by the PCAOB on May 16, 2005; and
  - Revisit and clarify what, if any, role the auditor should play in evaluating the company's process of assessing internal control effectiveness.

  The Commission will work closely with the PCAOB to ensure that the proposed revisions to AS No. 2 are in the public interest and consistent with the protection of investors.

- **SEC Oversight of PCAOB Inspection Program.** The PCAOB announced on May 1, 2006 that it would focus its 2006 inspections on whether auditors have achieved cost-saving efficiencies in the audits they have performed under AS No. 2, and on whether auditors have followed the guidance that the PCAOB issued in May and November 2005 urging them to do so. As part of the Commission's oversight of the PCAOB, the Commission staff inspects aspects of the PCAOB's operations, including its inspection program. Among other things, upon completion of the PCAOB's 2006 inspections, the staff will examine whether the PCAOB inspections of audit firms have been effective in encouraging implementation of the principles outlined in the PCAOB's May 1, 2006 statement.

- **Extension of Compliance for Non-Accelerated Filers.** In order to permit non-accelerated filers and their auditors to have the benefit of the management guidance that the SEC intends to issue, and to have the opportunity to evaluate and implement the revisions that the PCAOB plans to make to AS No. 2, the Commission expects to issue a short postponement of the effective date of the Commission's rules implementing Section 404 for non-accelerated filers. It is anticipated that any such postponement would nonetheless require all filers to comply with the management assessment required by Section 404(a) of Sarbanes-Oxley for fiscal years beginning on or after Dec. 16, 2006.

## C.   PROXIES

### 1.   THE PROBLEM (HEREIN OF COSTS OF SOLICITATION)

*P. 534 n.17, end note.*    In The Case for Shareholder Access to the Ballot, 59 Bus. Law. 43, 46 (2003), Professor Bebchuk summarized the incidence of contested proxy solicitations between 1996 and 2002:

| Year | Contested Solicita-tions | Contests Not over Election of Directors | Directors Contests over Sale, Acqui-sition, or Closed-End Fund Restructuring | Director Contests over Alternative Management Team |
|------|------|------|------|------|
| 2002 | 38 | 5 | 19 | 14 |
| 2001 | 40 | 8 | 16 | 16 |
| 2000 | 30 | 6 | 17 | 7 |
| 1999 | 30 | 10 | 7 | 13 |
| 1998 | 20 | 1 | 6 | 13 |
| 1997 | 29 | 12 | 12 | 5 |
| 1996 | 28 | 11 | 8 | 9 |
| TOTAL | 215 | 53 | 85 | 77 |

## 2. THE STATUTORY PROVISIONS AND GENERAL PROXY RULES

c. Coverage, Definitions, and Exemptions

***P. 539, new text, end page.*** In 2005 the Commission proposed amendments to Rules 14a-2, 14a-3, 14a-4, 14a-7, 14a-8, 14a-12, 14a-13, 14b-1, 14b-2, 14c-2, 14c-3, 14c-5, 14c-7, Schedule A, Schedule C, Form 10-K, Form 10-KSB, Form 10-Q, Form 10-QSB, and Form N-SAR to provide an alternative method for issuers and third persons to furnish proxy materials by posting them on the Internet. Shareholders would be given notice of the availability of the proxy materials and could obtain copies at no cost. These proposals would not apply to business combination transactions. All existing methods of furnishing proxy materials would continue to be available. Sec. Ex. Act Rel. 52,926, 86 SEC Dock. 2145 (2005) (proposal).

The proposal Release crisply summarized the immediate background of these proposals:

> In 2000, we discussed an "access equals delivery" model and an implied consent model as possible alternatives to the existing electronic delivery conditions. In our 2000 Interpretive Release, we described the "access equals delivery" model as one under which "investors would be assumed to have access to the Internet, thereby allowing delivery to be accomplished *solely* by an issuer posting a document on the issuer's or a third party's Web site." In that release, we also described the "implied consent" model as one that would allow an issuer to rely on electronic deliver if intended recipients did not affirmatively object when notified of the issuer's or intermediary's intention to deliver documents in an electronic format.
>
> We did not take action regarding either of those models in 2000. With the passage of five years and the increased use of the Internet as a means to quickly, reliably, and inexpensively disseminate information, we think it is again appropriate to consider the effect that technological developments have had on making

information available and propose an alternative model for furnishing proxy materials.

More than 10.7 million beneficial shareholders already have given their consent to electronic delivery of proxy materials and approximately 85% of their shares were voted electronically or telephonically during the 2005 proxy season. Moreover, recent data indicates that up to 75% of Americans have access to the Internet in their homes, and that this percentage is increasing steadily among all age groups.

In connection with our recent Securities Offering Reform effort, we adopted new Securities Act Rule 172, which implements an "access equals delivery" model in the context of final prospectus delivery. Under Rule 172, a final prospectus is deemed to precede or accompany a security for sale for purposes of Securities Act Section 5(b)(2) so long as the company offering the security files with the Commission a final prospectus meeting the requirements of Securities Act Section 10(a) as part of the registration statement pursuant to Securities Act Rule 424.

Investors will be able to access the electronically filed final prospectus on EDGAR, but no longer will receive a copy unless they request one.

Id. at 2148–2149.

The proposed rule changes were intended to similarly update the proxy system:

We are proposing amendments to the proxy rules to update our regulatory framework to take advantage of communications technology and provide an alternative proxy model that could reduce the printing and mailing costs associated with furnishing proxy materials to shareholders. The proposed amendments would provide an alternative method for furnishing proxy materials to shareholders based on a "notice and access" model. Under the proposals, an issuer would be able to satisfy its obligations under the Commission's proxy rules by posting its proxy materials on a specified, publicly-accessible Internet Web site (other than the Commission's EDGAR Web site) and providing shareholders with a notice informing them that the materials are available and explaining how to access those materials. These proposals are intended to establish procedures that would promote use of the Internet as a reliable and cost-efficient means of making proxy materials available to shareholders. The proposed amendments would provide a new alternative to existing methods of furnishing proxy materials, which would not be affected by the proposal....

The proposed amendments would require an issuer that is relying on the proposed "notice and access" model to provide a shareholder with a copy of the materials upon request (in papers or by e-mail, as requested). A soliciting person other than the issuer may choose not to provide a copy of its proxy materials to a requesting shareholder if the person is conducting a conditional "electronic only" proxy solicitation and soliciting proxy authority only from shareholders willing to electronically access the soliciting person's proxy materials.

Under the proposed "notice and access" model, the issuer would be able to send a notice to shareholders (the "Notice of Internet Availability of Proxy Materials" or "Notice") at least 30 days before the meeting, or if no meeting is to be held, at least 30 days before the date the votes, consents, or authorizations may be used to effect a corporate action, indicating that the issuer's proxy materials are available on a specified Internet Web site and explaining how to access those proxy materials. The Notice also would explain the procedure for requesting a copy of the materials, if a shareholder desires such a copy.

... The amendments would permit a soliciting person to choose to rely on the proposed model as a means of furnishing some proxy-related documents to shareholders and use other means, such as paper documents, with regard to other proxy-related materials. For example, an issuer could choose to use the "notice and access" model for its proxy statement and to furnish its annual report to security holders (commonly referred to as the "glossy annual report") in paper through the U.S. mail.

Id. at 2147.

Specifically the proposed alternative means would apply to:

- Notices of shareholder meetings;
- Schedule 14A proxy statements and consent solicitation statements;
- Proxy cards;
- Schedule 14C information statements;
- Annual reports to security holders;

- Additional soliciting materials; and
- Any amendments to such materials that are required to be furnished to shareholders.

Id. at 2149.

The proposal Release specifically stated with respect to the notice and access procedure:

To notify shareholders of the availability of the proxy materials on the specified Internet Web site, an issuer relying on the proposed "notice and access" model would have to send a Notice of Internet Availability of Proxy Materials to shareholders 30 days or more in advance of the shareholder meeting date or, if no meeting is to be held, 30 days or more in advance of the date that votes, consents, or authorizations may be used to effect the corporate actions to be voted on. The 30-day period is to provide shareholders with sufficient time to receive the Notice, request copies of the materials, if desired, and review the proxy materials prior to voting. We would view the Notice as additional soliciting material that would have to be filed with the Commission pursuant to Rule 14a-6(b) no later than the date it is first sent or given to shareholders.

The proposed Notice of Internet Availability of Proxy Materials and the notice of a shareholder meeting required under state corporation law could be combined together into a single document, unless prohibited by state law. The Notice could not be combined with any document other than the state law meeting notice. We believe that it is important for the Notice to be furnished in a way that brings it to each shareholder's attention. Therefore, whether or not combined with the state law meeting notice, the Notice of Internet Availability of Proxy Materials must be sent separately from other types of shareholder communications and may not accompany any materials other than the proxy card and return envelope.

The Notice of Internet Availability of Proxy Materials would have to include the following information in clear and understandable terms:

- A prominent legend in bold-face type that states:

**"Important Notice Regarding the Availability of Proxy Materials for the Shareholder Meeting to Be Held on [insert meeting date].**

- **This communication presents only an overview of the more complete proxy materials that are available to you on the Internet. We encourage you to access and review all of the important information contained in the proxy materials before voting.**

- **The [proxy statement] [information statement] [annual report to shareholders] [proxy card] are available at [insert Web site address].**

- **If you want to receive a paper or e-mail copy of these documents, you must request one. There is no charge to you for requesting a copy. Please make your request for a copy as instructed below on or before [insert a date that is two weeks or more before the meeting date] to facilitate timely delivery. If you hold your shares through a broker, bank, or other intermediary, you must request delivery of a copy of the proxy materials through that intermediary, but it likely will take longer to receive your materials through an intermediary than directly from the company."**

- The date, time and location of the meeting or, if corporate action is to be taken by written consent, the earliest date on which the corporation action may be effected;
- A clear and impartial identification of each separate matter intended to be acted upon and the issuer's recommendations regarding those matters, but no supporting statements;
- A list of the materials being made available at the specified Web site; and
- (1) a toll-free telephone number, and (2) an e-mail address where the shareholder can request a copy of the proxy materials.

Only the information specified above and, if it is being combined with the state law meeting notice, any information required by state law, could be included in the Notice. To ensure that the Notice is clear and understandable, it would have to meet substantially the same plain English principles as apply to key sections of Securities Act prospectuses pursuant to Securities Act Rule 421(d).

Id. at 2150.

The proposal Release also elaborated on the Internet Web site:

> All proxy materials to be furnished through the "notice and access" model, other than additional soliciting materials, would have to be posted on a specified Internet Web site by the time the issuer sends the Notice of Internet Availability of Proxy Materials to shareholders. These materials would have to remain on that Web site and be accessible to shareholders through the time of the related shareholder meeting, at no charge to the shareholder.... [T]he Notice must clearly identify the Internet Web site address at which the materials are available. The Internet Web site address must be specific enough to lead shareholders directly to the proxy materials, rather than to the home page or other section of the Web site on which the proxy materials are posted, so that shareholders do not have to browse the Web site to find the materials. The Internet Web site that an issuer uses to electronically furnish its proxy materials to shareholders must be a publicly accessible Internet Web site other than the Commission's EDGAR Web site.
>
> There are two primary reasons why we propose not to allow use of the EDGAR Web site for this purpose. First, issuers are not required to furnish their glossy annual reports to the Commission using the EDGAR system. Most issuers, therefore, furnish paper copies of these annual reports to the Commission. Even with respect to the issuers that choose to furnish the annual report to the Commission via EDGAR, they generally omit graphics included in the paper version, such as charts and tables, from their EDGAR submissions. Second, it is our view that electronically posted proxy materials should be presented on the Internet Web site in a format that provides a substantially identical version of those materials, including all charts, tables, graphics, and similarly formatted information, as otherwise furnished to shareholders in a different medium such as paper. Currently, the EDGAR system accepts documents only in ASCII or HTML format. Further, documents filed on EDGAR may omit or describe, but generally do not replicate, some disclosures, including charts and graphs. As a result, merely hyperlinking from the specified publicly accessible

Internet Web site to the filing on the Commission's EDGAR system would not satisfy the requirement.

Id. at 2154.

Notably the proposed proxy revisions also apply to intermediaries such as banks circulating materials to beneficial owners under Rules 14a-13, 14b-1, and 14b-2, id. at 2156–2159, and to soliciting persons other than issuers who proceed under Rules 14a-7 and 14a-12, id. at 2159–2162.

## 4.  CONTESTED SOLICITATIONS AND SECURITY HOLDER PROPOSALS

c.  Security Holder Proposals [Rule 14a-8]

*P. 573, new text, end page.*  In July 2003 the SEC Division of Corporation Finance published Staff Report: Review of the Proxy Process Regarding the Nomination and Election of Directors, 2003 Fed. Sec. L. Rep. (CCH) ¶86,938 (July 15, 2003), in response to a proposal of the American Federation of State, County, and Municipal Employees Pension Plan to require companies to include in their proxy materials the nominee of any shareholder or group of shareholders beneficially owning 3 percent or more of a company's outstanding common stock.

The Division recommended that the SEC seek public comment with respect to improved disclosure and conditional shareholder access to the nomination process. Id. at 87,886. With respect to conditional access, the Report specifically stated:

The Division recommends that the Commission propose and solicit public comment on new proxy rules that would allow a shareholder or a group of shareholders to place their nominees in a company's proxy materials within the following parameters:

- applicable state corporate law must provide the company's shareholders with the right to nominate a candidate for election as a director;

- neither the candidacy nor the election of a shareholder nominee may otherwise violate, or cause the company to violate, controlling state law, federal law or listing standards;
- the availability of a shareholder nomination process should be premised upon the occurrence of one or more triggering events that are objective criteria evidencing potential deficiencies in the proxy process such that shareholder views — especially those of a majority — may not otherwise be adequately taken into account;
- there should be appropriate standards for independence of shareholder nominees;
- there should be minimum standards with regard to shareholdings and the length of time those shares have been held by a nominating shareholder or shareholder group; and
- there should be limitations on the total number or percentage of permitted shareholder nominees.

Id. at 32–33.

In Sec. Ex. Act Rel. 48,626, 81 SEC Dock. 770 (2003) (proposal), the Commission proposed rules based on the Staff Report. The Commission proposed a new Rule 14a-11 that would permit a security holder holding individually or in a group that beneficially owns more than 5 percent of the registration securities to nominate one or more person for the board, subject to a 500 word limit or the statement of support, provided that:

(1) Applicable state law does not prohibit the registrant's security holders from nominating a candidate or candidates for election as a director;

(2) One or more of the following events has occurred during the calendar year in which the meeting that is the subject of the proxy statement is being held or during either of the preceding two calendar years:

(i) At least one of the registrant's nominees for the board of directors for whom the registrant solicited proxies received "withhold" votes from more than 35% of the votes cast at an annual meeting of security holders (or, in lieu of an annual meeting, a special meeting) held after January 1, 2004, at which directors were elected (provided, that this event will be deemed not to occur with regard to any contested election to which [Rule] 14a-12(c) applies or an election to which this section applies); or

(ii) A security holder proposal providing that the registrant become subject to [Rule] 14a-11 that was submitted pursuant to [Rule] 14a-8 by a security holder or group of security holders that held more than 1% of the securities entitled to vote on that proposal for at least one year as of the date the proposal was submitted and provided evidence of such holding to the registrant, received more than 50% of the votes cast on that proposal at an annual meeting of security holders (or, in lieu of an annual meeting, a special meeting) held after January 1, 2004.

Under proposed Rule 14a-11(d)(l) a registrant is not required to include more than one nominee if there are fewer than eight directors; two if there are more than eight but fewer than 20; and three, if there are more than 20 directors.

Proposed Rule 14a-11 represented the first SEC rule that would have permitted direct shareholder nomination of directors. As such it was a significant proposal. The proposal was susceptible to criticism for the temporal delays that the triggering events would portend. The proposal Release was notable for not addressing SEC authority to adopt a director nomination rule, an issue that wisely might have been raised given Business Roundtable v. SEC, 905 F.2d 406 (D.C. Cir. 1990). See generally ABA Task Force Report on Proposed Changes in Proxy Rules and Regulations Regarding Procedures for the Election of Corporate Directors, 59 Bus. Law. 109, 130–136 (2003).

On December 22, 2003 the Business Roundtable filed a 76 page Comment on the SEC's proposed election contest rules stressing its belief "that the Commission lacks the statutory authority to adopt the Proposed Election Contest Rules." Detailed Comments Accompanying Letter to Jonathan G. Katz from Business Round Table Dec. 22, 2003, re: File No. S7-19-03, at 1.

In Qwest Communications Int'l Inc., 2004–2005 Fed. Sec. L. Rep. (CCH) ¶78,922 (avail. Feb. 7, 2005), Alan Beller, Director, Division of Corporation Finance, signed a no action letter response signaling that the Commission would not adopt proposed Rule 14a-11. Earlier, in Sec. Ex. Act Rel. 48,626, 81 SEC Dock. 770 (2003) (proposal), the staff was reported to have informed the Commission of its intention to take the position that a proposal under Rule 14a-8(i)(8) to adopt the procedures in the proposed Rule 14a-11 could not be excluded. In the 2005 letter, "given the passage of time," the staff now concluded that a proposal that a corporation comply with Proposed Rule 14a-11 could be excluded under Rule 14a-8(i)(8).

### 5.   FALSE OR MISLEADING STATEMENTS [RULE 14a-9]

#### a.   In General

***P. 576, new text, end 1st sentence.***   See Makor Issues & Rights Ltd. v. Tellabs, Inc., 437 F.3d 588 (7th Cir. 2006) ("Mere sales puffery is not actionable under Rule 10b-5").

***P. 576 n.139, end note.***   A determination of *buried facts* is fact specific. Cf. Benzon v. Morgan Stanley Distrib., Inc., 420 F.3d 598, 608 (6th Cir. 2005) ("All of the information from which Plaintiffs' claims regarding Defendants' failure to make statements regarding the relative merits of different class shares are drawn is available in Defendants' prospectuses").

***P. 577 n.145, end note.***   In Nolte v. Capital One Fin. Corp., 390 F.3d 311, 315 (4th Cir. 2004), the Fourth Circuit interpreted *Virginia Bankshares* to require a pleading "that the opinion expressed was different from the opinion actually held by the speaker." Here an allegation that a bank executive feared a bank would be deemed undercapitalized was insufficient to plead that he believed the company was undercapitalized. Id. at 316.

#### b.   Materiality

***P. 582 n.155, end note.***   In Vernazza v. SEC, 327 F.3d 851, 860 (9th Cir. 2003), the court concluded that "[t]he Commission correctly determined that the petitioners had a duty to disclose any potential conflicts of interest accurately and completely" and to recognize that an investment adviser's Shareholder Servicing Agreement created such a potential conflict.

Cf. Derek L. DuBois, Sec. Ex. Act Rel. 48,332, 80 SEC Dock. 2403, 2405 (2003), a Commission opinion, in which it was held: "A prospective investor would consider it material that a salesperson who was recommending a particular investment was being compensated by a third party for doing so; as a result, the salesperson's recommendation might not be disinterested."

***P. 588 n.186, end note.*** In Kapps v. Torch Offshore, Inc., 379 F.3d 207, 213 (5th Cir. 2004), the court elaborated:

> Specifically, we hold that the definition of *material* under Section 11 is not strictly limited to information that is firm-specific and nonpublic. While all material information need not be included in the registration statement, an issuer is not free to make material misrepresentations, or to omit material information that is either required to be disclosed by law or that is necessary to disclose in order to prevent statements made in the registration statement from being misleading.

***P. 588 n.187, end note.*** In Gebhardt v. ConAgra Foods, Inc., 335 F.3d 824 (8th Cir. 2003), the court declined to dismiss a complaint on materiality grounds, stating in part:

> In addressing the circumstances of this case, the District Court held that "[i]n the total mix of information available to investors, the mere fact that ConAgra's revenues were overstated by 0.4 percent, during fiscal 1998–2000 was immaterial as a matter of law," and determined that the question of materiality could be decided against the plaintiffs as a matter of law.... In our view, the quantity of a revenue overstatement, in and of itself, is not sufficient to be dispositive of this issue. Instead, we look at the total mix of data available to investors, and place the misrepresented data in context. More than a revenue loss was involved here. There was also a loss in net income, a figure that may be of more significance to investors. Here, the complaint alleges that ConAgra overstated its net income for 1999 and 2000 by 8 percent.

It is hard to say that a discrepancy of this magnitude is immaterial as a matter of law. In order to take this decision away from the jury, the circumstances must make it obvious why a reasonable investor would not be concerned about the facts misrepresented. In *Parnes*, we found it rational to conclude that investors attracted to an investment with high risk and the potential of high return are not going to be fazed by a small increase in risk. 122 F.3d at 547. No such circumstances are obvious in this case, and they rarely will be at the pleadings stage.

Id. at 830. See also Stavros v. Exelon Corp., 266 F. Supp. 2d 833, 841–842 (N.D. Ill. 2003) (declining to hold that 1.5 percent earnings per share error was immaterial on a pretrial motion).

***P. 590 n.190, end 1st par.***    A court of appeals held that a reasonable jury could find a defendant criminally liable for insider trading when he exercised employee stock options after merger negotiations had begun. United States v. Mooney, 401 F.3d 940 (8th Cir. 2005).

In United States v. Mooney, 2004 Fed. Sec. L. Rep. (CCH) ¶92,874 at 94,154 (8th Cir. 2004), the court relied in part on call option purchases to conclude that a reasonable jury could find materiality. See also Media Gen., Inc. v. Tomlin, 387 F.3d 865, 870 (D.C. Cir. 2004) (testimony by counsel to a merger target that he would have wanted to know about expanded litigation claim was sufficient to defeat defendant motion to dismiss since "[a] major factor in determining whether information was material is the importance attached to it by those who know about it").

In contrast to SEC v. Sargent, 229 F.3d 68 (1st Cir. 2000), in SEC v. Happ, 392 F.3d 12 (1st Cir. 2004), sufficient circumstantial evidence was presented that defendant possessed and used material nonpublic information in deciding to sell stock when he did.

Whether omitted information is material may also involve the efficient market hypothesis. In Merck & Co. Sec. Litig., 432 F.3d 261, 268–271 (3d Cir. 2005), the court focused on the speed at which information was reflected in a stock price to analyze whether an omission was material. Citing Basic v. Levinson, 485 U.S. 224, 228 n.28 (1988), Burlington Coat Factory Sec. Litig.,

114 F.3d 1410, 1425 (3d Cir. 1997), and Oran v. Stafford, 226 F.3d 275, 282 (3d Cir. 2000), the court concluded that new publicly available information should be absorbed "immediately following disclosure," although not necessary instantaneously. 432 F.3d at 269.

## D.   TENDER OFFERS

## 2.   THE WILLIAMS ACT AND OTHER FEDERAL SECURITIES LAWS

### c.   Tender Offers [§14(d), Related Rules, and Schedules]

(iv) *Substantive Requirements*

***P. 643 n.107, end note.***    In WHX Corp., Sec. Ex. Act Rel. 47,980, 80 SEC Dock. 1153 (2003), the Commission found a violation of Rule 14d-10(a)(1) when shareholders, unable to provide a proxy vote at a shareholder meeting, could not participate in a tender offer.

On appeal the District of Columbia Court of Appeals, reversed. WHX Corp. v. SEC, 362 F.3d 854 (D.C. Cir. 2004). The court gave "great deference" to the SEC standard for issuing a cease and desist order, citing KMPG Peat Marwick LLP, 289 F.3d 109 (D.C. Cir. 2002), but found that application of that standard here was arbitrary and capricious in the court's view:

> WHX committed (at most) a single, isolated violation of the rule, it immediately withdrew the offending condition once the Commission had made its official position clear, and the Commission has offered no reason to doubt WHX's assurances that it will not violate the rule in the future. In light of these factors, none of which the Commission seems to have considered seriously, the imposition of the cease-and-desist order seems all the more gratuitous.

WHX Corp. at 861.

Rule 14d-10 has occasioned two major interpretative challenges in the courts.

First, *when* does a tender offer occur under the Rule? The courts are divided between those that favor a flexible or functional approach such as Epstein v. MCA, Inc., 50 F.3d 644 (9th Cir. 1995), *rev'd on other grounds sub nom.* Matsushita Elec. Indus. Corp. v. Epstein, 516 U.S. 367; Gerber v. Computer Assoc. Int'l, Inc., 303 F.3d 126 (2d Cir. 2002) and those that favor a more literal or bright line approach. See Lerro v. Quaker Oats Co., 84 F.3d 239 (7th Cir. 1996). Cf. Digital Island Sec. Litig., 357 F.3d 322 (3d Cir. 2004) (recognizing under *Lerro* that some payments made outside of the tender offer period may be so transparently fraudulent as to require them to be treated as made "during the tender offer"). The *Digital Island* case correctly recognizes that too rigid a rule can invite schemes to circumvent or "game" the rule. This does not appear to be consistent with the intent of the SEC in adopting Rule 14d-10, which appeared to cast a very wide net:

> Similarly, Section 14(d)(7) assures equality of treatment among all security holders who tender their shares by requiring that any increase in consideration offered to security holders be paid to all security holders whose shares are taken up during the offer. One of Congress' purposes in promulgating the provision was "to assure equality of treatment among all shareholders who tender their shares." These substantive provisions assume that offers will be made to all security holders and not just to a select few, and that offers will not be made to security holders at varying prices. Without the all-holders requirement and bestprice provision, the specific protections provided by Sections 14(d)(6) and (d)(7) would be vitiated because an offeror could simply address its offer either to a privileged group of security holders who hold the desired number of shares or to all security holders but for different considerations. The all-holders requirement and best-price provision both are consistent with Congressional intent and complement the pro rata and equal price protections of the Williams Act.

Sec. Ex. Act Rel. 23,421, 36 SEC Dock. 96, 99–100 (1986).

Second, does Rule 14d-10 also apply to employment contracts between bidders and target company executives or solely to share purchases? Cf. Walther, Employment Agreements and Tender Offers: Reforming the Problem Treatment of Severance Plans Under Rule 14d-10, 102 Colum. L. Rev. 774 (2002).

In 2005 the Commission proposed amendments to the tender offer best-price Rules 13e-4 and 14d-10. Sec. Ex. Act Rel. 52,968, 86 SEC Dock. 2394 (2005) (proposal).

Both Rules 13e-4(f)(8)(ii) and 14d-10(a)(2) were proposed to be amended to clarify that the best-price rules apply only to consideration offered and paid for securities tendered in a tender offer. This proposal was made in response to a conflict between courts that held that the best-price rule applies to all integral elements of a tender offer, including employment compensation, severance, and other employee benefits, see, e.g., Epstein v. MCA Inc., 50 F.3d 644 (9th Cir. 1995), *rev'd on other grounds sub nom.* Matsushita Elec. Indus. Co. v. Epstein, 516 U.S. 367 (1996), and courts that held that the best-price rule only applies to agreements between the time a tender offer formally commences and expires, see, e.g., Kramer v. Time Warner Inc., 937 F.2d 767 (2d Cir. 1991); Lerro v. Quaker Oats, 84 F.3d 239 (7th Cir. 1996); Digital Island Sec. Litig., 357 F.3d 322 (3d Cir. 2004).

The Commission neither subscribed to the integra-part nor to the bright-line test:

> We do not believe that the best-price rule should be subject to a strict temporal test. We also do not believe that all payments that are conditioned on or otherwise somehow related to a tender offer, including payments under compensatory or commercial arrangements that are made to persons who happen to be security holders, whether made before, during or after the tender offer period, should be subject to the best-price rule. Accordingly, we are proposing amendments to the best-price rule that do not follow the approach of either the integral-part or the bright-line test. Instead, the proposed amendments would refocus the determination as to potential violations of the best-price rule on whether any consideration paid to security holders for securities

tendered into an offer is the highest consideration paid to any other security holder for securities tendered into the tender offer.

The premise of the best-price rule is that bidders must pay consideration of equal value to all security holders for the securities that they tender in a tender offer. Accordingly, an analysis of the best-price rule must include a consideration of whether any security holders have been paid additional or different consideration for the securities they tendered in the offer.

Our proposed amendments recognize that if purchases of securities are deemed to be made as part of a tender offer, then the consideration paid for all securities tendered in the offer must satisfy the best-price rule. We propose to amend the best-price rule to establish clearly that it applies with respect to the consideration offered and paid for securities tendered in the tender offer. Specifically, we propose to revise the best-price rule to state that a bidder shall not make a tender offer unless "[t]he consideration paid to any security holder for securities tendered in the tender offer is the highest consideration paid to any other security holder for securities tendered in the tender offer." In doing so, the clause "for securities tendered in the tender offer" would replace the current clauses "pursuant to the tender offer" and "during such tender offer" to clarify the intent of the best-price rule.

Id. at 2398–2399.

The proposal is more precise in its use of the phrase "for securities tendered" rather than "pursuant to" a tender offer. Consideration paid for other arrangements, including compensation and commercial arrangements, accordingly would not be within the scope of the best-price rules.

Augmenting this proposed amendment was a proposed specific exemption to Rule 14d-10(c) for:

> The negotiation, execution or amendment of an employment compensation, severance or other employee benefit arrangement, or payments made or to be made or benefits granted or to be granted according to such arrangements, with respect to employees and directors of the subject company, where the amount payable under the arrangement: (i) relates solely to past services performed or future services to be performed or refrained from performing, by the employee or director (and matters incidental

157

thereto), and (ii) is not based on the number of securities the employee or director owns or tenders.

We believe that amounts paid pursuant to employment compensation, severance or other employee benefit arrangements should not be considered when calculating the price paid for tendered securities. These payments are made for a different purpose.

Id. at 2400.

The Commission also proposed a compensation committee safe harbor in Rule 14d-10(c) for bidders and subject companies who enter employment compensation, severance, and employee benefits arrangements during a third-party tender offer subject to Rule 14d-10:

> The safe harbor provision would allow the compensation committee or a committee performing similar functions of the subject company's or bidder's board of directors, depending on whether the subject company or the bidder is the party to the arrangement, to approve an employment compensation, severance or other employee benefit arrangement and thus have it deemed to be an arrangement within the exemption of the proposed rule. The proposed safe harbor would require that the compensation committee or the committee performing similar functions be comprised solely of independent directors. Specifically, the proposals would add the following sentence to new proposed Rule 14d-10(c)(3):
>
>> For purposes of paragraph (c)(2) of this section, pursuant to this non-exclusive safe harbor, an arrangement shall be deemed an employment compensation, severance or other employee benefit arrangement if it is approved as meeting the requirements of paragraphs (c)(2)(i) and (ii) of this section by the compensation committee of the subject company's or bidder's (depending on whether the subject company or bidder is a party to the arrangement) board of directors. If that company's board of directors does not have a compensation committee, the arrangement shall be deemed an employment compensation, severance or other employee benefit arrangement if it is so approved by the committee of that board of directors that performs functions similar to a compensation committee. In each circumstance, the

arrangement shall be deemed an employment compensation, severance or other employee benefit arrangement only if the approving compensation committee or the committee performing similar functions is comprised solely of independent directors.

Id. at 2402.

With respect to determining independence, the proposed revision would:

Include an instruction to Rule 14d-10(c)(3) providing that if the bidder or the subject company, as the case may be, is a listed issuer whose securities are listed on a registered national securities exchange or in an automated inter-dealer quotation system of a national securities association that has independence requirements for compensation committee members, the independence standards for compensation committee members as defined in the listing standards applicable to listed issuers should be used. Alternatively, if the bidder or the subject company is not a listed issuer, in determining whether a member of the compensation committee is independent, the bidder or subject company would use a definition of independence of a national securities exchange or a national securities association, so long as whatever definition is chosen is used consistently for all members of the compensation committee.

Id. at 2403.

## F.   SARBANES-OXLEY ACT AMENDMENTS

### 1.   PROHIBITIONS ON LOANS

*P. 726, new note 0, end 1st sentence.*    In 2004 the Commission adopted Rule 13k-1 to exempt an issuer that is a foreign bank or its parent from the §13(k) prohibition on insider lending. Sec. Ex. Act Rel. 48,481, 81 SEC Dock. 107 (2003) (proposal); 49,616, 82 SEC Dock. 2538 (2004) (adoption).

CHAPTER 7

# REGULATION OF THE SECURITIES MARKETS

## A. STRUCTURE OF THE SECURITIES MARKETS

### 1. INTRODUCTION

*P. 739, new text after 2d par.* In the aftermath of Richard Grasso's resignation as NYSE Chair, and a major enforcement action against NYSE specialists, questions concerning the NYSE system of governance received renewed attention. See, e.g., Cohen, Craig & Dugan, NYSE Trading Probe Took Late, Sharp Turn, Wall St. J., Oct. 17, 2003, at C1; see also Craig, Kelly & Dugan, NYSE Traders Are Subject of Investigation, Wall St. J., Mar. 4, 2004, at C1.

John Reed, former co-chair of Citigroup, was named interim chair of the NYSE in September 2003. Thomas & Labaton, New Roles and New Faces at the New York Stock Exchange, N.Y. Times, Oct. 17, 2003 at C1; Reed Defends Self-Regulation for NYSE, Outlines Plans for Election of New Board, 35 Sec. Reg. & L. Rep. (BNA) 1732 (2003).

In November Reed proposed and the NYSE membership approved several proposals to change NYSE governance. These proposals were subject to SEC review and approval. Reed proposed eight candidates for election to the reconstituted board: Madeleine K. Albright, Herbert M. Allison, Jr., Euan D. Baird, Marshall N. Carter, Shirley Ann Jackson, James S. McDonald,

Robert B. Shapiro, and Sir Dennis Weatherstone. These new members were intended to serve until June 2004 after which the entire board would stand for election each June.

The Reed proposals to amend the NYSE Constitution envisioned both a streamlined board of directors with 6 to 12 directors and a board of executives, appointed by the board of directors, comprised of approximately 20 constituent representatives, balanced among the major broker-dealer firms, the floor community, lessor members, institutional investors, large public funds, and listed companies. The board of directors would select the Chairman and the CEO each June, although the Reed proposal did not resolve whether this would be one or two persons. The board of directors would meet no less than four times a year, Art. IV §6 of Proposed NYSE Constitution, and was empowered to delegate specified powers to committees or the board of executives. Art. IV §14. The board of directors would have authority for rulemaking, supervision, and listing of securities. Art. VIII. It would also be responsible for disciplinary proceedings, Art. IX, membership fees, Art. X, and arbitration, Art. XI.

Under the proposed Constitution, the Nominating and Governance, Human Resources and Compensation, Audit, and Regulatory Oversight and Regulatory Budget committees were required to consist solely of members of the board of directors. Art. IV §12(a).

There are also new proposed joint committees comprising both members of the board of directors and board of executives to address regulation and enforcement and listing standards. Art. IV §12(b).

The board of directors and board of executives were authorized further to meet in joint sessions several times a year.

The board of executives was intended to provide "reasonably balanced representation of the many communities that come together in the Exchange." Art. V §2(a). Cf. §6(b)(3) of Securities Exchange Act. The Chairman of the board of directors would also be Chairman of the board of executives. If there is a separate CEO he or she would also be a member of the board of executives.

The Board of Executives members (other than the Chairman and Chief Executive Officer) shall be appointed by the Board at its annual organizational meeting and shall consist of (i) at least six individuals who are either the chief executive or a principal executive officer of a member organization that engages in a business involving substantial direct contact with securities customers, (ii) at least two individuals who are either the chief executive or a principal executive officer of a specialist member organization, (iii) at least two individuals, each of whom spends a majority of his or her time on the Floor of the Exchange, and has as a substantial part of his or her business the execution of transactions on the Floor of the Exchange for other than his or her own account or the account of his or her member organization, but who shall not be registered as a specialist, (iv) at least two individuals who are lessor members who are not affiliated with a broker or dealer in securities, (v) at least four individuals who are either the chief executive or a principal executive officer of an institution that is a significant investor in equity securities, at least one of whom shall be a fiduciary of a public pension fund, and (vi) at least four individuals who are either the chief executive or a principal executive officer of a listed company.... If the Board increases the size of the Board of Executives it shall strive to maintain approximately the same balance between Industry Members of the Board of Executives and other members of the Board of Executives as is represented above.

Art. V §2(b).

The board of executives shall meet at least six times each year.
Art. V §6(a).

The Reed proposal envisioned permitting the board of directions to fashion the role of the Chair. However, in Art. VI §2, the Restated Constitution does provide:

The Chairman shall preside at all meetings of the Board and of the Board of Executives and shall decide all questions of order, subject, however, to an appeal to the Board; provided, however, that if the Chairman is also the Chief Executive Officer, he or she shall not participate in executive sessions of the Board. If the Chairman is not the Chief Executive Officer, he or she shall act as liaison officer between the Board and the Chief Executive

163

Officer. In addition to his or her usual duties, the Chairman shall make an Annual Report on the Exchange's activities to a Plenary Session.

Art. VI §1 specifies additional officers, including the Chief Regulatory Officer, one or more Vice Presidents (one or more of whom may be designated as Executive Vice Presidents or as Senior Vice Presidents or by other designations), a Secretary, a Treasurer, a Controller, and such other officers as the CEO may propose, subject to the approval of the board. Any office may be occupied by more than one individual.

The board of directors was also intended to maintain other advisory committees. NYSE Proxy Notice of Special Meeting at 8 (Nov. 4, 2003).

Reed emphasized the transparency of the revised board of directors:

(1) Prior to the Annual Meeting, we will publish a proxy statement disclosing the Board Committee charters and the Committee reports on their activities for the year; membership on the Board, on the Board of Executives, and on the various standing and advisory Committees; the facts establishing each Board member's independence, including any non-director relationship between Board members and the NYSE itself and any material relationships among Board members; and Board compensation.

(2) We will publicly disclose information regarding the means by which members and investors may communicate with the NYSE's non-management directors.

(3) The annual report of the Human Resources & Compensation Committee will detail compensation decisions for the top five officers, the existence of any contracts for these individuals and the compensation for the top management team as a whole. The Committee will detail the competitive comparisons and performance judgments that guided their recommendations.

(4) The Nominating & Governance Committee will explain its nominations and make public the procedures that are in place to ensure that appropriate potential nominees are found and considered.

(5) The Board of Directors will detail the considerations that lead to membership on the Board of Executives, and the current membership. A report of the activities of the Board of Executives will be included in the proxy statement.

(6) The various advisory committees of the NYSE will be identified and described, and their members listed in the proxy statement.

(7) An annual report detailing the charitable activities of or on behalf of the Exchange, including the activities of the NYSE Foundation, will be included with the proxy statement.

(8) A report disclosing NYSE political activities, including a list of political contributions made by any NYSE PAC, will be made available prior to the annual meeting.

John Reed Letter to NYSE Members, Nov. 4, 2003, at 3–4.

Two days earlier the *Wall Street Journal* published a front page article describing a 40 page SEC staff report that sharply criticizes the NYSE for laxity in the investigation and discipline of specialists. The Staff Report allegedly concluded that over 22 billion shares were improperly traded over three years, costing investors $155 million. Solomon & Craig, SEC Blasts Big Board Oversight of "Specialist" Trading Firms, Wall St. J., Nov. 3, 2003, at A1. Subsequently the California Public Employees Retirement System (CalPERS) sued the NYSE and seven specialist firms over these practices. CalPERS Sues NYSE, Specialist Firms, Claiming Trading Practices Hurt Investors, 35 Sec. Reg. & L. Rep. (BNA) 2128 (2003); Two NYSE Specialist Firms Settle SEC, Exchange Allegations, 36 Sec. Reg. & L. Rep. (BNA) 331 (2004).

In December 2003 the SEC approved the NYSE reorganization as proposed. Sec. Ex. Act Rel. 48,946, 81 SEC Dock. 2676, 2685 (2003). The Commission concluded its approval of the NYSE reorganization somewhat tentatively:

> The Commission believes that the revised NYSE governance structure is one, but not the only, model for SRO governance consistent with the Act that would provide independence between the business side of the Exchange and its regulatory operations. Other self-regulatory structures or allocations of regulatory duties among SROs may offer advantages and disadvantages in terms of

expertise, effectiveness, responsiveness, costs and, ultimately, investor protection. In considering the NYSE proposal, some commenters have advocated the complete separation of market and SRO functions. In the Commission's view, the complete structural separation of the NYSE's—or any other SRO's—regulatory function cannot be accomplished by an individual SRO, but would require Commission or Congressional action on a market-wide basis.

The Commission is considering a regulatory initiative to assess possible steps to strengthen the framework for the governance of SROs. In addition, the Commission will continue to consider ways to improve the transparency of the governance procedures of all SROs. In this context, some of the transparency topics the Commission may examine include increasing the disclosure of information relating to compensation of SRO directors, officers and employees; regulatory performance (*e.g.*, number of enforcement actions); types and amounts of fines levied; financial information and financial results; and the operation of key committees.

Id. at 2690.

In 2004, the Commission published a detailed rule proposal with respect to stock market governance, Sec. Ex. Act Rel. 50,699, 84 SEC Dock. 444 (2004) (proposal), as well as a related Concept Release. Cf. Seligman, Cautious Evolution or Perennial Irresolution: Stock Market Self-Regulation during the First Seventy Years of the Securities and Exchange Commission, 59 Bus. Law. 1347 (2004).

The Concept Release emphasized the inherent conflicts between SRO functions and SRO members, market operations, listed issuers, and shareholders:

## 1. INHERENT CONFLICTS WITH MEMBERS

The SROs are responsible for promulgating and enforcing rules that govern all aspects of their members' securities business, including their financial condition, operational capabilities, sales practices, and the qualifications of their personnel. In fulfilling these functions, the SROs conduct examinations on the premises of their members, monitor financial and other operational reports, investigate potential violations of rules, and bring disciplinary proceedings when appropriate. In addition, SROs must surveil trading on any markets they operate to detect rule violations and other improper practices, such as insider trading and market manipulation. Unchecked conflicts in the dual role of regulating and serving can result in poorly targeted SRO rulemaking, less extensive SRO rulemaking, and under zealous enforcement of SRO rules against members.... If [the SRO] regulatory staff is disinclined to regulate members, self-regulation will fail. Thus, to be effective, an SRO must be structured in such a way that regulatory staff is unencumbered by inappropriate business pressure.

Pressures that inhibit effective regulation and discourage vigorous enforcement against members can arise for a variety of reasons, including member domination of SRO funding, member control of SRO governance, and member influence over regulatory and enforcement staff. In addition, the economic importance of certain SRO members may create particularly acute conflicts, especially in light of the consolidation of some of the largest securities firms. For example, the number of NYSE specialist firms, which are control to the NYSE's auction trading model, has dropped from 27 in 1999 to 7 in 2002. One NYSE specialist firm in 2003 accounted for over 28% of total NYSE trading volume....

Thus, the current situation appears to be one in which a declining number of member firms are increasingly important to the business interests of their regulator SROs. The anecdotal evidence cited above could indicate that SROs have become more dependent on large members for their funding, potentially enabling those members to wield significant influence with respect to their regulator SROs. This creates the potential for failures by SROs to enforce rules against these members, especially when compared to enforcement against other smaller or less economically influential members, and SRO failures to develop rules that would disrupt the business practices of important members.

The PCX's proposal in 2001 to enter into an arrangement in which ArcaEx would become the PCX's equity trading facility presented a particularly complicated situation in which an SRO would be affiliated with a member. In the ArcaEx Approval Order, the Commission examined a variety of issues related to self-regulation, including the regulatory responsibilities of the

PCX under the new structure and the potential for inherent conflicts to be exacerbated when an SRO is affiliated with a member. In addition, the Commission imposed certain requirements with respect to PCX and ArcaEx that were designed to ensure that the various functions of the affiliated brokerdealer were properly regulated.

In an ArcaEx Approval Order, the Commission discussed the PCX's proposal that Wave Securities LLC ("Wave"), a wholly owned subsidiary of ArcaEx, would be a registered broker-dealer and a member of both the PCX and the NASD. Wave would have two primary functions with respect to Arca-Ex. Specifically, Wave would act as an introducing broker for customers that were not PCX members and would provide sponsored access to ArcaEx. Wave would also provide an optional routing service for ArcaEx, and, as necessary, would route orders to other market centers from ArcaEx.

Under Section 6(b)(5) of the Exchange Act, the rules of a national securities exchange must not be designed to permit unfair discrimination between customers, issuers, brokers, or dealers. The Commission noted in the ArcaEx Approval Order that the potential for unfair discrimination may be heightened if a national securities exchange or its affiliate owns or operates a broker-dealer. This is because, the Commission stated, the financial interests of the exchange may conflict with its responsibilities as an SRO regarding the affiliated broker-dealer. Moreover, the Commission described the conflict of interest that may arise if a national securities exchange (or an affiliate) provides advantages to its broker-dealer that are not available to other members, or provides a feature to all members that was designed to give its broker-dealer a special advantage. These advantages, such as greater access to information, improved speed of execution, or enhanced operational capabilities in dealing with the exchange, might constitute unfair discrimination under the Exchange Act, the Commission concluded. Thus, the Commission required that the PCX not serve as the self-regulatory organization primarily responsible for examining the Wave broker-dealer. . . .

## 2. INHERENT CONFLICTS WITH MARKET OPERATIONS

In addition to conflicts with members, an SRO's regulatory obligations may conflict with the interests of its own or its affiliate's market operations. The SROs that operate markets ...

are responsible for promulgating rules that govern trading in their markets; establishing the necessary systems and procedures to monitor such trading; identifying instances of suspicious trading, such as potential insider trading and market manipulation; and enforcing the Exchange Act, the rules thereunder, and their own rules. If an SRO identifies potential misconduct involving persons or entities within its jurisdiction, the SRO is responsible for conducting a further investigation and bringing a disciplinary action when appropriate. . . .

As competition among markets grows, the markets that SROs operate will continue to come under increased pressure to attract order flow. This business pressure can create a strong conflict between the SRO regulatory and market operations functions. Because increasing inter-market competition has provided members ... with increasing flexibility as to where to direct order flow, SRO staff may be less inclined to enforce vigorously SRO rules that would cause large liquidity providers to redirect order flow. ...

While regulatory staff is responsible for carrying out self-regulatory obligations, they are also a component of a competitive business organization. As inter-market competition increases, regulatory staff may come under pressure to permit market activity that attracts order flow to their market. Market operations staff may also be less likely to cooperate and communicate with regulatory staff if they think such cooperation or communication will hinder their effort to attract order flow. . . .

Another concern is the potential for SRO regulatory staff, in the course of developing rules and examining members, to become overly dependent on members for their understanding of market practices and to lose their independent perspective concerning these practices. A potential loss of objectivity could accompany the greater knowledge and expertise that result from having SRO regulatory staff interwoven with SRO market operations.

Also, SROs may have a tendency to abuse their SRO status by over-regulating members that operate markets that compete with the SRO's own market for order flow. Indeed, among other reasons, these concerns led the Commission to require the NASD to establish the Alternative Display Facility ("ADF"). Exchange Act rule 11Ac1-1 requires that SRO members communicate their best bids and offers to an SRO and in the late 1990s broker-dealer choice as to where to post quotes in Nasdaq securities was effectively limited to Nasdaq. Thus, certain users of Nasdaq were concerned that they would be put at a distinct competitive disadvantage if they were compelled to provide their best bids and offers to the exclusive Securities Information Processor ("SIP") for Nasdaq securities through the new SuperMontage system. These users argued that, not only would their quotes be subject to a competing market's trading rules, but that the situation would be rife for abuse because of Nasdaq functioning both as a regulator and competitor of the ECNs. Thus, before permitting the launch of Nasdaq's SuperMontage, the Commission required that the NASD provide an alternative, the ADF, to Nasdaq's Super-Montage on which to quote Nasdaq securities....

### 3.   INHERENT CONFLICTS WITH ISSUERS

Another potential SRO conflict is with listed issuers. The SROs promulgate and administer listing standards that govern the securities that may be traded in their markets. For corporate securities, these rules include minimum financial qualifications and reporting requirements for their issuers. Obtaining a listing on a prominent SRO market provides corporate issuers with enhanced visibility and prestige in the eyes of investors, as well as the appearance of a well-operated and well-regulated trading market for their securities. An active market for secondary trading serves not only its shareholders, but also the corporation itself through enhanced capital-raising capacities.

SRO listing standards also have a major role in corporate governance, particularly since the passage of the Sarbanes-Oxley Act....

As issuers are offered new alternatives as to markets on which to list their securities, SROs face increasing competitive pressure to gain and retain listings. As with SRO competition for members and order flow, competition for issuers may cause an SRO to fail to discharge its self-regulatory responsibilities properly. This can take the form of admitting to trading issuers that fail to satisfy initial listing standards; delaying the delisting of issuers that no longer satisfy maintenance standards; failing to enforce listing standards (including the new issuer corporate governance standards); and reducing (or even eliminating) listing fees. This competition also can reveal itself in an unwillingness to restrict issuer activities or impose requirements that may be more stringent than similar rules of competitor SROs. . . .

### 4.   INHERENT CONFLICTS WITH SHAREHOLDERS

Another significant conflict of interest for SRO responsibilities is with SRO shareholders. SRO demutualization raises the concern that the profit motive of a shareholder-owned SRO could detract from proper self-regulation. For instance, shareholder owned SROs may commit insufficient funds to regulatory operations or use their disciplinary function as a revenue generator with respect to member firms that operate competing trading systems or whose trading activity is otherwise perceived as undesirable. Moreover, as with the inherent conflicts discussed above, this conflict can be exacerbated by increased intermarket competition.

A variety of ownership controls for demutualized SROs can potentially prevent some of these conflicts. Indeed, as previously noted, this concept release is being published in conjunction with the SRO Governance and Transparency Proposal, which would, if adopted, impose a variety of restrictions, including an effective restriction on revenue from regulatory operations being used to pay dividends to shareholders.

Id. at 624–631. See also id. at 633–646 (recent intermarket surveillance and funding stresses on SRO regulation).

To ensure fair administration of SRO governance, the Commission proposed identical new Rule 6a-5 applicable to national securities exchanges and new Rule 15Aa-3 applicable to registered securities associations:

The proposals would apply to exchanges and associations minimum governance standards that are commensurate with standards required of listed issuers. Among other provisions, the proposed rules would require an exchange's or association's governing board to be composed of a majority of independent directors, with key board committees to be composed solely of independent directors. . . .

The proposed governance rules also would require each exchange and association to separate its regulatory function from its market operations and other commercial interests, whether through functional or organizational separation. Although a premise underlying self-regulation is that regulation works best when it is carried out in proximity to the regulated activity, it is equally important that there be sufficient independence within the self-regulatory process to adequately check undue interference or influence from the persons or entities being regulated. In the Commission's view, the proposed rules would help insulate the regulatory activities of an exchange or association from the conflicts of interest that otherwise may arise by virtue of its market operations.

In addition, the proposed rules would require an exchange or association to establish ownership and voting limitations on the interest of its members that are brokers or dealers in the exchange, association, or a facility of the exchange or association through which the member is permitted to effect transactions. Members who trade on an exchange or through a facility of an exchange or association have traditionally had ownership interests in such exchange or facility. Recent developments, including the trend towards demutualization, have raised the concern that a member's interest could become so large as to cast doubt on whether the exchange or association could fairly and objectively exercise its self-regulatory responsibilities with respect to that member.... The Commission believes that the proposed rules would help mitigate the conflicts of interest that could occur if a member were to control a significant stake in its regulator, and are necessary and appropriate to help ensure that an exchange or association can effectively carry out its statutory obligations under Section 6(b) or 15A(b) of the Exchange Act, respectively.

Id. at 455–456.

Proposed Rules 6a-5 and 15Aa-3 apply respectively to each national securities exchange and generally to each of its regulatory subsidiaries. Proposed Rule 6a-5(a); Proposed Rule 15Aa-3(a). There are exceptions for a national securities exchange registered under §6(g)(1) and a limited purpose national securities association under §15A(k)(1).

Proposed Rules 6a-5 and 15Aa-3 would impose identical substantive requirements with respect to each covered exchange and covered securities association.

Proposed Rules 6a-5(c)(1) and 15Aa-3(c)(1) would expressly require that the board of each national securities exchange and registered securities association be composed of a majority of independent directors. The proposal Release further notes: "SROs, of course, can elect to implement a greater proportion of independent directors." Id. at 458. A footnote notes that the NYSE has done so. Id. at 458 n.94.

Currently the exchanges, the NASA, and the Nasdaq divide their boards between industry, non-industry, and public directors. Under this construct:

> An *industry* director is generally an individual who is an officer, director or employee of a broker or dealer or an affiliate of a broker or dealer, a consultant or employee of the exchange itself, or an exchange permit holder. *See, e.g.*, NASD Bylaws, Articles I(n) and I(o) and Phlx Bylaws, Article I, Section 1-1(m).
>
> A *non-industry* director may be an individual who has some relationship with the SRO or the financial services industry; thus, a non-industry director could not be considered truly *public*. For example, officers and employees of issuers listed on the exchange are considered non-industry directors. *See, e.g.*, Phlx Bylaws, Article I, Section 1-1(t) and CHX Bylaws, Article III, Section 10(1).
>
> A *public* director is generally an individual who has no material business relationship with a broker or dealer or with the exchange or association. *See, e.g.*, NASD Bylaws, Articles I(ee) and I(ff); Phlx Bylaws, Article I, Section 1-1(y); and CHX Bylaws, Article III, Section 10(2).

Id. at 458. A number of exchanges require that at least 50 percent of the board be composed of public and non-industry directors. Id. at 458–459.

The SEC rule proposals notably alter this allocation to require a majority of each covered securities exchange and securities association be the equivalent to *public* directors. Proposed Rules 6a-5(c)(2) and 15Aa-3(c)(2) provide:

> No director may qualify as an independent director unless the Board affirmatively determines that the director has no material relationship with the national securities exchange or any affiliate

of the national securities exchange. The Board must make this determination upon the director's nomination or appointment to the Board and thereafter no less frequently than annually and as often as necessary in light of the director's circumstances.

More significantly proposed Rules 6a-5(b)(12) and 15Aa-3(b)(13) elaborately provide:

> The term *independent director* means a director who has no material relationship with the national securities exchange or any affiliate of the national securities exchange, any member of the national securities exchange or any affiliate of such member, or any issuer of securities that are listed or traded on the national securities exchange or a facility of the national securities exchange. A director is not independent if any of the following circumstances exist:

> (i) The director, or an immediate family member, is employed by or otherwise has a material relationship with the national securities exchange or any affiliate of the national securities exchange, or within the past three years was employed by or otherwise had a material relationship with the national securities exchange or any affiliate of the national securities exchange.

> (ii) The director is a member or is employed by or affiliated with a member or any affiliate of a member or, within the past three years was a member or was employed by or affiliated with a member or any affiliate of a member, or the director has an immediate family member that is, or within the past three years was, an executive officer of a member or any affiliate of a member.

> (iii) The director, or an immediate family member, has received during any twelve month period within the past three years more than $60,000 in payments from the national securities exchange or any affiliate of the national securities exchange or from a member or any affiliate of a member, other than the following:

> (A) Compensation for Board or Board committee service;

> (B) Compensation to an immediate family member who is not an executive officer of the national securities exchange or any affiliate of the national securities exchange or of a member of any affiliate of a member; and

174

(C) Pension and other forms of deferred compensation for prior service, provided such compensation is not contingent in any way on continued service.

(iv) The director, or an immediate family member, is a partner in, or controlling shareholder or executive officer of any organization to which the national securities exchange or any affiliate of the national securities exchange made, or from which the national securities exchange or any affiliate of the national securities exchange received, payments for property or services in the current or any of the past three full fiscal years that exceed two percent of the recipient's consolidated gross revenues for that year, or $200,000, whichever is more, other than the following:

(A) Payments arising solely from investments in the securities of the national securities exchange or any facility or affiliate of the national securities exchange; or

(B) Payments under non-discretionary charitable contribution matching programs.

(v) The director, or an immediate family member, is, or within the past three years was, an executive officer of an issuer of securities listed or primarily traded on the national securities exchange or a facility of the national securities exchange.

(vi) The director, or an immediate family member, is, or within the past three years was, employed as an executive officer of another entity where any of the national securities exchange's executive officers serves on that entity's compensation committee.

(vii) The director, or an immediate family member, is a current partner of the outside auditor of the national securities exchange or any affiliate of the national securities exchange, or was a partner or employee of the outside auditor of the national securities exchange or any affiliate of the national securities exchange who worked on the national securities exchange's or any affiliate's audit, at any time within the past three years.

(viii) In the case of a director that is a member of the Audit Committee, such director (other than in his or her capacity as a member of the Audit Committee, the Board, or any other Board committee), accepts, directly or indirectly, any consulting, advisory, or other compensatory fee from the national securities exchange, any affiliate of the national securities exchange, any member, or affiliate of a member, other than fixed amounts of pension and other forms of deferred compensation for prior service, provided such compensation is not contingent in any way on continued service.

Other definitions amplify the independent director definition.

An *immediate family member*, under proposed Rules 6a-5(b)(11) and 15Aa-3(b)(12) "means a person's spouse, parents, children, and siblings, whether by blood, marriage, or adoption, or anyone residing on such person's home."

*Compensation*, as defined in proposed Rules 6a-5(b)(6) and 15Aa-3(b)(7):

> means any form of compensation and any material perquisites awarded, or that are to be awarded, whether or not set forth in any written documents, to any executive officer of the national securities exchange, including, without limitation, salary, bonus, pension, deferred compensation, compensation awarded pursuant to any incentive plan or equity-based plan, or any other plan, contract, authorization or arrangement pursuant to which cash or securities may be received.

However, "[t]he Commission believes that compensation received as deferred compensation for prior service should not by itself exclude a director from being considered independent." Id. at 460.

Those requirements "are similar to criteria that are contained in SRO listing standards, which recently were approved by the Commission and are designed to address similar governance concerns and the conflicts of interest that can arise between a company's management and its public shareholders." Id. at 461.

There are other independent board requirements. Each covered securities exchange or covered securities association is required to establish policies and procedures that require each director to inform the exchange or association of the existence of any relationship or interest that may reasonably be considered to bear on whether the director is an independent director. Proposed Rules 6a-5(c)(3) and 15Aa-3(c)(3). See also proposed Rules 6a-5(c)(9) and 15Aa-3(c)(9) (covered exchange or association also must establish procedures for interested persons to communicate their concerns regarding any matter within the authority or jurisdiction of a standing committee directly to the independent directors).

At least 20 percent of the total number of directors must be selected by members. Proposed Rules 6a-5(c)(4) and 15Aa-3(c)(4). At least one director must be a representative of the issuers and at least one must be representative of investors. Neither of these directors may be associated with an exchange or association member or a broker-dealer. Proposed Rules 6a-5(c)(5) and 15Aa-3(c)(5). These provisions are intended to be consistent with the requirements of *fair representation* and *issuer and investor representation* requirements of the Securities Exchange Act §§6(b)(3) and 15A(b)(4). The proposal Release further elaborates:

> This requirement is not intended to prohibit exchanges and associations from having boards composed solely of independent directors. If an exchange's or association's board is composed wholly of independent directors, the candidate or candidates selected by members would have to be independent. This *20% standard* for member candidates comports with previously-approved SRO rule changes that raised the issue of fair representation. The Commission preliminarily believes that the proposed 20% requirement strikes a proper balance by giving members a practical voice in the governance of the exchange or association and the administration of its affairs, without jeopardizing the overall independence of the board.

Id. at 462.

When the board of a covered exchange or association considers any matter that is recommended or otherwise within the jurisdiction of a Standing Committee, a majority of the directors who vote on the matter must be independent directors. Proposed Rules 6a-5(c)(6) and 15Aa-3(c)(6). The proposal Release elaborates: "For example, assume an exchange has a board composed of nine independent directors and eight non-independent directors. If two independent directors do not participate in a board meeting but all the non-independent directors participate in such meeting, the matter could be voted upon only by the seven independent directors present and six of the eight non-independent directors present." Id. at 462.

Following the models of the new NYSE and Nasdaq listing requirements and the recent NYSE governance changes, the Commission is proposing that each covered exchange and covered association, at a minimum, have five Standing Committees: Nominating, Governance, Compensation, Audit, and Regulatory Oversight. Proposed Rules 6a-5(e)(1) and 15Aa-3(e)(1). A footnote, however, somewhat softens this requirement by explaining:

> An SRO would not be precluded from allowing a single committee to carry out the functions of two Standing Committees as long as the committee consisted solely of independent directors, *e.g.*, the functions of the Nominating Committee and the Governance Committee could be carried out by a single committee. Also, to the extent that a Standing Committee of the exchange or association carries out responsibilities on behalf of a regulatory subsidiary, the regulatory subsidiary would not be required to have a Standing Committee that performs the same functions. *See* proposed Rules 6a-5(a) and 15Aa-3(a).

Id. at 463 n.155.

The responsibilities of the Audit and Regulatory Oversight Committees are defined broadly in Rules 6a-5(i)(2), 6a-5(j)(2), 15Aa-3(i)(2), and 15Aa-3(j)(2) and provide in the securities exchange version:

> The Audit Committee must have written a charter that addresses the Audit Committee's purpose and responsibilities, which, at a minimum, must be to assist the Board in oversight of the integrity of the national securities exchange's financial statements; the national securities exchange's compliance with related legal and regulatory requirements; and the qualifications and independence of the national securities exchange's auditor, including direct responsibility for the hiring, firing, and compensation of the auditor; overseeing the auditor's engagement; meeting regularly in executive session with the auditor; reviewing the auditor's reports with respect to the national securities exchange's internal records; pre-approving all audit and nonaudit services performed by the auditor; determining the budget and staffing of

the national securities exchange's internal audit department; and establishing procedures for the receipt of complaints regarding accounting, internal accounting controls, or auditing matters of the national securities exchange and the confidential submission by employees of the national securities exchange of concerns regarding questionable accounting or auditing matters. . . .

The Regulatory Oversight Committee must have a written charter that addresses the Regulatory Oversight Committee's purpose and responsibilities, which, at a minimum, must be to assure the adequacy and effectiveness of the regulatory program of the national securities exchange; assess the exchange's regulatory performance; determine the regulatory plan, programs, budget, and staffing for the regulatory functions of the exchange; assess the performance of, and recommend compensation and personnel actions involving, the Chief Regulatory Officer and other senior regulatory personnel to the Compensation Committee; monitor and review regularly with the Chief Regulatory Officer matters relating to the exchange's surveillance, examination, and enforcement units; assure that the exchange's disciplinary and arbitration proceedings are conducted in accordance with the exchange's rules and policies and any other applicable laws or rules, including those of the Commission; prior to the exchange's approval of an affiliated security for listing, certify that such security meets the exchange's rules for listing; and approve reports filed with the Commission as required by Regulation AL. . . .

Each Standing Committee must have the authority to direct and supervise any matter within the scope of its duties and to obtain advice and assistance from independent legal counsel and other advisors as it deems necessary. Proposed Rules 6a-5(e)(2) and 15Aa-3(e)(2). Each covered securities exchange and each covered securities association must provide sufficient resources, "as determined by each Standing Committee" to permit the Standing Committee to fulfill its responsibilities, including retaining independent legal counsel and other advisors. Proposed Rules 6a-5(g)(3) and 15Aa-3(e)(3).

Each Standing Committee, other than the Governance Committee, would be required to conduct an annual performance self-evaluation. Proposed Rules 6a-5(f)(5), 6a-5(h)(3), 6a-5(i)(3),

6a-5(j)(6), 15Aa-3(f)(3), 15Aa-3(h)(3), 15Aa-3(i)(3), and 15A-3(j)(6). The Governance Committee would be required to conduct an evaluation of the exchange or association as a whole. Proposed Rules 6a-5(g)(3) and 15Aa-3(g)(3). Similarly each Standing Committee would be required to have a written charter addressing the Committee's purpose and responsibilities. See Proposed Rules 6a-5(f)(2), 6a-5(g)(2), 6a-5(h)(2), 6a-5(i)(2), 6a-5(j)(2), 15Aa-3(f)(2), 15Aa-3(g)(2), 15Aa-3(h)(2), 15Aa-3(i)(2), and 15Aa-3(j)(2).

In addition, any committee, subcommittee, or panel that is responsible for conducting hearings, rendering decisions, and imposing sanctions with respect to disciplinary matters would be subject to the jurisdiction of the Regulatory Oversight Committee. Although the Regulatory Oversight Committee would be required to be composed solely of independent directors, the Commission believes that, to satisfy the fair representation requirement, the exchange or association must provide for member participation on any committee, subcommittee, or panel that is responsible for conducting hearings, rendering decisions, and imposing sanctions with respect to member disciplinary matters. In order to satisfy this requirement, the proposal would require that at least 20% of the members of any such committee, subcommittee, or panel be members of the exchange or association.

Each covered securities exchange or covered association would be permitted to establish other committees of the board as it determines to be appropriate. If, however, additional Committees, such as an Executive Committee, act on behalf of the board, the Committee would be required to be composed of a majority of independent directors. Proposed Rules 6a-5(k)(i) and 15Aa-3(k)(l). The proposal Release added: "In addition, the Commission is proposing that at least 20% of the persons serving on any committee that is not a Standing Committee and any committee, subcommittee, or panel that is subject to the jurisdiction of a Standing Committee, and that is responsible for providing advice with respect to trading rules or disciplinary rules, be members of the exchange or association." Id. at 466.

Under the proposed Rules, the independent directors are required to meet regularly in executive session, proposed Rules 6a-5(d)(1) and 15Aa-3(d)(1), which is defined by proposed Rules

180

6a-5(b)(9) and 15Aa-3(b)(10), to mean "a meeting of the independent directors of the Board, without the presence of management ... or the directors who are not independent directors." The proposed Rules, however, do not specify a minimum frequency for meetings in executive session. More generally the independent directors, as with the Standing Committees, have authority to direct and supervise inquiries brought to their attention within the scope of their duties, to obtain advice and assistance from independent legal counsel and other advisors, and to be provided sufficient funding and other resources, as determined by the independent directors, to fulfill their responsibilities. Proposed Rules 6a-5(d)(2)-(3) and 15Aa-3(d)(2)-(3).

The proposed Rules do not require the separation of the board Chair from the CEO, but do require if an SRO voluntarily chooses separation, that the Chair be an independent director. Proposed Rule 6a-5(m)(1) and 15Aa-3(m)(1). The proposal Release explained:

> The proposed rules, including the provision related to the Chairman and CEO, are designed to foster a greater degree of independent decision-making by the governing body of an exchange or association. However, while recognizing the benefits of independence, the Commission understands that some SROs may perceive efficiencies in having one person serve as Chairman and CEO, and therefore the Commission is not proposing to prohibit this arrangement. In this regard, the Commission notes that both the NYSE and BSE currently have separate individuals serving as the Chairman and as the CEO of the exchange, although the exchanges' governing documents do not expressly require this separation.

Id. at 467. If the Chair and CEO are the same individual, the board would be required to designate an independent director as a *lead director* to preside over executive sessions. Proposed Rules 6a-5(m)(3) and 15Aa-3(m)(3).

While the SEC does not propose to separate the board Chair and CEO, it does propose a more far reaching separation of regulatory and market operations. Under proposed Rules 6a-5(n) and 15Aa-3(n) each covered securities exchange or covered association is required to establish policies and procedures to assure the

independence of its regulatory program from its market operations and other commercial interests. Proposed Rule 6a-5(n)(1)
and 15Aa-3(n)(1). This can either be done by (i) structurally separ-
ating market operations from other commercial interests by means
of separate legal entities or (ii) functional separation within the
same legal entity. Proposed Rules 6a-5(n)(3) and 15Aa-3(n)(3). In
either case, the proposed Rules would require that the board
appoint a Chief Regulatory Officer to administer the regulatory
program and that the Chief Regulatory Officer report directly to
the Regulatory Oversight Committee. The proposal Release
explained:

> The Commission believes that its proposal to require the struc-
> tural or functional separation of the regulatory functions and the
> market operations and other commercial interests of the exchange
> or association, together with the creation of a fully independent
> Regulatory Oversight Committee and the appointment of a Chief
> Regulatory Officer who would administer the regulatory program
> and report directly to the Regulatory Oversight Committee, are
> designed to manage more effectively the inherent conflicts of
> interest in our self-regulatory system and a particular structure
> for this separation — focusing on the ends rather than the means —
> the proposed rules would provide exchanges and associations with
> a measure of flexibility in determining how best to achieve the
> result of functional independence of the regulatory program.

Id. at 468.

In December 2005 the NYSE merged with Archipelago Holdings, Inc. The merger provided the NYSE with an electronic
trading platform and was the largest merger in history between
securities exchanges.

Two days later the Nasdaq entered into a definitive agreement
with Instinet. Big Board, Archipelago Members Approve Merger
to Form For-Profit NYSE Group Inc., 37 Sec. Reg. & L. Rep.
(BNA) 2026 (2005). See also SEC Approves Rule Changes
Needed to Effectuate NYSE/Archipelago Merger, 38 id. 362
(2006); NYSE, Archipelago Merger Complete; New For-Profit
Company to Begin Trading, 38 id. 414.

## 2.   THE STOCK MARKETS

c.   The Consolidated Reporting System

(iii)   *Regulation NMS*

*P. 746, new text, end page.*   In 2004 the Commission proposed a new Regulation NMS to codify its existing national market system rules and to adopt four new rules addressing: (1) Trade Through Transactions; (2) Market Access; (3) Subpenny Quotes; and (4) Market Data. Sec. Ex. Act Rel. 49,325, 82 SEC Dock. 758 (2004) (proposal).

The Commission articulated the rationale for Regulation NMS broadly:

> If adopted, the proposals collectively would constitute a significant upgrade of the NMS regulatory framework and address a variety of issues that have arisen in recent years. The NMS needs to be enhanced and modernized, not because it has failed investors, but because it has been so successful in promoting growth, efficiency, innovation, and competition that many of its old rules now are outdated. Since the NMS was created nearly thirty years ago, trading volume has exploded, competition among market centers has intensified, and investor trading costs have shrunk dramatically. Each of the major milestones in the development of the NMS — including the creation of the consolidated system for disseminating market information in the 1970s, the incorporation of The Nasdaq Stock Market, Inc. ("Nasdaq") securities into the NMS in the 1980s, and the adoption of the Order Handling Rules in the 1990s — has successively generated enormous benefits for investors.
>
> In the 2000s, improvements to the NMS have continued to benefit investors. In particular, the rescission of New York Stock Exchange, Inc. ("NYSE") Rule 390, trading in penny increments, and public disclosure of order execution quality have set the stage for exceptionally vigorous competition among market centers, particularly to provide the best prices for orders of less than block size (10,000 shares). Since November 2001, for example (the first month for which all markets were required to disclose

their execution quality), the effective spreads paid by investors seeking liquidity in the NMS have declined steadily across all markets by a cumulative total of more than 40%. In November 2003 alone, these reduced spreads resulted in cumulative investor savings of more than $340 million, or more than $4.0 billion on an annualized basis. Importantly, small investors seeking direct participation in the U.S. securities markets have shared fully in these savings, and indeed have been the biggest beneficiaries of NMS improvements....

The objectives for the NMS set forth in the Exchange Act are well known — efficiency, competition, price transparency, best execution, and direct interaction of investor orders. Each of these objectives is essential, yet they sometimes conflict with one another in practice and can require delicate balancing. In particular, the objective of market center competition can be difficult to reconcile with the objective of investor order interaction. We want to encourage innovation and competition by the many individual market centers that collectively make up the NMS, while at the same time assuring that each of these parts contributes to a system that, as a whole, generates the greatest benefits for investors — not their market intermediaries.

The Commission therefore has sought to avoid the extremes of, on the one hand, isolated market centers and, on the other hand, a totally centralized system that loses the benefits of vigorous competition and innovation among market centers. To achieve the appropriate degree of integration, the Commission primarily has relied on two tools: (1) transparency of the best prices through the consolidated display of quotes and trades from all NMS market centers; and (2) intermarket "rules of the road" that establish a basic framework within which competition among NMS market centers can flourish on terms that ultimately benefit investors. Today's proposals are intended to continue this strategy.

In particular, the proposals are designed to address a variety of problems that generally fall within three categories:

(1) the need for uniform rules that promote equal regulation of, and free competition among, all types of market centers;

(2) the need to update antiquated rules that no longer reflect current market conditions; and

(3) the need to promote greater order interaction and displayed depth, particularly for the very large orders of institutional investors.

Id. at 762.

In late 2004, the Commission reproposed Regulation NMS. Sec. Ex. Act Rel. 50,870, 84 SEC Dock. 1431 (2004) (proposal). See also In Move Likely to Stall NYSE Plans, SEC Reproposes Market Structure Rules, 36 Sec. Reg. & L. Rep. (BNA) 2221 (2004). By then, the Commission reported: "The NMS encompasses the stocks of more than 5000 listed companies, which collectively represent more than $14 trillion in U.S. market capitalization." 84 SEC Dock. at 1433.

While many of the original regulated NMS proposals were retained in reproposed Regulation NMS, the reproposal did include several significant changes:

(1) The Trade Through Rule (proposed Rule 611): The proposed Rule now focuses on *trading centers*, rather than *order execution facilities*. By definition a *trading center* is defined in reproposed Rule 600(b)(78) to mean a national securities exchange, a national securities association that operates an SRO trading facility, an ATS, an exchange marketmaker, an OTC marketmaker, and a block position ("any other broker or dealer that executes orders internally by trading as principal or crossing orders as agent").

A *trade through* is defined in reproposed Rule 600(b)(77) to mean "the purchase or sale of an NMS stock during regular trading hours, either as principal or agent, at a price that is lower than a protected bid or higher than a protected offer."

The basic goal of preventing trade throughs is retained in reproposed Rule 611(a), unless an exception can be identified in reproposed Rule 611(b). Significantly reproposed Rule 611(b) eliminates the controversial *opt out* exception, but would extend the scope of the reproposed Rule 611 trade through Rule beyond the best limit order on a market's books.

As with the original proposal, the Commission powerfully favors markets with automatic execution over manual markets.

(2) Access Rule (proposed Rule 610): The reproposal was more precise in achieving the three basic goals articulated in the initial proposed Rule 610:

> Rule 610 is designed to promote access to quotations in three ways. First, it would enable the use of private linkages offered by a variety of connectivity providers, rather than mandating a collective linkage facility such as ITS, to facilitate the necessary access to quotations. The lower cost and increased flexibility of connectivity in recent years has made private linkages a feasible alternative to hard linkages, absent barriers to access. Using private linkages, market participants may obtain indirect access to quotations displayed by a particular trading center through the members, subscribers, or customers of that trading center. To promote this type of indirect access, Rule 610 would prohibit a trading center from imposing unfairly discriminatory terms that would prevent or inhibit the access of any person through members, subscribers, or customers of such trading center.
>
> Second, reproposed Rule 610 would limit the fees that any trading center can charge (or allow to be charged) for accessing its protected quotations to no more than $0.003 per share....
>
> Finally, reproposed Rule 610 would require SROs to establish and enforce rules that, among other things, prohibit their members from engaging in a pattern of displaying quotations that lock or cross the automated quotations of other trading centers. Trading centers would be allowed, however, to display automated quotations that lock or cross the *manual* quotations of other trading centers.

Id. at 1437–1438.

(3) Sub-penny Rule (reproposed Rule 612): Reproposed Rule 612 included only minor changes from the initial proposal. Reproposed Rule 612(a) would prohibit subpenny quotes in NMS stocks over $1.

(4) Market Data Rules and Plan Amendments (reproposed Rules 601 and 603): As with the initial proposal the Commission reproposes a formula for allocating revenues generated by market data fees to SRO participants, but simplifies the initial proposal.

In April 2005, the Commission adopted Regulation NMS. Sec. Ex. Act Rel. 51,808, 85 SEC Dock. 1642 (2005) (adoption). See Norris, SEC Expands Best-Price Rule on Stock Trading, N.Y. Times, Apr. 7, 2005, at C1, quoting the author; Over Dissent of Two Commissioners SEC Adopts Market Structure Regulation, 37 Sec. Reg. & L. Rep. (BNA) 621 (2005). Regulation NMS was adopted by a 3-2 vote over the dissent of Commissioners Atkins and Glassman, prompting a detailed response to the dissent, see id. at 1785–1794, which was unusual, if not a novelty, in an SEC rule adoption.

Three themes dominated the adoption Release. First, the Commission has a strong preference for electronic rather than manual markets. See, e.g., "The new formula eliminates any allocation of revenues for manual quotations." Id. at 1653. This may prove to be the most enduring consequence of Regulation NMS by stimulating an acceleration of new trading technologies and market structures. Second, the Release otherwise expressed a general unwillingness to address fundamental market structure issues such as market linkages. A footnote explained: "Nearly all commenters, both those supporting and opposing the need for an intermarket trade-through rule, agreed that the current ITS trade-through provisions are seriously outdated and in need of reform." Id. at 1656. This significantly understates the long articulated critique that ITS itself is "seriously outdated and in need of reform," which contributed to dissatisfaction with Regulation NMS for tending to side with the New York Stock Exchange (NYSE), which has been the most fervent advocate of ITS. The failure to effectively study or prescribe a new system of linkages is the most fundamental weakness of Regulation NMS. Third, Regulation NMS appropriately did move to equalize standards that applied to traditional stock markets such as the NYSE with those applicable to electronic markets such as the Nasdaq and ECNs.[1] This was an intent of the Securities Act Amendments of 1975, and long overdue.

---

[1] The author should note that he is a member of the Board of Governors of the NASD, which owns an equity interest in the Nasdaq. The views stated here are solely those of the author, writing as an independent scholar, and do not articulate the views of the Nasdaq.

Regulation NMS largely adopted the December 2004 reproposal Release, with some modifications and a detailed rationale,
no doubt designed to withstand potential judicial challenge.

Of primary importance was Rule 611, now called the Order
Protection Rule in place of the earlier term, the Trade Through
Rule. The adoption Release aptly explained: "Clearly, the Order
Protection Rule was most controversial and attracted the most
public comment and attention, yet the breadth of support in the
record for the Rule is compelling." Id. at 1645–1646. The adoption Release, for example, noted that 1689 commenters on the
proposal and reproposal favored a uniform trade through rule
without an opt out exception, while only 448 opposed a uniform
trade through rule. Id. at 1656. The Commission explained:

> Why did a broad spectrum of commenters, many of which have
> extensive experience and expertise regarding the inner workings
> of the equity markets, support the Order Protection Rule and its
> emphasis on the principle of best price? They based their support
> on two fundamental rationales, with which the Commission fully
> agrees. First, strengthened assurance that orders will be filled at
> the best prices will give investors, particularly retail investors,
> greater confidence that they will be treated fairly when they parti-
> cipate in the equity markets. Maintaining investor confidence is an
> essential element of well-functioning equity markets. Second, pro-
> tection of the best displayed and accessible prices will promote
> deep and stable markets that minimize investor transaction costs.
> More than 84 million individual Americans participate, directly or
> indirectly, in the U.S. equity markets. The transaction costs asso-
> ciated with the prices at which their orders are executed represent
> a continual drain on their long-term savings. Although these costs
> are difficult to calculate precisely, they are very real and very
> substantial, with estimates ranging from $30 billion to more than
> $100 billion per year. Minimizing these investor costs to the great-
> est extent possible is the hallmark of efficient markets, which is a
> primary objective of the NMS.

Id. at 1646.

The Order Protection Rule was adopted essentially as reproposed in December 2004 with a new exception for specified
*Stopped Orders* added in Rule 611(b)(9). As adopted:

Rule 611 can be divided into three elements: (1) the provisions that establish the scope of the Rule's coverage, most of which are set forth in the definitions of Rule 600(b); (2) the operative requirements of paragraph (a) of Rule 611, which, among other things, mandate the adoption and enforcement of written policies and procedures that are reasonably designed to prevent trade throughs on that trading center of protected quotations and, if relying on an exception, that are reasonably designed to assure compliance with the terms of the exception; and (3) the exceptions set forth in paragraph (b) of Rule 611....

### 1. Scope of Rule

... In general, the Rule addresses trade-throughs of protected quotations in NMS stocks by trading centers. A *trading center* is defined in Rule 600(b)(78) as a national securities exchange or national securities association that operates an SRO trading facility, an ATS, an exchange market maker, and OTC market maker, or any other broker or dealer that executes orders internally by trading as principal or crossing orders as agent. This last phrase is intended particularly to cover block petitioners. An *NMS stock* is defined in paragraphs (b)(47) and (b)(46) of Rule 600 as a security, other than an option, for which transaction reports are collected, processed and made available pursuant to an effective national market system plan. This definition effectively covers stocks listed on a national securities exchange and stocks included in either the National Market or SmallCap tiers of Nasdaq. It does not include stocks quoted on the OTC Bulletin Board or elsewhere in the OTC market.

The term *trade-through* is defined in Rule 600(b)(77) as the purchase or sale of an NMS stock during regular trading hours, either as principal or agent, at a price that is lower than a protected bid or higher than a protected offer. Rule 600(b)(57), which defines a *protected bid* or *protected offer*, includes three main elements: (1) an automated quotation; (2) displayed by an automated trading center; and (3) that is the best bid or best offer of an exchange, the NASDAQ Stock Market, or an association other than the NASDAQ Stock Market (currently, the best bid or offer of the NASD's ADF).

As discussed above, an *automated quotation* is defined in Rule 600(b)(3) as a quotation displayed by a trading center that: (1) permits an incoming order to be marked as immediate-or-cancel; (2) immediately and automatically executes an order marked as immediate-or-cancel against the displayed quotation up to its full size; (3) immediately and automatically cancels any unexecuted portion of an order marked as immediate-or-cancel without routing the order elsewhere; (4) immediately and automatically transmits a response to the sender of an order marked as immediate-or-cancel indicating the action taken with respect to such order; and (5) immediately and automatically displays information that updates the displayed quotation to reflect any change to its material terms.

Consequently, a quotation will not qualify as *automated* if any human intervention after the time an order is received is allowed to determine the action taken with respect to the quotation. The term *immediate* precludes any coding of automated systems or other type of intentional device that would delay the action taken with respect to a quotation. . . .

. . . [A]n *automated trading center* is defined in Rule 600(b)(4) as a trading center that: (1) has implemented such systems, procedures, and rules as are necessary to render it capable of displaying quotations that meet the requirements for an automated quotation set forth in paragraph (b)(3) of this section; (2) identifies all quotations other than automated quotations as manual quotations; (3) immediately identifies its quotations as manual quotations whenever it has reason to believe that it is not capable of displaying automated quotations; and (4) has adopted reasonable standards limiting when its quotations change from automated quotations to manual quotations, and vice versa, to specifically defined circumstances that promote fair and efficient access to its automated quotations and are consistent with the maintenance of fair and orderly markets. The requirement of reasonable standard for switching the automated/manual status of quotations is designed to preclude practices that would cause confusion among market participants concerning the status of a trading center's quotations or that would inappropriately advantage the members or customers of a trading center at the expense of the public.

The third element of the definition of *protected bid* and *protected offer* identifies which automated quotations are protected under the Order Protection Rule. Specifically, Rule 600(b)(57) provides that an automated quotation displayed by an automated trading center that is the BBO [Best Bid or Offer] of an exchange SRO, the BBO of Nasdaq, or the BBO of the NASD (*i.e.*, the ADF) qualifies as a protected quotation. Thus, only a single, accessible best bid and best offer for each of the exchange SROs, Nasdaq, and the NASD is protected under the Order Protection Rule. A best bid and best offer must be accessible by routing an order to a single market destination (*i.e.*, currently, either to a single exchange execution system, a single Nasdaq execution system, or a single ADF participant).

### 2. Requirement of Reasonable Policies and Procedures

Paragraph (a)(1) of Rule 611 requires a trading center to establish, maintain, and enforce written policies and procedures that are reasonably designed to prevent trade-throughs on that trading center of protected quotations in NMS stocks that do not fall within an exception set forth in paragraph (b) of Rule 611 and, if relying on such an exception, that are reasonably designed to assure compliance with the terms of the exception. In addition, paragraph (a)(2) of Rule 611 requires a trading center to regularly surveil to ascertain the effectiveness of the policies and procedures required by paragraph (a)(1) and to take prompt action to remedy deficiencies in such policies and procedures. . . .

### 3. Exceptions

Rule 611(b) sets forth a variety of exceptions addressing transactions that may fall within the definition of a tradethrough, but which are not subject to the operative requirements of the Rule. The exceptions primarily are designed to achieve workable intermarket price protection and to facilitate certain trading strategies and order types that are useful to investors, but also are consistent with the principle of price protection.

Paragraph (b)(1) excepts a transaction if the trading center displaying the protected quotation that was traded through was experiencing a failure, material delay, or malfunction of its systems or equipment when the trade-through occurred. . . .

Paragraph (b)(8) of Rule 611 sets forth an exception for flickering quotations. It excepts a transaction if the trading center displaying the protected quotation that was traded through had displayed, within one second prior to execution of the tradethrough, a best bid or best offer, as applicable, for the NMS stock with a price that was equal or inferior to the price of the trade-through transaction. This exception thereby provides a *window* to address false indications of trade-throughs that in actuality are attributable to rapidly moving quotations. It also potentially will reduce the number of instances in which a trading center must alter its normal trading procedures and route orders to other trading centers to comply with Rule 611. The exception is thereby intended to promote more workable intermarket price protection.

Paragraphs (b)(5) and (b)(6) of Rule 611 set forth exceptions for intermarket sweep orders. An intermarket sweep order is defined in Rule 600(b)(30) as a limit order that meets the following requirements: (1) when routed to a trading center, the limit order is identified as an intermarket sweep order, and (2) simultaneously with the routing of the limit order identified as an intermarket sweep order, one or more additional limit orders, as necessary, are routed to execute against the full displayed size of all protected quotations with a superior price. These additional limit orders must be marked as intermarket sweep orders to allow the receiving market center to execute the order immediately without regard to better-priced quotations displayed at other trading centers (by definition, each of the additional limit orders would meet the requirements for an intermarket sweep order).

Paragraph (b)(5) allows a trading center immediately to execute any order identified as an intermarket sweep order. It therefore need not delay its execution for the updating of the betterpriced quotations at other trading centers to which orders were routed simultaneously with the intermarket sweep order. Paragraph (b)(6) allows a trading center itself to route intermarket sweep orders and thereby clear the way for immediate internal executions at the trading center. This exception particularly will facilitate the immediate execution of block orders by dealers on behalf of their institutional clients. Specifically, if a dealer wishes to execute internally a customer order at a price that would trade through one or more protected quotations on other trading centers, the dealer will be able to do so if it simultaneously routes one or more intermarket sweep orders to execute against the full displayed size of each such better-priced protected quotations. If there is only one better-priced protected quotation, then the dealer is only required to route an intermarket sweep order to execute against that protected quotation.

Paragraph (c) of Rule 611 requires that the trading center, broker, or dealer responsible for the routing of an intermarket sweep order take reasonable steps to establish that orders are properly routed in an attempt to execute against all applicable protected quotations. A trading center, broker, or dealer is required to satisfy this requirement regardless whether it routes the order through its own systems or sponsors a customer's access through a third-party vendor's systems....

The exception in paragraph (b)(7) of Rule 611 will facilitate other types of orders that often are useful to investors—benchmark orders. It excepts the execution of an order at a price that was not based, directly or indirectly, on the quoted price of an NMS stock at the time of execution and for which the material terms were not reasonably determinable at the time the commitment to execute the order was made. A common example of a benchmark order is a VWAP order. Assume a broker-dealer's customer decides to buy a stock at 9:00 a.m. before the markets open for normal trading. The customer submits, and the brokerdealer accepts, an order to buy 100,000 shares at the volume-weighted price of the stock from opening until 1:00 p.m. At 1:00 p.m., the national best offer in the stock is $20.00, but the relevant volume-weighted average price (in a rising market) is $19.90. The broker-dealer would be able to rely on the benchmark order exception to execute the order at $19.90 at 1:00 p.m., without regard to better-priced protected quotations at other trading centers. Of course, any transactions effected by the broker-dealer during the course of the day to obtain sufficient stock to fill the benchmark order would remain subject to Rule 611. The benchmark exception also would encompass the execution of an order that is benchmarked to a market's single-priced opening, as the Commission would not interpret such an opening price to be the *quoted price* of the NMS stock at the time of execution.

Paragraph (b)(9) of Rule 611 provides an exception for the execution of certain stopped orders. Specifically, the exception applies to the execution by a trading center of a stopped order where the price of the execution of the order was, for a stopped buy order, lower than the national best bid at the time of execution or, for a stopped sell order, higher than the national best offer at the time of execution....

Finally, paragraph (b) of Rule 611 includes a variety of other exceptions: (1) transactions other than *regular way* contracts; (2) single-price opening, reopening, or closing transactions; and (3) transactions executed at a time when protected quotations were crossed. The crossed quotation exception would not apply when a protected quotation crosses a non-protected (*e.g.*, manual) quotation. The exception for single-priced reopenings will only apply to single-priced reopening transactions after a trading halt conducted pursuant to a trading center rule. To qualify, the reopening process must be transparent and provide for the queuing and ultimate execution of multiple orders at a single equilibrium price.

Id. at 1693–1696.

Given criticism of the proposed Uniform Order Protection Rule as unnecessary to maintain market quality in the Nasdaq, not earlier subject to a trade through rule, the Commission conducted studies to compare trade through rates in the Nasdaq or the NYSE. Specifically stock studies found that overall trade through rates for Nasdaq stocks were 7.9 percent of total volume of traded shares, compared to 7.2 percent for NYSE stocks. Id. at 1658. When NYSE block trades and other noncovered transactions are eliminated, NYSE trade throughs are reduced to approximately 2.3 percent of total share volume. Id. at 1658.

With respect to the argument that the Nasdaq had superior execution quality, the adoption Release responded at length:

> The staff studies indicate that the execution quality statistics submitted by commenters on the original proposal are flawed. The claimed large and systematic disparities between Nasdaq and NYSE effective spreads disappear when an analysis of execution quality more appropriately controls for differences in stocks, order types, and order sizes....
>
> First, the effective spread analyses submitted by commenters do not, in a number of respects, reflect appropriately the comparative costs in Nasdaq and NYSE stocks. They were presented in terms of *cents-per-share* and therefore failed to control for the varying level of stock prices between Nasdaq stocks and NYSE stocks in the S&P 500. Lower priced stocks naturally will tend to have lower spreads in terms of cents-per-share than higher priced stocks, even when

such cents-per-share spreads constitute a larger percentage of stock price and therefore represent transaction costs for investors that consume a larger percentage of their investment. By using cents-per-share statistics, commenters did not adjust for the fact that the average prices of Nasdaq stocks are significantly lower than the average prices of NYSE stocks. For example, the average price of Nasdaq stocks in the S&P 500 in January 2004 was $34.14, while the average price of NYSE stocks was $41.32.

The effective spread analyses submitted by commenters also were weakened by their failure to address the much lower fill rates of orders in Nasdaq stocks than orders in NYSE stocks. The commenters submitted *blended* statistics that encompassed both market orders and marketable limit orders. The effective spread statistics for these order types are not comparable, however, because market orders do not have a limit price that precludes their execution at prices inferior to the prevailing market price at time of order receipt. In contrast, the limit price of marketable limit orders often precludes an execution, particularly when there is a lack of liquidity and depth at the prevailing market price. For example, the fill rates for marketable limit orders in Nasdaq stocks generally are less than 75%, and often fall below 50% for larger order sizes.

Accordingly, investors must accept trade-offs when deciding whether to submit market orders or marketable limit orders (particularly when the limit price equals the current market price). Use of a limit price generally assures a narrower spread by precluding an execution at an inferior price. By precluding an execution, however, the limit price may cause the investor to *miss the market* if prices move away (for example, if prices rise when an investor is attempting to buy). Effective spreads for marketable limit orders therefore represent transaction costs that are conditional on execution, while effective spreads for market orders much more completely reflect the entire implicit transaction cost for a particular order. Market orders represent only approximately 14% of the blended flow of market and marketable limit orders in Nasdaq stocks (reflecting the fact that ECNs now dominate Nasdaq order flow and limit orders represent the vast majority of ECN order flow). In contrast, market orders represent approximately 36% of the blended order flow in NYSE stocks. Accordingly, the effective spread statistics for marketable limit orders, and particularly for orders in Nasdaq stocks, must be considered in conjunction with the fill rate for such orders—while a narrow spread is good, the benefits are greatly limited if investors are unable to obtain an execution at that spread. The analyses presented by the commenters, however, did not address the respective fill rates for Nasdaq stocks and NYSE stocks or reflect the inherent differences in measuring the transaction costs of market orders and marketable limit orders. . . .

For Nasdaq stocks, the Rule 11Ac1-5 statistics reveal very low fill rates for larger sizes of marketable limit orders (*e.g.*, 2000 shares or more), which generally fall below 50% for most Nasdaq stocks. Contrary to the assertion of some commenters, certainty of *execution* for large marketable limit orders clearly is not a strength of the current market for Nasdaq stocks. Certainty of a fast response is a strength, but much of the time the response to large orders will be a *no fill* at any given trading center. . . .

Accordingly, the Commission's concern with fill rates for larger orders in Nasdaq stocks is not that they are lower than those for NYSE stocks, but that they are very low in absolute terms—often falling well below 50%.

Id. at 1665–1667.

To make the Order Protection Rule effective, it is limited to automated quotations. "The Commission agrees with commenters that providing protection to manual quotations ... potentially would lead to undue delays in the routing of investor orders, thereby not justifying the benefits of price protection." Id. at 1673. Rule 600(b)(3) adopted the definition of automated quotation as proposed, in essence limiting such quotations to those displayed by a trading center that can (1) act on an incoming order; (2) respond to the send of the order; and (3) update the quotation. See id. at 1674.

In response to commenter concerns that the original trade through rule could not be implemented in a workable manner, particularly for high volume stocks, the Commission made modifications to the original rule:

> First and most importantly, as included in the reproposal and as adopted today, only automated trading centers, as defined in Rule 600(b)(4), that are capable of providing immediate responses

to incoming orders are eligible to have their quotations protected. Moreover, an automated trading center is required to identify its quotations as manual (and therefore not protected) whenever it has reason to believe that it is not capable of providing immediate responses to orders. Thus, a trading center that experiences a systems problem, whether because of a flood of orders or otherwise, must immediately identify its quotations as manual....

The adopted Order Protection Rule ... provides a *self-help* remedy that will allow trading centers to bypass the quotations of a trading center that fails to meet the immediate response requirement. Rule 611(b)(1) sets forth an exception that applies to quotations displayed by trading centers that are experiencing a failure, material delay, or malfunction of its systems or equipment. To implement this exception consistent with the requirements of Rule 611(a), trading centers will have to adopt policies and procedures reasonably designed to comply with the selfhelp remedy. Such policies and procedures will need to set forth specific objective parameters for dealing with problem trading centers and for monitoring compliance with the self-help remedy, consistent with Rule 611. Given current industry capabilities, the Commission believes that trading centers should be entitled to bypass another trading center's quotations if it repeatedly fails to respond within one second to incoming orders attempting to access its protected quotations. Accordingly, trading centers will have the necessary flexibility to respond to problems at another trading center as they occur during the trading day.

Id. at 1677.

The Commission declined, however, to create a categorical exemption for actively traded stocks:

> The Commission recognizes that commenters have raised a serious concern regarding implementation of the Order Protection Rule, particularly for many Nasdaq stocks that are very actively traded and whose trading is spread across many different individual trading centers. An exemption for active stocks, however, would be particularly inconsistent with the investor protection objectives of the Order Protection Rule because these also are the stocks that have the highest level of investor participation.

Id. at 1680.

The Commission limited the scope of protected quotations to the Market Best Bid and Offer (BBO) rather than a Voluntary Depth Alternative, which likely would have been more difficult and costly to implement. Id. at 1688.

The Commission characterized the benefits of strengthened order protection in these terms:

> The Commission believes that the benefits of strengthening price protection for exchange-listed stocks (*e.g.*, by eliminating the gaps in ITS coverage of block positioners and 100-share quotes) and introducing price protection for Nasdaq stocks will be substantial, although the total amount is difficult to quantify. One objective, though quite conservative, estimate of benefits is the dollar amount of quotations that annually are traded through. The Commission staff's analysis of trade-through rates indicates that over 12 billion shares of displayed quotations in Nasdaq and NYSE stocks were traded through in 2003, by an average amount of 2.3 cents for Nasdaq stocks and 2.2 cents for NYSE stocks. These traded-through quotations represent approximately $209 million in Nasdaq stocks and $112 million in NYSE stocks, for a total of $321 million in bypassed limit orders and inferior prices for investors in 2003 that could have been addressed by strong trade-through protection. The Commission believes that this $321 million estimated *annual* benefit, particularly when combined with the benefits of enhanced investor confidence in the fairness and orderliness of the equity markets, justifies the one-time costs of implementation and ongoing annual costs of the Order Protection Rule. ...
>
> The Order Protection Rule can be expected to generate other categories of benefits that are not quantified in the $321 million estimate, such as the benefits that can be expected to result from increased use of limit orders, increased depth, and increased order interaction.

Id. at 1691–1692.

Buttressing the Order Protection Rule is Rule 610, the Access Rule. Rule 610 was essentially adopted as proposed, with the adoption Release stating:

> All SROs that trade exchange-listed stocks currently are linked through ITS, a collective intermarket linkage facility. ITS provides

a means of access to exchanges and Nasdaq by permitting each market to send a *commitment to trade* through the system, with receiving markets generally having up to 30 seconds to respond. ITS also provides access to quotations of participants without fees and establishes uniform rules to govern quoting practices. Although ITS promotes access among participants that is uniform and free, it also is often slow and limited. Moreover, it is governed by a unanimous vote requirement that has at times impeded innovation in the system or its set of rules.

In contrast, there is no collective intermarket linkage system for Nasdaq stocks. Instead, access is achieved primarily through private linkages among individual trading centers. This approach has demonstrated its benefits among electronic markets; it is flexible and can readily incorporate technological advances as they occur. There is no intermarket system, however, that offers free access to quotations in Nasdaq stocks. Nor are the trading centers for Nasdaq stocks subject to uniform intermarket standards governing their quoting and trading practices. The fees for access to ECN quotations in Nasdaq stocks, as well as the absence of standards for quotations that lock and cross markets, have been the source of disputes among participants in the market for Nasdaq stocks for many years. Moreover, access problems have arisen with respect to small market centers operating outside of an SRO trading facility and markets like the Amex that engage in manual trading of Nasdaq stocks. Access problems also have arisen with respect to intentional barriers to access, especially involving fees.

Rule 610 reflects the Commission's determination that fair and efficient access to markets can be achieved without a collective intermarket linkage facility such as ITS, if baseline intermarket rules are established. The rule adopts a private linkage approach for all NMS stocks with modifications to address the most serious problems that have arisen with this approach in the trading of Nasdaq stocks.

Id. at 1700–1701.

Rule 610 first prohibits certain forms of discrimination against nonmembers:

Rules 610(a) and (b) further the goal of fair and efficient access to quotations primarily by prohibiting trading centers from unfairly discriminating against nonmembers or nonsubscribers that attempt to access their quotations through a member or subscriber of the trading center. Market participants can either become members or subscribers of a trading center to obtain direct access to its quotations, or they can obtain indirect access by *piggybacking* on the direct access of members or subscribers. These forms of access are widely used today in the market for Nasdaq stocks (as well as to a lesser extent in the market for exchange-listed stocks). Instead of every market participant establishing separate linkages with every trading center, many different private firms have entered the business of linking with a wide range of trading centers and then offering their customers access to those trading centers through the private firms' linkages. Competitive forces determine the types and costs of these private linkages. . . .

The Commission does not believe that the private linkage approach adopted today will seriously undermine the value of membership in SROs that offer valuable services to their members. First, the fact that markets will not be allowed to impose unfairly discriminatory terms on non-members who obtain indirect access to quotations through members does not mean that non-members will obtain *free* access to quotations. Members who provide piggyback access to non-members will be providing a useful service and presumably will charge a fee for such service. The fee will be subject to competitive forces and likely will reflect the costs of SRO membership, plus some element of profit to the SRO's members. As a result, nonmember that frequently make use of indirect access are likely to contribute to the costs of membership in the SRO market. Moreover, the unfair discrimination standard of Rule 610(a) will apply only to access to quotations, not to the full panoply of services that markets generally provide only to their members. These other services will be subject to the more general fair access provisions applicable to SROs and     large ECNs, as well as statutory provisions that govern SRO rules.

On the other hand, any attempt by an SRO to charge differential fees based on the non-member status of the person obtaining indirect access to quotations, such as whether it is a competing market maker, would violate the anti-discrimination standard of Rule 610. . . .

Other types of differential fees, however, would not violate the anti-discrimination standard of Rule 610. Fees with volume-based

discounts or fees that are reasonably based on the cost of providing a particular service will be permitted, so long as they do not
vary based on the non-member status of a person obtaining indirect access to quotations. For example, a member providing indirect access could be given a volume discount on the full amount of
its volume, including the volume accounted for by persons obtaining indirect access to quotations.

Id. at 1701–1703.

The Commission under Rule 610(b)(1) requires ADF participants to bear the costs of providing the necessary connectivity to
facilitate access to their quotations. "Specifically, under reproposed Rule 610(b)(1) those ATSs and market makers that choose
to display quotations in the ADF would bear the responsibility of
providing a level and cost of access to their quotations that is
substantially equivalent to the level and cost of access to quotations displayed by SRO trading facilities." Id. at 1704.

Small ADFs will be exempt from this connectivity requirement
because Rule 301(b)(3) of Regulation ATS only requires an ATS
to display its quotations in a consolidated quotation or stream in
those securities for which its trading volume equals 5 percent of
total trading volume. Id. at 1705. The NASD as *gatekeeper*
for ADF will need to make an affirmative determination that
existing ADF participants are in compliance with Rule 610. Id.
at 1707.

Separately, in Rule 610(c) the Commission adopted a flat
$0.003 per share limitation on access fees:

> The limitation is intended to achieve several objectives. First, Rule
> 610(c) promotes the NMS objective of equal regulation of markets
> and broker-dealers by applying equally to all types of trading
> centers and all types of market participants.... although ECNs
> and other types of trading centers, including SROs, may currently
> charge access fees, market makers have not been permitted to
> charge any fee for counterparties accessing their quotations. The
> Commission believes, however, that it is consistent with the Quote
> Rule for market makers to charge fees for access to their quota-
> tions, so long as such fees meet the requirements of Rule 610(c). In
> particular, market makers will be permitted to charge fees for

executions of orders against their quotations, irrespective of whether the order executions are effected on an SRO trading facility or directly by a market maker.

Second, the adopted fee limitation is designed to preclude individual trading centers from raising their fees substantially in an attempt to take improper advantage of strengthened protection against trade-throughs and the adoption of a private linkage regime. In particular, the fee limitation is necessary to address *outlier* trading centers that otherwise might charge high fees to other market participants required to access their quotations by the Order Protection Rule. It also precludes a trading center from charging high fees selectively to competitors, practices that have occurred in the market for Nasdaq stocks. In the absence of a fee limitation, the adoption of the Order Protection Rule and private linkages could significantly boost the viability of the outlier business model....

The $0.003 cap will limit the outlier business model. It will place all markets on a level playing field in terms of the fees they can charge and the rebates they can pass on to liquidity providers. Some markets might choose to charge lower fees, thereby increasing their ranking in the preferences of order routers. Others might charge the full $0.003 and rebate a substantial proportion to liquidity providers. Competition will determine which strategy is most successful....

The Commission notes the $0.003 fee limitation is consistent with current business practices, as very few trading centers currently charge fees that exceed this amount. It appears that only two ECNs currently charge fees that exceed $0.003, charging $0.005 for access through the ADF. These ECNs currently do not account for a large percentage of trading volume. In addition, while a few SROs have large fees on their books for transactions in ETFs that exceed a certain size (*e.g.*, 2100 shares), it is unlikely that these fees generate a large amount of revenues.

Id. at 1709–1710.

The fee limitation cap applies "to manual quotations that are best bids and offers to the same extent it applies to covered automatic quotations." Id. at 1710.

The cap, however, only applies to best bid and offer quotations and will not apply to other trading center quotations, such as depth of book quotations. Id. at 1710.

Rule 610(d) requires each national securities exchange and national securities association to establish written rules that require its members to avoid quotations that lock or cross any covered quotation in an NMS stock. The Commission explained:

> When two market participants are willing to trade at the same quoted price, giving priority to the first-displayed automated quotation will encourage posting of quotations and contribute to fair and orderly markets. The basic principle underlying the NMS is to promote fair competition among markets, but within a system that also promotes interaction between all of the buyers and sellers in a particular NMS stock. Allowing market participants simply to ignore accessible quotations in other markets and routinely display locking and crossing quotations is inconsistent with this principle. The Rule will, however, not prohibit automated quotations from locking or crossing manual quotations, thereby permitting market participants to reflect information regarding the inaccessibility of a particular trading center's quotations.

Id. at 1712.

Rule 612, the Subpenny Rule, which prohibits subpenny quoting in quotations above $1.00 per share, was adopted in December 2004 with minor amendments. Id. at 1716–1726. The rationale for Rule 612 was articulated succinctly:

> Rule 612 will deter the practice of stepping ahead of exposed trading interest by an economically insignificant amount. Limit orders provide liquidity to the market and perform an important pricesetting function. The Commission is concerned that, if orders lose execution priority because competing orders step ahead for an economically insignificant amount, liquidity could diminish.

Id. at 1720.

In adopting Rule 612, the Commission did retain the power by order to exempt any person, security, or quotation, if future circumstances warranted. Id. at 1720.

For trades not subject to the subpenny quote restriction, a provision was adopted limiting a quotation under $1.00 per share to four decimal places. "Thus, under new Rule 612, a quotation of $0.9987 × $1.00 is permitted but a quotation of $0.9987 × $1.0001 is not." Id. at 1723.

Rule 612 does not prohibit subpenny trading, for example, a subpenny execution resulting from a midpoint or volume weighted algorithm, see id. at 1724, nor does Rule 612 apply to options. Id. at 1725.

In adopting Regulation NMS, the Commission wrote that "[t]he Exchange Act rules and joint-SRO Plans for disseminating market information to the public are the heart of NMS." Id. at 1726. In 2004 Market Data Networks collected $434.1 million in revenues derived from market data fees. Id. at 1726. The adoption Release added:

> Moreover, the U.S. equity markets are not alone in their reliance on market data revenues as a substantial source of funding. All of the other major world equity markets currently derive large amounts of revenues from selling market information, despite having significantly less trading volume and less market capitalization than the NYSE and Nasdaq. To illustrate, the following table sets forth the respective market information revenues, dollar value of trading, and market capitalization for the largest world equity markets in 2003:

| | Data Revenues (millions) | Trading Volume (trillions) | Market Capitalization (trillions) |
|---|---|---|---|
| London | $180 | $3.6 | $2.5 |
| NYSE | $172 | $9.7 | $11.3 |
| Nasdaq | $147 | $7.1 | $2.8 |
| Deutsche Bourse | $146 | $1.3 | $1.1 |
| Euronext | $109 | $1.9 | $2.1 |
| Tokyo | $60 | $2.1 | $3.0 |

Id. at 1730.

The Commission adopted its Allocation Amendment to each SRO Plan with modifications from both the original proposal and December 2004 reproposal:

> The adopted formula reflects a two-step process. First, a Network's distributable revenues (*e.g.*, $150 million) will be allocated among the many individual securities (*e.g.*, 3000) included in the Network's data stream. Second, the revenues that are allocated to an individual security (*e.g.*, $200,000) will be allocated among the SROs based on measures of the usefulness to investors of the SRO's trades and quotes in the security. The Allocation Amendment provides that, notwithstanding any other provision of a Plan, its SRO participants shall receive an annual payment for each calendar year that is equal to the sum of the SRO's Trading Shares and Quoting Shares in each Network security for the year. These two types of Shares are dollar amounts that are calculated based on SRO trading and quoting activity in each Network security.

Id. at 1739.

The Commission elaborated:

> Commenters on the original proposal generally believed that the originally proposed formula was complex and may have been difficult to implement efficiently. They particularly noted that the proposed NBBO Improvement Share was difficult to understand and had the potential to be abused through gaming behavior. The Commission agreed with these commenters and has modified the reproposed formula and adopted formula accordingly. Given that only automated quotations will be entitled to earn an allocation under the adopted formula, the originally proposed NBBO Improvement Share, as well as the proposed cutoff of credits for manual quotations left alone at the NBBO, have been deleted from the reproposed formula and remain deleted in the adopted formula. The elimination of these two elements greatly reduces the complexity of the adopted formula and promotes more efficient implementation of the formula. In addition, the 15% of the Security Income Allocation that was allocated to the NBBO Improvement Share in the proposed formula now has been

shifted to the Quoting Share to assign an even allocation of revenues between trading and quoting.

Id. at 1733.

Generalizing the Commission explained:

The current Plan formulas allocate revenues based on the number of trades (Networks A and B) or on the average number of trades and share volume of trades (Network C) reported by SROs. By focusing solely on trading activity (and particularly by rewarding the reporting of many trades no matter how small their size), these formulas have contributed to a variety of distortive trade reporting practices, including wash sales, shredded trades, and SRO print facilities. To address these practices and to establish a more broad-based measure of an SRO's contribution to the consolidated trade stream, the proposed formula provided that an SRO's Trading Store in a particular stock would be calculated by taking the average of the SRO's percentage of total dollar volume in the stock and the SRO's percentage of qualified trades in the stock. A *qualified trade* was defined as having a dollar volume of $5000 or more. . . .

Several commenters on the original proposal believed that small trades contribute to price discovery and should be entitled to earn at least some credit in the calculation of the number of qualified trades. The Commission agreed and included in the reproposed formula a provision that awards a fractional proportion of a qualified report for trades of less than $5000. The adopted formula also includes this provision. Thus, a $2500 trade will constitute ½ of a qualified transaction report. This approach greatly reduces the potential for large allocations attributable to shredded trades, while recognizing the contribution of small trades to price discovery. . . .

The proposed formula included a Security Income Allocation, pursuant to which a Network's total distributable revenues would be allocated among each of the Network's stocks based on the square root of dollar volume. The square root function was intended to adjust for the highly disproportionate level of trading in the very top tier of Network stocks. A few hundred stocks (*e.g.*, the top 5%) are much more heavily traded than the other thousands of Network stocks. . . .

With one modification, the Commission has retained the square root function in the adopted formula to allocate distributable Network revenues more appropriately among all of the stocks included in a Network. Although the extent to which Network stocks are tiered according to trading volume varies among the three Networks, it is quite pronounced in each of them. The use of the square root function reflects the Commission's judgment that, on average and not necessarily in every particular case, information about a $50,000 trade in a stock with an average daily trading volume of $500,000 is marginally more useful to investors than a $50,000 trade in a stock with an average daily trading volume of $500 million. Markets that provide price discovery in less active stocks serve an extremely important function for investors in those stocks. Price discovery not only benefits those investors who choose to trade on any particular day, but also benefits those who simply need to monitor the status of their investment. Efficient secondary markets support buy-andhold investors by offering them a ready opportunity to trade at any time at a fair price if they need to buy or sell a stock. Indeed, this enhanced assurance is one of the most important contributions of secondary markets to efficient capital-formation and to reducing the cost of capital for listed companies. The square root function allocates revenues to markets that perform this function for less-active stocks by marginally increasing their percentage of market data revenues, while still allocating a much greater dollar amount to more actively traded stocks.

With respect to very inactively traded stocks, however, the adopted formula modifies the reproposed square root allocation by limiting the revenues that can be allocated to a single Network security to an amount that is no greater than $4 per qualified transaction report. The amount that exceeds this $4 limitation will be reallocated among all Network securities in direct proportion to their dollar volume of trading (which is heavily weighted toward the most actively traded stocks). The Commission is adopting this $4 limitation to respond to commenters' concerns about the potential for abusive quoting behavior in extremely inactive stocks by anyone seeking to game the Quoting Share allocation.

Id. at 1736–1737.

The Commission, as in the December 2004 reproposal, followed the Advisory Committee on Market Information, chaired by the author, and limited mandatory quotations in new Rule 603(c) to basic quotation information (price, size, and market center identification of the NBBO). The Commission rescinded the prohibition earlier in former Rule 11Aa3-1 (redesignated as Rule 601) on SROs disseminating their trade reports independently. "Under adopted Rule 601, members of an SRO will continue to be required to transmit trades to the SRO (and the SROs would continue to transmit trades to the Networks pursuant to the Plans), but such members also will be free to distribute their own data independently, with or without fees." Id. at 1741.

The Commission retains the market data consolidation model, see id. at 1742, but substantially revises the consolidated display requirement:

> It incorporates a new definition of *consolidated display* (set forth in adopted Rule 600(b)(13)) that is limited to the prices, sizes, and market center identifications of the NBBO and *consolidated last sale information* (which is defined in Rule 600(b)(14)). The consolidated information on quotations and trades must be provided in an equivalent manner to any other information on quotations and trades provided by a securities information processor or broker-dealer. Beyond disclosure of this basic information, market forces, rather than regulatory requirements, will be allowed to determine what, if any, additional data from other market centers is displayed. In particular, investors and other information users ultimately will be able to decide whether they need additional information in their displays.
>
> In addition, adopted Rule 603(c) narrows the contexts in which a consolidated display is required to those when it is most needed — a context in which a trading or order-routing decision could be implemented. For example, the consolidated display requirement will continue to cover broker-dealers who provide on-line data to their customers in software programs from which trading decisions can be implemented. Similarly, the requirement will continue to apply to vendors who provide displays that facilitate order routing by broker-dealers. It will not apply, however,

> when market data is provided on a purely informational website that does not offer any trading or order-routing capability.

Id. at 1742.

The balance of Regulation NMS generally renumbered rules adopted under §11A of the Securities Exchange Act as part of Regulation NMS:

- Rule 600: NMS Security Designation and Definitions (replaces Exchange Act Rule 11Aa2-1, which the Commission is rescinding, and incorporates definitions from the existing NMS rules and the new rules adopted today):
- Rule 601: Dissemination of Transaction Reports and Last Sale Data with Respect to Transactions in NMS Stocks (renumbers and renames Exchange Act Rule 11Aa3-1, the substance of which is being modified);
- Rule 602: Dissemination of Quotations in NMS Securities (renumbers and renames Exchange Act Rule 11Ac1-1 (*Quote Rule*), the substance of which remains largely intact);
- Rule 603: Distribution, Consolidation, and Display of Information with Respect to Quotations for and Transactions in NMS Stocks (renumbers and renames Exchange Act Rule 11Ac1-2 (*Vendor Display Rule*), the substance of which is being modified substantially);
- Rule 604: Display of Customer Limit Orders (renumbers Exchange Act Rule 11Ac1-4 (*Limit Order Display Rule*), the substance of which remains largely intact);
- Rule 605: Disclosure of Order Execution Information (renumbers Exchange Act Rule 11Ac1-5, the substance of which remains largely intact);
- Rule 606: Disclosure of Order Routing Information (renumbers Exchange Act Rule 11Ac1-6, the substance of which remains largely intact);
- Rule 607: Customer Account Statements (renumbers Exchange Act Rule 11Ac1-3, the substance of which remains largely intact);

209

- Rule 608: Filing and Amendment of National Market System Plans (renumbers Exchange Act Rule 11Aa3-2, the substance of which remains largely intact);
- Rule 609: Registration of Securities Information Processors: Form of Application and Amendments (renumbers Exchange Act Rule 11Ab2-1, the substance of which remains largely intact).

Id. at 1743.

The Commission also made conforming amendments to several other SEC rules, including Securities Act Rule 144; Securities Exchange Act Rules 0-10, 3a51-1, 3b-16, 10a-1, 10b-10, 10b-18, 12a-7, 12f-1, 12f-2, 15b9-1, 15c2-11, 19c-3, 19c-4, and 31; as well as Regulation ATS Rules 300 and 301 and Rule 17a-7 of the Investment Company Act.


### 3.   THE OVER-THE-COUNTER MARKET


#### a.   Nasdaq

***P. 758, new text, end carryover par.*** Earlier in 2006 the SEC approved the application of Nasdaq. SEC approval was conditioned on the satisfaction of several conditions for Nasdaq before commencing operations as an exchange. These included:

- Nasdaq must join the various national market system plans and the Intermarket Surveillance Group.
- The NASD must determine that its control of Nasdaq through its Preferred Class D share is no longer necessary because the NASD can fulfill through other means its obligations with respect to non-Nasdaq exchange-listed securities under the Exchange Act, the rules adopted thereunder, and the various national market system plans.
- The Commission must declare effective certain regulatory plans to be filed by Nasdaq.

- Nasdaq must file, and the Commission must approve, an agreement pursuant to Section 17d-2 of the Exchange Act that allocates to the NASD regulatory responsibility with respect to certain activities of common members.

SEC Rel. 2006-9 (Jan. 13, 2006). See also Sec. Ex. Act Rel. 52,049, 85 SEC Dock. 3069 (2005) (NASD Notice of Proposed Rule Changes to Reflect Nasdaq's Separation Upon Anticipated Approval of Nasdaq's Application to Be a National Securities Exchange).

### c.   Order Execution

*P. 763 n.100, end note.*   In 2003 the Commission approved a post-trade anonymity feature in SuperMontage. Sec. Ex. Act Rel. 48,527, 81 SEC Dock 291 (2003) (approval).

In Domestic Sec., Inc. v. SEC, 333 F.3d 239 (D.C. Cir. 2003), the court rejected a petition to review the alternative display facility in SuperMontage because the SEC order was supported by substantial evidence and was not arbitrary or capricious.

### 4.   OPTIONS MARKETS

### a.   Stock Options

*P. 763, new n.101.1, end page.*   In 2003 the Commission approved a post-trade anonymity feature in SuperMontage. Sec. Ex. Act Rel. 48,527, 81 SEC Dock 291 (2003) (approval).

## C.   SECURITIES ASSOCIATIONS

### 2.   THE NATIONAL ASSOCIATION OF SECURITIES DEALERS

*P. 788 n.4 end note.*   The Second Circuit has held that the NASD, a private SRO, is not a state actor subject to due process requirements. See Desiderio v. NASD, 191 F.3d 198, 206–207 (2d Cir. 1999); Perpetual Sec., Inc. v. Tang, 290 F.3d 132, 127–139 (2d Cir. 2002). Cf. D'Alessio v. SEC, 380 F.3d 112, 121–122, n.12 (2d Cir. 2004) (reserving question with respect to NYSE).

The Second Circuit, however, has concluded that the statutory requirement in the Securities Exchange Act of a "fair procedure" will subject SROs to a due process requirement that the decision-maker be impartial. Id. at 121 (concluding that NYSE Hearing Panel could be impartial even if defendants were suing senior Exchange officials).

Similarly the Second Circuit has held that the personal recusals of SEC Commissioners is "sufficient to cure any impropriety in appearance of impropriety with respect to the Commission proceedings." MFS Sec. Corp. v. SEC, 380 F.3d 611, 618–620 (2d Cir. 2004). Unlike an SRO, the Fifth and Fourteenth Amendments do apply to the SEC and do require a tribunal free of personal bias. Ibid.

## D.   BROKERAGE COMMISSION RATE REGULATION

### 1.   ANTITRUST GENERALLY

*P. 797 n.25, end note.*   In MFS Sec. Corp. v. NYSE, Inc., 142 Fed. Appx. 541 (2d Cir. 2005), the Second Circuit affirmed a dismissal of an antitrust case alleging a group boycott. In the context of a self-regulatory organization operating under the Securities Exchange Act, a plaintiff has to satisfy the rule of reason and allege anticompetitive effects. Here the plaintiff alleged none.

In contrast, in Billing v. Credit Suisse First Boston, 426 F.3d 130 (2d Cir. 2005), the court held that the federal securities laws did not completely repeal the antitrust laws when the plaintiff alleged a conspiracy involving book building in several underwritings.

## 2. Commission Rate Regulation

*P. 802 n.39, end note.* By 2002 Greenwich Associates estimated that $4.5 billion of the $12.7 billion paid in commissions by mutual funds and other institutional investors was for research and other items purchased with soft dollars. Oster & Lauricella, Mutual Funds' Soft Fees Getting a Hard Look, Wall St. J., Dec. 26, 2003, at C1.

In February 2004 the SEC unanimously voted to outlaw directed brokerage arrangements in which mutual funds use brokerage commissions to pay broker-dealers for selling fund shares. SEC Proposes Directed-Brokerage Ban, Adopts New Fee-Disclosure Requirements, 36 Sec. Reg. & L. Rep. (BNA) 293 (2004).

The Report of the NASD Mutual Fund Task Force on Soft Dollars and Portfolio Transactions (Nov. 11, 2004) unanimously recommended retaining the §28(e) safe harbor, but that the SEC should narrow its interpretation of the scope of §28(e) to better tailor the Section to the type of soft dollar services that benefit the adviser' clients rather than the adviser.

In 2005 the Commission proposed a new interpretation of §28(e). Sec. Ex. Act Rel. 52,635, 86 SEC Dock. 1235 (2005) (proposal). The proposal Release explained in part:

> In light of recent developments in client commission practices, evolving technologies, marketplace developments, and the observations of the staff in examinations of industry participants, we have revisited our previous guidance as to the meaning of the phrase "brokerage and research services" in Section 28(e). After careful consideration, we are proposing a revised interpretation that would replace Sections II and III of the 1986 Release. Specifically, we are providing guidance with respect to: (i) the appropriate framework for analyzing whether a particular service falls within the "brokerage and research services" safe harbor; (ii) the eligibility criteria for "research"; (iii) the eligibility criteria for "brokerage"; and (iv) the appropriate treatment of "mixed-use" items. We also discuss the money manager's statutory requirement to make a good faith determination that the commissions paid are reasonable in relation to the value of the brokerage and research

services received. Finally, we provide guidance on third-party research and commission-sharing arrangements.

Section 28(e) applies equally to arrangements involving client commissions paid to full service broker-dealers that provide brokerage and research services directly to money managers, and to third-party research arrangements where the research services and products are developed by third parties and provided by a broker-dealer that participates in effecting the transaction. Today, it remains true that, if the conditions of the safe harbor of Section 28(e) are met, a money manager does not breach his fiduciary duties solely on the basis that he uses client commissions to pay a broker-dealer more than the lowest available commission rate for a bundle of products and services provided by the broker-dealer (*i.e.*, anything more than "pure execution"). . . .

Taking into account the legislative history of Section 28(e) and our prior guidance, the analysis of whether a particular product or service falls within the safe harbor should involve three steps. First, the money manager must determine whether the product or service falls within the specific statutory limits of Section 28(e)(3)(A), (B), or (C) (*i.e.*, whether it is an eligible product or service under the safe harbor). Second, the manager must determine whether the eligible product or service actually provides lawful and appropriate assistance in the performance of his investment decision-making responsibilities. Finally, the manager must make a good faith determination that the amount of client commissions paid is reasonable in light of the value of products or services provided by the broker-dealer. . . .

### Eligibility Criteria for "Research Services" under Section 28(e)(3); Lawful and Appropriate Assistance

The eligibility criteria that govern "research services" are set forth in Section 28(e)(3) of the Exchange Act:

> For purposes of the safe harbor, a person provides . . . *research services* insofar as he —
>
> (A) furnishes *advice*, either directly or through publications or writings, as to the value of securities, the advisability of investing in, purchasing, or selling securities, and the availability of securities or purchasers or sellers of securities;

(B) furnishes *analyses* and *reports* concerning issuers, industries, securities, economic factors and trends, portfolio strategy, and the performance of accounts; ...

In determining that a particular product or service falls within the safe harbor, the money manager must conclude that it constitutes "advice," "analyses," or "reports" within the meaning of the statute and that its subject matter falls within the categories specified in Section 28(e)(3)(A) and (B). With respect to the subject matter of potential "research services," we note that the categories expressly listed in Section 28(e)(3)(A) and (B) also "subsume" other topics related to securities and the financial markets. Thus, for example, a report concerning political factors that are interrelated with economic factors could fall within the scope of the safe harbor. The form (*e.g.*, electronic or paper) of the research is irrelevant to the analysis of eligibility under the safe harbor.

In evaluating the statutory language, the Commission notes that an important common element among "advice," "analyses," and "reports" is that each reflects substantive content—that is, the expression of reasoning or knowledge. Thus, in determining whether a product or service is eligible as "research" under Section 28(e), the money manager must conclude that it reflects the expression of reasoning or knowledge and relates to the subject matter identified in Section 28(e)(3)(A) or (B). Traditional research reports analyzing the performance of a particular company or stock clearly would be eligible under Section 28(e). Certain financial newsletters and trade journals also could be eligible research services if they relate to the subject matter of the statute. Quantitative analytical software and software that provides analyses of securities portfolios would be eligible under the safe harbor if they reflect the expression of reasoning or knowledge relating to subject matter that is included in Section 28(e)(3)(A) and (B). Seminars or conferences where the content satisfies the above criteria also would be eligible.

In contrast, products or services that do not reflect the expression of reasoning or knowledge, including products with inherently tangible or physical attributes (such as telephone lines or office furniture), are not eligible as research under the safe harbor. We do not believe that these types of products and services could be said to constitute "advice," "analyses," or "reports" within the meaning of the statute. Applying this guidance, a money

215

manager's operational overhead expenses would not constitute eligible "research services." For example, travel expenses, entertainment, and meals associated with attending seminars would not be eligible under the safe harbor. Similarly, office equipment, office furniture and business supplies, telephone lines, salaries (including research staff), rent, accounting fees and software, website design, e-mail software, internet service, legal expenses, personnel management, marketing, utilities, membership dues, professional licensing fees, and software to assist with administrative functions such as managing back-office functions, operating systems, and word processing are examples of other overhead items that do not meet the statutory criteria for research (or brokerage) set forth in this release and are not eligible under the safe harbor.

Computer hardware and computer accessories, while they may assist in the delivery of research, would not be eligible "research services" because they do not reflect substantive content related in any way to making decisions about investing. Similarly, the peripherals and delivery mechanisms associated with computer hardware, including telecommunications lines, transatlantic cables, and computer cables, are outside the "research services" safe harbor.

As noted above, even if the manager properly concludes that a particular product or service is an "analysis," "advice," or "report" that reflects the expression of reasoning or knowledge, it would be eligible research only if the subject matter of the product or service falls within the categories specified in Section 28(e)(3)(A) and (B). Thus, for example, consultants' services may be eligible for the safe harbor if the consultant provides advice with respect to portfolio strategy, but such services would not be eligible if the advice relates to the managers' internal management or operations.

With respect to data services — such as those that provide market data or economic data — we believe that such services could fall within the scope of the safe harbor as eligible "reports" provided that they satisfy the subject matter criteria. In the 1986 Release, we included market data services within the safe harbor, finding that they serve "a legitimate research function of pricing securities for investment and keeping a manager informed of market developments." Because market data contain aggregations of information on a current basis related to the subject matter identified in the statute, and in light of the history of Section 28(e), our interpretation would conclude that market data, such as stock quotes, last sale prices, and trading volumes, contain substantive content and constitute "reports concerning ... securities" within the meaning of Section 28(e)(3)(B), and thus would be eligible as "research services" under the safe harbor. Similarly, other data would be eligible under the safe harbor if they reflect substantive content—that is, the expression of reasoning or knowledge—related to the subject matter identified in the statute. For example, we believe that company financial data and economic data (such as unemployment and inflation rates or gross domestic product figures) would be eligible as research under Section 28(e). . . .

### Eligibility Criteria for "Brokerage" under Section 28(e)(3); Lawful and Appropriate Assistance

Under Section 28(e)(3)(C) of the Act, a person provides "brokerage ... services" insofar as he or she:

> effects securities transactions and performs functions incidental thereto (such as clearance, settlement, and custody) or required in connection therewith by rules of the Commission or a self-regulatory organization of which such person is a member or in which such person is a participant.

Section 28(e)(3)(C) describes the brokerage products and services that are *eligible* under the safe harbor. In addition to activities required to effect securities transactions, Section 28(e)(3)(C) provides that functions "incidental thereto" are also eligible for the safe harbor, as are functions that are required by Commission or self-regulatory organization ("SRO") rules. Clearance and settlement services in connection with trades effected by the broker are explicitly identified as eligible incidental brokerage services. Therefore, the following post-trade services relate to functions incidental to executing a transaction and are eligible under the safe harbor as "brokerage services": post-trade matching; exchange of messages among broker-dealers, custodians, and institutions; electronic communication of allocation instructions between institutions and broker-dealers; and routing settlement instructions to custodian banks and broker-dealers' clearing agents. Similarly, services that are required by the Commission or SRO rules are eligible under the safe harbor. For example, in certain circumstances, the use of electronic confirmation and affirmation of institutional trades is required in connection with settlement processing. . . .

Guided by the statute and legislative history, we believe that Congress intended "brokerage" services under the safe harbor to relate to the execution of securities transactions. In our view, brokerage under Section 28(e) should reflect historical and current industry practices that execution of transactions is a process, and that services related to execution of securities transactions begin when an order is transmitted to a broker-dealer and end at the conclusion of clearance and settlement of the transaction. We believe that this temporal standard is an appropriate way to distinguish between "brokerage services" that are eligible under Section 28(e) and those products and services, such as overhead, that are not eligible. Specifically, for purposes of the safe harbor, we believe that brokerage begins when the money manager communicates with the broker-dealer for the purpose of transmitting an order for execution and ends when funds or securities are delivered or credited to the advised account or the account holder's agent. Unlike brokerage, research services include services provided before the communication of an order. Thus, advice provided by a broker before an order is transmitted may fall within the research portion of the safe harbor, but not the brokerage portion of the safe harbor.

Under this temporal standard, communications services related to the execution, clearing, and settlement of securities transactions and other incidental functions, *i.e.*, connectivity service between the money manager and the broker-dealer and other relevant parties such as custodians (including dedicated lines between the broker-dealer and the money manager's order management system; lines between the broker-dealer and order management systems operated by a third-party vendor; dedicated lines providing direct dial-up service between the money manager and the trading desk at the broker-dealer; and message services used to transmit orders to broker-dealers for execution) are eligible under Section 28(e)(3)(C). In addition, trading software operated by a broker-dealer to route orders to market centers and algorithmic trading software is [*sic*] "brokerage."

On the other hand, order management systems ("OMS") used by money managers to manage their orders (including OMS developed in-house at the manager and those obtained from third-party vendors) and hardware, such as telephones or computer terminals, are not eligible for the safe harbor as "brokerage" because they are not sufficiently related to order execution and fall outside the temporal standard for "brokerage" under the safe harbor. Products and services such as trade analytics, surveillance systems, or compliance mechanisms, do not qualify as "brokerage" in the safe harbor because they are not integral to the execution of orders by the broker-dealers, *i.e.*, they fall outside the temporal standard described above. Moreover, error correction trades or related services in connection with errors made by money managers are not related to the initial trade for a client within the meaning of Section 28(e)(3)(C) because they are separate transactions to correct the manager's error, not to benefit the advised account, and thus error correction functions are not eligible "brokerage services" under the safe harbor. The products and services described in this paragraph are properly characterized as "overhead" and are ineligible under Section 28(d).

### "Mixed-Use" Items

... [T]he 1986 Release introduced the concept of "mixed use." Where a product obtained with client commissions has a mixed use, a money manager faces an additional conflict of interest in obtaining that product with client commissions. The 1986 Release stated that where a product has a mixed use, a money manager should make a reasonable allocation of the cost of the product according to its use, and emphasized that the money manager must keep adequate books and records concerning allocations in order to make the required good faith determination. Moreover, the allocation determination itself poses a conflict of interest for the money manager that should be disclosed to the client. It appears that, in practice, some managers may have made questionable mixed-use allocations and failed to document the bases for their allocation decisions. Lack of documentation makes it difficult for the manager to make the required good faith showing of the reasonableness of the commissions paid in relation to the value of the portion of the item allocated as brokerage and research under Section 28(e), and also makes it difficult for compliance personnel to ascertain the basis for the allocation.

We continue to believe that the "mixed-use" approach is appropriate. In that connection, we reiterate today the Commission's guidance provided in the 1986 Release regarding the mixed-use standard: "The money manager must keep adequate books and records concerning allocations so as to be able to make the required good faith showing." ... [T]he mixed-use approach requires a money manager to make a reasonable allocation of the cost of the product according to its use. For example, an allocable portion of the cost of portfolio performance evaluation services or reports may be eligible as research, but money managers must use their own funds to pay for the allocable portion of such services or reports that is used for marketing purposes.

### The Money Manager's Good Faith Determination as to Reasonableness Under Section 28(e)

Section 28(e) requires money managers who are seeking to avail themselves of the safe harbor to make a good faith determination that the commissions paid are reasonable in relation to the value of the brokerage and research services received. The Commission reaffirms the money manager's essential obligation under Section 28(e) to make this good faith determination. The burden of proof in demonstrating this determination rests on the money manager. . . .

### Third-Party Research and Commission-Sharing Arrangements

Third-party research arrangements can benefit advised accounts by providing greater breadth and depth of research. First, these arrangements can provide money managers with the ability to choose from a broad array of independent research products and services. Second, the manager can use third-party arrangements to obtain specialized research that is particularly beneficial to their advised accounts.

### Research Services Must Be "Provided by" the Broker-Dealer

Section 28(e) requires that the broker-dealer receiving commissions must "provide" brokerage or research services. The Commission has interpreted this to permit money managers to use client

220

commissions to pay for research produced by someone other than the executing broker-dealer, in certain circumstances (referred to as "third-party research"). The essential feature of the "provided by" element is that the broker-dealer has the direct legal obligation to pay for the research. The Commission also has clarified that research provided in third-party arrangements is eligible under Section 28(e) even if the money manager participates in selecting the research services or products that the broker-dealer will provide. The third party may send the research directly to the broker's customer so long as the broker-dealer has the obligation to pay for the services. In contrast, a money manager may not rely upon Section 28(e) if he uses the broker-dealer merely to pay an obligation that he has incurred with a third party. The 1998 OCIE Report discussed instances in which some money managers had entered into such arrangements whereby broker-dealers paid for research or brokerage services for which the money managers were obligated to pay. The Commission reminds money managers and broker-dealers that these arrangements are not eligible for the Section 28(e) safe harbor.

### "Effecting" Transactions

Section 28(e) requires that the broker-dealer providing the research also be involved in "effecting" the trade. The inclusion of this element in Section 28(e) was principally intended to preclude the practice of paying "give-ups." Specifically, when brokerage commissions were fixed before 1975, a "give-up" was a payment to another broker-dealer of a portion of the commission required to be charged by the executing broker-dealer. The broker-dealer receiving the give-up may have had no role in the transaction generating the commission, and it may not even have known where or when the trade was executed. Because the portion of the commission "given up" is a charge above the cost of execution on client accounts and because the broker-dealer receiving the "give-up" did nothing in connection with the securities trade to benefit investors, the Commission found that these arrangements violated the securities laws. In enacting Section 28(e), Congress addressed the issue of give-ups by indicating that the provision did not apply when the money manager made payment to one broker-dealer for the services performed by another broker-dealer. In the 1986 Release, the Commission indicated that payment of a part of a commission to a broker-dealer who is a "normal and legitimate correspondent" of the executing or clearing broker-dealer would not necessarily be a "give-up," outside the protection of Section 28(e).

Some investment managers today use "commission-sharing" arrangements to execute trades with one broker-dealer and obtain research or other services from a different broker-dealer. In some commission-sharing arrangements, the introducing broker-dealer accepts orders from its customers and then may execute the trade and provide research, while a second broker-dealer clears and settles the transaction. In other commission-sharing arrangements, an "introducing" broker-dealer retains a portion of the commission, and has little, if any, role in accepting customer orders or in executing, clearing, or settling any portion of the trade. Rather, another broker-dealer (often called the "clearing broker") executes, clears, and settles the trade, receiving a portion of the commission for its services. In some instances, the introducing broker is unaware of the daily trading activity of its customers because the orders are sent by the money manager directly (and only) to the clearing broker-dealer.

Where more than one broker-dealer is involved in a commission-sharing arrangement, the Commission takes the view that the "introducing broker [must be] engaged in securities activities of a more extensive nature than merely the receipt of commissions paid to it by other broker-dealers for 'research services' provided to money managers."

Commission-sharing arrangements typically involve clearing agreements pursuant to SRO rules. These SRO rules require that introducing and clearing firms contractually agree to allocate enumerated functions, but do not mandate how the functions should be divided (*i.e.*, they do not specify the functions that must be done by the introducing broker-dealer or clearing broker-dealer). We note, however, that a clearing agreement that satisfies SRO rule requirements does not necessarily satisfy the criteria of Section 28(e). Each broker-dealer must play a role in effecting securities transactions that goes beyond the mere provision of research services to money managers. The nature of the activities actually performed by each broker-dealer determines whether the commission-sharing arrangement qualifies under Section 28(e).

In connection with commission-sharing arrangements, each party to the arrangement must determine if it is contributing to a violation of law, including whether the involvement of multiple parties to the trade is necessary to effecting the trade, beneficial to the client, and appropriate in light of all applicable duties. In particular, as discussed above, the broker-dealer involved in effecting the trade must also be legally obligated to pay for the third-party research or brokerage service (*i.e.*, the "provided by" requirement).

The following elements are necessary for a commission-sharing arrangement under which research and brokerage services are provided under the safe harbor:

- The commission-sharing arrangement must be part of a normal and legitimate correspondent relationship in which each broker-dealer is engaged in securities activities of a more extensive nature than merely the receipt of commissions paid to it by other broker-dealers for research services provided to money managers (*i.e.*, "effecting securities transactions" requirement). Based on the Commission's experience, we believe that, at a minimum, this means that the introducing broker-dealer must: (1) be financially responsible to the clearing broker-dealer for all customer trades until the clearing broker-dealer has received payment (or securities), *i.e.*, the introducing broker-dealer must be at risk to the clearing broker-dealer for its customers' failure to pay; (2) make and/or maintain records relating to its customer trades required by Commission and SRO rules, including blotters and memoranda of orders; (3) monitor and respond to customer comments concerning the trading process; and (4) generally monitor trades and settlements; and
- A broker-dealer effecting the trade (if not providing research and brokerage services directly) must be legally obligated to a third-party producer of research or brokerage services to pay for the service ultimately provided to a money manager (*i.e.*, "provided by" requirement).

Id. at 1242–1252.

# CHAPTER 8

# REGULATION OF BROKERS, DEALERS, AND INVESTMENT ADVISERS

## A. BROKER-DEALER REGISTRATION

### 8. RESEARCH ANALYSTS

#### a. The Global Settlement

***P. 841, new n.109.1, end 2d par.*** In Merrill Lynch & Co., Inc. Research Reports, 272 F. Supp. 2d 243 (S.D.N.Y. 2003), the late Judge Milton Pollack dismissed with prejudice an action against a proprietary mutual fund that invested in the common stock of companies covered by Merrill Lynch analyst researches, in part, because the court did not find that the defendants had a duty to disclose specified omitted information.

In affirming Judge Pollack's decision, the Second Circuit in Lentell v. Merrill Lynch & Co., Inc., 396 F.3d 161 (2d Cir. 2005), *cert. denied*, 126 S. Ct. 421, assumed a less vituperative tone and relied upon the plaintiff's failure to adequately plead loss causation:

> Plaintiffs allege that when they invested, there were relying on the integrity of the market (including the fraudulent recommendations and omissions made by Merrill Lynch during the putative

class periods), that the shares plummeted, and that their investments became virtually worthless. To plead loss causation, the complaints must allege facts that support an inference that Merrill's misstatements and omissions concealed the circumstances that bear upon the loss suffered such that plaintiffs would have been spared all or an ascertainable portion of that loss absent the fraud. As the district court found, no such allegations are made. *Merrill Lynch*, 273 F. Supp. 2d at 367-68. There is no allegation that the market reacted negatively to a corrective disclosure regarding the falsity of Merrill's *buy* and *accumulate* recommendations and no allegation that Merrill misstated or omitted risks that did lead to the loss. This is fatal under Second Circuit precedent....

As noted, to establish loss causation, "a plaintiff must allege ... that the *subject* of the fraudulent statement or omission was the cause of the actual loss suffered." *Suez Equity*, 250 F.3d at 95 (emphasis added). It is alleged that Merrill's *buy* and *accumulate* recommendations were false and misleading with respect to 24/7 Media and Interliant, and that those recommendations artificially inflated the value of 24/7 Media and Interliant stock. However, plaintiffs do not allege that the subject of those false recommendations (that investors should buy or accumulate 24/7 Media and Interliant stock), or any corrective disclosure regarding the falsity of those recommendations, is the cause of the *decline* in stock value that plaintiffs claim as their loss. Nor do plaintiffs allege that Merrill Lynch concealed or misstated any risks associated with an investment in 24/7 Media or Interliant, some of which presumably caused plaintiffs' loss. Plaintiffs therefore failed to allege loss causation, as that requirement is set out in *Emergent Capital*, *Castellano*, and *Suez Equity*.

Id. at 175.

In Merrill Lynch & Co., Inc., 273 F. Supp. 2d 351 (S.D.N.Y. 2003), Judge Pollack also dismissed claims against Merrill Lynch for the opinions expressed by its Internet research group. This case was striking for its tone. Judge Pollack wrote in part:

The record clearly reveals that plaintiffs were among the high-risk speculators who, knowing full well or being properly chargeable with appreciation of the unjustifiable risks they were undertaking in the extremely volatile and highly untested stocks at issue, now hope to twist the federal securities laws into a scheme of cost-free speculators' insurance. Seeking to lay the blame for the enormous Internet Bubble solely at the feet of a single actor, Merrill Lynch, plaintiffs would have this court conclude that the federal securities laws were meant to underwrite, subsidize, and encourage their rash speculation in joining a freewheeling casino that lured thousands obsessed with the fantasy of Olympian riches, but which delivered such riches to only a scant handful of lucky winners. Those few lucky winners, who are not before the court, now hold the monies that the unlucky plaintiffs have lost — fair and square — and they will never return those monies to plaintiffs. Had plaintiffs themselves won the game instead of losing, they would have owed not a single penny of their winnings to those they left to hold the bag (or to defendants).

Notwithstanding this — the federal securities laws at issue here only fault those who, *with intent to defraud,* make a *material* misrepresentation or omission of *fact* (not opinion) in connection with the purchase or sale of securities that *causes* a plaintiff's losses. Considering all of the facts and circumstances of the cases at bar, and accepting all of plaintiffs' voluminous inflammatory and improperly generalized allegations as true, this court is utterly unconvinced that the misrepresentations and omissions alleged in the complaints have been sufficiently alleged to be cognizable misrepresentations and omissions made with the intent to defraud. Plaintiffs have failed to adequately plead that defendant and its former chief internet analyst *caused* their losses. The facts and circumstances fully within this court's proper province to consider on a motion to dismiss show beyond doubt that plaintiffs brought their own losses upon themselves when they knowingly spun an extremely high-risk, high-stakes wheel of fortune.

Id. at 358. See also Merrill Lynch & Co., Inc. Research Reports, 289 F. Supp. 2d 416 (S.D.N.Y. 2003) (dismissal of similar complaints); Merrill Lynch & Co., Inc. Research Reports, 289 F. Supp. 2d 429 (S.D.N.Y. 2003).

In July 2003 Citigroup, Inc. and J. P. Morgan Chase & Co. agreed to pay approximately $305 million to settle federal and state charges that they structured transactions by Enron in a way that allowed Enron to falsely characterize loan proceeds as cash from operations. Citigroup, J. P. Morgan Chase Settle Charges

They Helped Enron Commit Fraud, 35 Sec. Reg. & L. Rep. (CCH) 1285 (2003).

### b.　NASD and NYSE Rules

*P. 843 n.111, end note.*　In 2003 the SEC approved the NYSE and NASD rules. Sec. Ex. Act Rel. 48,252, 80 SEC Dock. 2179 (2003) (approval). See also Responses to Frequently Asked Questions Concerning Regulation Analyst Certification, 2003 Fed. Sec. L. Rep. (CCH) ¶86,955 (Aug. 6, 2003).

Early in 2005, the Commission approved further amendments to the NYSE and NASD rules that restrict research analyst activities. Sec. Ex. Act Rels. 51,358, 84 SEC Dock. 3571 (2005) (proposed NYSE Rule 472(b) and NASD Rule 2711(c)); 51,593, 85 SEC Dock. 739 (2005) (approval). The new restrictions, which were inspired by the global settlement, prohibit research analyst participation in road shows; three way conversations with research analysts, investors, *and* investment bankers or executives of a corporate issuer; research analyst sales or marketing activities; and require fair, balanced, and not misleading research analyst written or oral communications.

## C.　INVESTMENT ADVISERS

### 2.　Definition of *Investment Adviser*

### b.　Exclusions

(iv)　*Brokers and Dealers*

*P. 894, new par. after carryover par.*　In 2005, the Commission adopted Rule 202(a)(11)-1 after earlier having adopted most of the proposed Rule on a temporary basis in Rule 202(a) (11)T.

Inv. Adv. Act Rels. 2340, 84 SEC Dock. 2208 (2005) (proposed Rule 202(a)(11)-1); 2339, 84 SEC Dock. 2204 (2005) (adoption of Rule 202(a)(11)T); 2376, 85 SEC Dock. 474 (2005) (adoption of Rule 202(a)(11)-1).

In 1999, the Commission had proposed a rule under §202(a) (11) to respond to the introduction of fee based brokerage and discount brokerage programs by full service brokers. Inv. Adv. Rel. 1841, 70 SEC Dock. 2486 (1999) (proposed Rule). The 2005 proposal Release explained:

> Fee-based brokerage programs provide customers a package of brokerage services — including execution, investment advice, custodial and recordkeeping services — for a fee based on the amount of assets on account with the broker-dealer (*i.e.*, an asset-based fee) or a fixed fee. Asset-based fees generally range from 1.10 percent to 1.50 percent of assets. A broker-dealer may be deemed to have received special compensation solely because the broker or dealer would not be deemed to have received special compensation solely because the broker or dealer charges a commission, mark-up, mark-down, or similar fee for brokerage services that is greater than or less than one it charges another customer. This provision was designed to permit full-service broker-dealers to offer discounted brokerage, including electronic trading, without having to treat fullprice, full-service brokerage customers as advisory clients.

Inv. Adv. Rel. 2340, 84 SEC Dock. at 2210–2211.

The Commission received over 1700 comment letters on the proposal, with broker-dealers strongly supporting the new approach and investment advisers fervently opposing it:

> Broker-dealers commenting on the rule strongly supported it. They asserted that fee-based brokerage programs benefitted customers by aligning the interests of representatives with those of their customers. According to some of these broker-dealers, the application of the Advisers Act would discourage the introduction of fee-based programs by imposing what these brokerage firms viewed to be a duplicative and unnecessary regulatory regime....

A large number of investment advisers — in particular, financial planners — and a few consumer groups submitted letters strongly opposed to the proposed rule.... Many of these commenters asserted that the adoption of the rule would deny investors important protections provided by the Act, in particular, the fiduciary duties and disclosure obligations to which advisers are held.

Id. 85 SEC Dock. at 478–479.

After several years of reconsideration, the Commission proposal largely sided with the broker-dealers:

We continue, however, to believe that fee-based brokerage has the potential to provide significant benefits to brokerage customers. Our reproposal therefore reflects our belief that when broker-dealers offer advisory services as part of the traditional package of brokerage services, broker-dealers ought not to be subject to the Advisers Act merely because they re-price those services. The reproposal also reflects our belief that broker-dealers should be permitted to offer both full-service brokerage and discount brokerage services without triggering application of the Advisers Act. The reproprosal also reflects our belief that a broker-dealer providing discretionary advice would be deemed to be an investment adviser under the Advisers Act.

Id. 84 SEC Dock. at 2213.

Conceptually, the Commission based its position in its interpretation of history:

Broker-dealers have traditionally provided investment advice that is substantial in amount, variety, and importance to their customers. This was well understood in 1940 when Congress passed the Advisers Act. The broker-dealer exception in the Act was designed not to except broker-dealers whose advice to customers is minor or insignificant, but rather to avoid additional and duplicative regulation of broker-dealers, which were regulated under provisions of the Exchange Act that had been enacted six years earlier. The exception also differentiated between advice provided by brokerdealers to customers as part of a package of traditional brokerage services for which customers paid fixed commissions — which was not covered by the Advisers Act, and advice provided through broker-dealer's special advisory departments for which customers separately contracted and paid a fee —which was covered by the Act.... [T]he Advisers Act was written in such a way to cover feebased programs because the fee would constitute *special compensation*, it does not appear to have been Congress' intent to apply the Act to cover broker-dealers providing advice as part of the package of brokerage services they provide under fee-based brokerage programs.

The Advisers Act was enacted in an era when broker-dealers were paid fixed commission rates for the traditional package of services (including investment advice), and Congress understood *special compensation* to mean non-commission compensation. There is no evidence that the *special compensation* requirement was included in section 202(a)(11)(C) for any purpose beyond providing an easy way of accomplishing the underlying goal of excepting only advice that was provided as part of the package of traditional brokerage services. In particular, neither the legislative history of section 202(a)(11)(C) nor the broader history of the Advisers Act as a whole, considered in light of contemporaneous industry practice, suggests that, in 1940, Congress viewed the form of compensation for the services at issue — commission versus fee-based compensation — as having any *independent* relevance in terms of the advisory services the Act was intended to reach.

Id. at 2214–2215.

The Commission also acknowledged that fee-based brokerage programs were now offered by most large broker-dealers and held over $254 billion in customer assets, meaning that there had been a significant growth in the number of broker-dealers that were now covered by both the Securities Exchange and Investment Advisers acts. Id. at 2215.

Proposed Rule 202(a)(11)-1(a)(1) was similar to the 1999 Proposal, except that the disclosure obligation in proposed Rule 202(a)(11)-1(a)(iii) was amplified:

(a) A broker or dealer registered with the Commission under section 15 of the Securities Exchange Act of 1934:

(1) Will not be deemed to be an investment adviser based solely on its receipt of special compensation, provided that:

(i) The broker or dealer does not exercise investment discretion, as that term is defined in section 3(a)(35) of the Exchange Act, over accounts from which it receives special compensation;

(ii) Any investment advice provided by the broker or dealer with respect to accounts from which it receives special compensation is solely incidental to the brokerage services provided to those accounts; and

(iii) Advertisements for, and contracts, agreements, applications and other forms governing, accounts for which the broker or dealer receives special compensation include a prominent statement that the accounts are brokerage accounts and not advisory accounts; that, as a consequence, the customer's rights and firm's duties and obligations to the customer, including the scope of the firm's fiduciary obligations, may differ; and must identify an appropriate person at the firm with whom the customer can discuss the differences.

The 1999 proposed disclosure requirement only required a broker-dealer to disclose that fee based accounts are brokerage accounts. The 2005 proposal Release explained:

We received a great deal of comment that this disclosure was inadequate to permit customers and prospective customers to understand the differences between advisory and brokerage accounts, including the differences in fiduciary duties owed to investors by advisers and brokers. In response, we have reproposed significantly expanded disclosure in order to focus investors on the differences between the two types of accounts.

Id. at 2212.

Temporary Rule 202(a)(11)T(a) in contrast, was identical to proposed Rule 202(a)(11)-1(a), except that it did not include the language of proposed Rule 202(a)(11)-1(a)(iii) and had no disclosure requirement.

Proposed Rule 202(a)(11)-1 was not purely deregulatory. The proposed Rule 202(a)(11)-1(b) exclusion from the Investment Advisers Act was not available for any account over which a broker-dealer exercises investment discretion, without regard, as before, as to whether the broker-dealer had enough other discretionary accounts. The Commission elaborated:

> We believe that such an approach may be preferable for several reasons. First, it better ensures that the Advisers Act is applied where investors have the sort of relationship with a broker-dealer that we have long recognized the Act was intended to reach. Second, it is consistent with the longstanding view, which would be codified in reproposed rule 202(a)(11)-1(c), that a broker-dealer is an investment adviser solely with respect to those accounts for which the broker-dealer provides services or receives compensation that subject the broker-dealer to the Advisers Act. Third, unlike the existing staff approach, the proposed rule provides a bright-line test for the availability of the section 202(a)(11)(C) exception. It thereby clarifies that provision at a time when the line between advisory and brokerage services is blurring and the original *bright line* of special compensation has ceased to function as a reliable indicator of the services the Act was designed to reach. Finally, the proposed interpretation would result in all discretionary accounts being treated as advisory accounts without regard to the form of broker compensation and would therefore be consistent with the design of reproposed rule 202(a)(11)-1 as a whole.

Id. at 2221.

The Commission acknowledged that there is an open question as to whether the legislative history of §202(a)(11)(c) supported proposed Rule 202(a)(11)-1(b). Id. at 2222.

The Committee also sought comment as to whether it should issue an interpretative position with regard to the term *solely incidental to* in proposed Rule 202(a)(11)-1. Id. at 2223–2226.

In the adoption Release the Commission went further and defined *solely incidental to* in Rule 202(a)(11)-1(b):

> A broker or dealer provides advice that is not solely incidental to the conduct of its business as a broker or dealer within the meaning of section 202(a)(11)(C) of the Advisers Act or to the brokerage services provided to accounts from which it receives special compensation within the meaning of paragraph (a)(1)(i) of this section

if the broker or dealer (among other things, and without limitation):

(1) Charges a separate fee, or separately contracts, for advisory services;

(2) Provides advice as a part of a financial plan or in connection with providing financial planning services and;

    (i)   holds itself out generally to the public as a financial planner or as providing financial planning services;

    (ii)  delivers to the customer a financial plan; or

    (iii) represents to the customer that the advice is provided as part of a financial plan or in connection with financial planning services; or

(3) Exercises investment discretion, as that term is defined in paragraph (d) of this section, over any customer accounts.

This was a major clarification of the often blurry line between broker-dealers, investment advisers, and financial planners. The adoption Release explained:

> In general, investment advice is "solely incidental to" the conduct of a broker-dealer's business within the meaning of section 202(a)(11)(C) and to "brokerage services" provided to accounts under the rule when the advisory services rendered are in connection with and reasonably related to the brokerage services provided. This is consistent with the language Congress chose and the legislative history of the Advisers Act, including contemporaneous industry practice, which indicates Congress' intent to exclude broker-dealers providing advice as part of traditional brokerage services. It is also consistent with the Commission's contemporaneous construction of the Advisers Act as excepting broker-dealers whose investment advice is given "*solely as an incident* of their regulation business." ...
>
> In a new section (b) of the rule, we are identifying three general circumstances under which we believe the provision of advisory services by a broker-dealer would not be solely incidental to brokerages. ...

## 1. SEPARATE CONTRACT OR FEE

Our rule contains a provision that a broker-dealer that separately contracts with a customer for investment advisory services (including financial planning services) cannot be considered to be providing advice that is solely incidental to its brokerage....

Similarly, advisory services are not solely incidental to brokerage services when those services are rendered for a separate fee. Charging a separate fee reflects the recognition that such services are provided independently of brokerage services and, therefore, cannot be considered to be solely incidental to brokerage services....

## 2. FINANCIAL PLANNING

Under rule 202(a)(11)-1(b)(2), a broker-dealer would not be providing advice solely incidental to brokerage if it provides advice as part of a financial plan or in connection with providing planning services and: (i) holds itself out generally to the public as a financial planner or as providing financial planning services; or (ii) delivers to its customer a financial plan or financial planning services. As a result, when the advice described above is provided, a broker-dealer that advertises (or otherwise generally lets it be known that it is available to provide) financial planning services must register under the Act (unless an exemption from registration is available)....

## 3. HOLDING OUT

We have decided not to include in rule 202(a)(11)-1 any other limitations on how a broker-dealer may hold itself out or titles it may employ without complying with the Advisers Act. Many commenters argued that we should prohibit broker-dealers from calling themselves financial advisors, financial consultants or other similar names. The commenters asserted such titles are inconsistent with the broker-dealer exception for advice that is solely incidental to brokerage. Other commenters, however, argued that, in many instances, such titles are fully consistent with the services provided to brokerage customers, whether fee-based or commission-based, and should not be proscribed. . . .

We believe the better approach, which we are adopting today, is to require broker-dealers to inform clients clearly that they are entering into a brokerage, and not an advisory, relationship. The customer disclosure requirements, which we discuss above, must be included in all customer documents for fee-based brokerage accounts. We encourage brokers to consider making similar disclosure in other communications.


### 4.   DISCRETIONARY ASSET MANAGEMENT

Under the rule we adopt today, discretionary investment advice is not "solely incidental to" brokerage services within the meaning of the rule (or to the business of a broker-dealer within the meaning of section 202(a)(11)(C) and, accordingly, brokers and dealers are not excepted from the Act for any accounts over which they exercise investment discretion as that term is defined in section 3(a)(35) of the Exchange Act (except that investment discretion granted by a customer on a temporary or limited basis is excluded). The rule terminates the existing staff approach, under which a discretionary account is subject to the Act only if the broker-dealer has enough *other* discretionary accounts to trigger the Act. Under the new rule, the exception provided by section 202(a)(11)(C) is unavailable for any account over which a broker-dealer exercises investment discretion, regardless of the form of compensation and without regard to how the broker-dealer handles other accounts.

We believe that a broker-dealer's authority to effect a trade without first consulting a client is qualitatively distinct from simply providing advice as part of a package of brokerage services. When the broker-dealer has discretion, it is not only the source of advice, it is also the person with the authority to make investment decisions relating to the purchase or sale of securities on behalf of the broker-dealer's clients. This quintessentially supervisory or managerial character warrants the protection of the Advisers Act because of the "special trust and confidence inherent" in such relationships. Most commenters addressing the issue, including those representing investors, advisers, brokerdealers, and others, generally agreed with us....

Several commenters, however, persuade us that defining "discretionary authority" by reference to section 3(a)(35) of the Exchange Act, would as a practical matter preclude many forms of limited discretion commonly exercised by broker-dealers assisting customers with otherwise non-discretionary brokerage accounts. We believe that such an effect would not benefit brokerage customers, nor would it be necessary to achieve the purpose of the rule. Therefore, the final rule permits broker-dealers to exercise investment discretion on a temporary or limited basis without becoming ineligible for the exception under the rule. In such cases, the customer is granting discretion primarily for execution purposes and is not seeking to obtain discretionary supervisory services. Such discretion must be limited to a transaction or series of transactions and not extend to setting investment objectives or policies for the customer. For example, we would view a broker-dealer's discretion to be temporary or limited within the meaning of rule 202(a)(11)-1(d) when the broker-dealer is given discretion:

- As to the price at which or the time to execute an order given by a customer for the purchase or sale of a definite amount or quantity of a specified security;
- On an isolated or infrequent basis, to purchase or sell a security or type of security when a customer is unavailable for a limited period of time not to exceed a few months;
- As to cash management, such as to exchange a position in a money market fund for another money market fund or cash equivalent;
- To purchase or sell securities to satisfy margin requirements;
- To see specific bonds and purchase similar bonds in order to permit a customer to take a tax loss on the original position;
- To purchase a bond with a specified credit rating and maturity; and
- To purchase or sell a security or type of security limited by specific parameters established by the customer.

## 5.  WRAP FEE SPONSORSHIP

Broker-dealers often serve as sponsors of wrap fee programs, under which broker-dealers effect securities transactions for one or more portfolio managers, which may be independent investment advisers. The sponsoring broker-dealer may provide wrap fee program clients with asset allocation models or with advice about selecting one or more of the portfolio managers in the program. The portfolio managers typically have discretionary authority over the client's assets. Traditionally, we have not viewed the sponsor's asset allocation or portfolio manager selection advice as incidental to the brokerage transactions initiated by the portfolio manager and executed by the sponsor. In our Reproposing Release, however, we asked whether such broker-dealers may have available the exception provided by rule 202(a)(11)-1 if, among other things, the portfolio manager selection and asset allocation services could be viewed as solely incidental to the sponsor's business of brokerage. Commenters urged the Commission to reaffirm its interpretation that portfolio manager selection and asset allocation services involved in wrap fee programs are advisory services that are not solely incidental to brokerage services, and we do so here today.

Id. at 2214–2215.

Rule 202(a)(11)-1 otherwise was generally substantively adopted as proposed.

!In Rule 202(a)(11)-1(a) the earlier proposed Rule 202(a)(11)-1(a)(i) addressing investment discretion was removed and treated as discussed above in Rule 202(a)(11)-1(b) and (d). Rule 202(a)(11)-1(d) defines *investment discretion* as having the same meaning as that in §3(a)(35) of the Securities Exchange Act "except that it does not include investment discretion granted by a customer on a temporary or limited basis."

Rule 202(a)(11)-1(a) both requires a broker-dealer who receives special compensation for investment advice to do so solely incidental to brokerage services and satisfy the rewritten advertisement prohibition in Rule 202(a)(11)-1(a)(ii) to avoid application of the Investment Advisers Act. Rule 202(a)(11)-1(a)(ii) now employs plain English and provides:

> Advertisements for, and contracts, agreements, applications and other forms governing, accounts for which the broker or dealer receives special compensation include a prominent statement that: "Your account is a brokerage account and not an advisory account. Our interests may not always be the same as yours. Please ask us questions to make sure you understand your rights and our obligations to you, including the extent of our obligations to disclose conflicts of interest and to act in your best interest. We are paid both by you and, sometimes, by people who compensate us based on what you buy. Therefore, our profits, and our salesperson' compensation, may vary by product and over time." The prominent statement also must identify an appropriate person at the firm with whom the customer can discuss the differences.

Rule 202(a)(11)-1(a)(2), which addresses discount brokerage programs and Rule 202(a)(11)-1(c), which only requires broker-dealers to register as an investment adviser with respect to accounts for which it receives nonexcluded special compensation were adopted as proposed.

# CHAPTER 9
# FRAUD

## A. COMMON LAW AND SEC *FRAUD*

### 2. THE RELATION BETWEEN SEC *FRAUD* CONCEPTS AND COMMON LAW DECEIT

*P. 913 n.32, end note.* Judge Alito phrased matters succinctly: "It is well known that the federal securities laws provide broader fraud protection than the common law, having been enacted in response to the common law's perceived failure at stamping out fraud in the securities markets." MBIA Ins. Corp. v. Royal Indem. Co., 426 F.3d 204, 218 (3d Cir. 2005).

## B. ISSUERS AND *INSIDERS*

### 4. THE FRAUD ELEMENT

#### b. Issuers Activities

(ii) *Regulation FD*

*P. 957, end text.* Twenty-two law professors, including the author, signed a brief defending Regulation FD when a defendant, Siebel Systems, Inc., as well as the Chamber of

Commerce, challenged the SEC authority to adopt the Regulation. SEC v. Siebel Sys., Inc., No. 04 (CV 5130m (GBD)) (S.D.N.Y. Mar. 10, 2005) (Law Professors Brief as *Amicus Curiae* in Opposition to Motion to Dismiss); Plitch, Law Professors Back Reg. FD, Take SEC Side vs. Challenge, Dow Jones Newswire, Mar. 11, 2005.

Subsequently, without addressing the Commission's authority to adopt Regulation FD or its constitutionality, the court granted the defendant's motion to dismiss on the ground that the statements that the SEC alleged violated Regulation FD did not support the Commission's claim that Siebel, or its senior officers, privately disclosed material nonpublic information. SEC v. Siebel Sys., Inc., 384 F. Supp. 2d 694 (S.D.N.Y. 2005).

## 6.   SCIENTER

***P. 1025 n.327, end note.***    In Ottmann v. Hanger Orthopedic Group, Inc., 353 F.3d 338, 344 (4th Cir. 2003), the Fourth Circuit definitively stated: "[W]e therefore agree with our sister circuits that a securities fraud plaintiff may allege scienter by pleading not only intentional misconduct, but also recklessness."

## 7.   SCOPE OF RULE 10b-5

### b.   In Connection with a Purchase or Sale

***P. 1047 n.418, end note.***    In Smith v. Pennington, 352 F.3d 884 (4th Cir. 2003), a de facto beneficiary or plan participant, who had no control over trust investments, was denied standing to sue.

In Mutual Funds Inv. Litig., 384 F. Supp. 2d 845, 854–855 (D. Md. 2005), Judge Motz questioned whether *Blue Chip Stamps* should ban holders of mutual fund shares who suffered dilution because of market timing and late trades.

## 8.　RULE 14e-3

***P. 1051 n.442, end note.***　In SEC v. Ginsburg, 362 F.3d 1292, 1304 (11th Cir. 2004), the court held:

> In this case there was a meeting between executives, which was followed by due diligence procedures, a confidentiality agreement, and by a meeting between Ginsburg and Olds—from which Ginsburg realized that the deal had to go down fast. These activities, which did result in a tender offer, were substantial steps for purposes of Rule 14e-3. Were it otherwise, liability could be avoided by taking care to tip only before the formal steps finalizing the acquisition are completed, leaving a substantial gap between the acquisition of inside information and the regulation of its disbursement.

## 9.　SPECIAL *INSIDER TRADING* SANCTIONS

### a.　Disgorgement

***P. 1054 n.464, end note.***　In SEC v. JT Wallenbrock & Assocs., 440 F.3d 1109, 1114 (9th Cir. 2006), the court held that "it would be unjust to permit the defendants to offset against the investor dollars they received the expenses of running the very business they created to defraud those investors into giving the defendants the money in the first place."

In SEC v. Great White Marine & Recreation, Inc., 428 F.3d 553 (5th Cir. 2005), the court proceeded with a disgorgement proceeding and dismissed a subsequently initiated involuntary bankruptcy proceeding.

In SEC v. Smyth, 420 F.3d 1225 (11th Cir. 2005), the Eleventh Circuit reversed the District Court's denial of an evidentiary hearing concerning the appropriate disgorgement amount and remanded for further proceedings.

## C.   BROKERS AND DEALERS

### 1.   UNREASONABLE SPREADS

#### a.   The *Shingle* Theory and Markups

***P. 1071 n.34, end note.***   Excessive markups have been found in municipal cases when markups ranged from 1.42 to 5.64 percent in challenged transactions. Mark D. Anderson, Sec. Ex. Act Rel. 48,352, 80 SEC Dock. 2567, 2568 (2003). Excessive markups were also found with respect to treasury notes (in amounts of 2.75–3.87 percent); Treasury strips (2.99–4.01 percent; agency specified pool securities (2.29–4.01 percent); collateralized mortgage obligations (1.42–4.02 percent). Id. at 2570-2571.

### 3.   DUTY TO INVESTIGATE AND THE SUITABILITY DOCTRINE

#### a.   Penny Stock Suitability Requirements [Rule 15g-9]

***P. 1093, end carryover par.***   In 2005 the Commission adopted amendments to the *penny stock* Rules. Sec. Ex. Act Rel. 51,983, 85 SEC Dock. 2605 (2005) (adoption). Rule 3a51-1(a) was amended to address exclusions from the initial concept that a penny stock involves any equity security. Under Rule 3a51-1(a)(1) a security is excluded from the definition of a *penny stock* if it is registered or approved for registration upon notice of issuance on a national securities exchange that has been continuously registered since April 20, 1992 (when Rule 3a51-1 was adopted) and the exchange has maintained quantitative listing standards that are substantially similar to or stricter than the listing standards that were in place on that exchange on January 8, 2004. Alternatively, under Rule 3a51-1(a)(2) a security would be excluded from the definition of a *penny stock* if the security is registered or approved for registration upon notice of issuance on an exchange or listed or approved for listing on an automated quotation system sponsored by a registered national association that:

(i) Has established initial listing standards that meet or exceed the following criteria:
    (A) The issuer shall have:
        (1) Stockholders' equity of $5 million;
        (2) Market value of listed securities of $50 million for 90 consecutive days prior to applying for the listing (market value means the closing bid price multiplied by the number of securities listed); or
        (3) Net income of $750,000 (excluding extraordinary or non-recurring items) in the most recently completed fiscal year or in two of the last three most recently completed fiscal years;
    (B) The issuer shall have an operating history of at least one year or a market value of listed securities of $50 million (market value means the closing bid price multiplied by the number of securities listed);
    (C) The issuer's stock, common or preferred, shall have a minimum bid price of $4 per share;
    (D) In the case of common stock, there shall be at least 300 round lot holders of the security (a round lot holder means a holder of a normal unit of trading);
    (E) In the case of common stock, there shall be at least 1 million publicly held shares and such shares shall have a market value of at least $5 million (market value means the closing bid price multiplied by the number of publicly held shares, and shares held directly or indirectly by an officer or director of the issuer and by any person who is the beneficial owner of more than 10 percent of the total shares outstanding are not considered to be publicly held);
    (F) In the case of a convertible debt security, there shall be a principal amount outstanding of at least $10 million;
    (G) In the case of rights and warrants, there shall be at least 100,000 issued and the underlying security shall be registered on a national securities exchange or listed on

an automated quotation system sponsored by a registered national securities association and shall satisfy the requirements of paragraph (a) or (e) of this section;

(H) In the case of put warrants (that is, instruments that grant the holder the right to sell to the issuing company a specified number of shares of the company's common stock, at a specified price until a specified date), there shall be at least 100,000 issued and the underlying security shall be registered on a national securities exchange or listed on an automated quotation system sponsored by a registered national securities association and shall satisfy the requirements of paragraph (a) or (e) of this section;

(I) In the case of units (that is, two or more securities traded together), all component parts shall be registered on a national securities exchange or listed on an automated quotation system sponsored by a registered national securities association and shall satisfy the requirements of paragraph (a) or (e) of this section; and

(J) In the case of equity securities (other than common and preferred stock, convertible debt securities, rights and warrants, put warrants, or units), including hybrid products and derivative securities products, the national securities exchange or registered national securities association shall establish quantitative listing standards that are substantially similar to those found in paragraphs (a)(2)(i)(A) through (a)(2)(i)(I) of this section; and

(ii) Has established quantitative continued listing standards that are reasonably related to the initial listing standards set forth in paragraph (a)(2)(i) of this section, and that are consistent with the maintenance of fair and orderly markets.

This represents an attempt to preserve the *status quo* for existing markets, 85 SEC Dock. at 2608, rather than an attempt to require uniform standards across all markets and exchanges, which the adoption Release characterized as "inappropriate because it would require the Commission, as opposed to the markets, to establish listing standards." Id. at 2608.

The Commission also eliminated the former Rule 3a51-1(f), which excluded specified securities quoted or authorized for quotation on Nasdaq "because we believe it no longer serves any purpose." Id. at 2608.

A new Rule 3a51-1(f) excluded penny stock futures products listed on a national securities exchange or an automated quotation system sponsored by a registered national securities association. This approach is consistent with the treatment of options under Rule 3a51-1(c).

The Commission eliminated the exclusion in Rule 3a51-1(a) for Amex's Emerging Company Marketplace for the straightforward reason that the market no longer exists.

Rule 15g-2(a) was modestly amended. The Rule earlier required a customer before effecting a penny stock transaction to be furnished a document containing information delineated in Schedule 15G. As amended Rule 15g-2(a) no longer requires that the customer manually sign and date an acknowledgment of receipt of the disclosure document, but merely sign and date the acknowledgment. More significantly Rule 15g-2(b) now requires a two business day waiting period after a penny stock disclosure document has been sent either electronically or by mail or by other means before a penny stock transaction can be effected. Id. at 3194.

A corresponding amendment was made to Rule 15g-9 to prohibit a broker-dealer from executing a penny stock transaction until at least two business days after the broker-dealer has sent the suitability statement required by Rule 15g-9(b) and the agreement to a penny stock transaction required by Rule 15g-9(a)(2)(ii). Id. at 3194–3197.

The Commission also adopted amendments to the Schedule 15G penny stock disclosure document, largely to modernize the document and make it easier to read. Id. at 3197–3200.

## D.  FRAUD BY INVESTMENT ADVISERS

*P. 1108, new par. of text after carryover indented quotation.*  In 2003 the Commission adopted Rule 206(4)-7 to require each investment adviser to adopt and implement written policies and procedures reasonably designed to prevent violation of the Investment Adviser Act by the adviser or any of its supervised persons. Inv. Adv. Rel. 2204, 81 SEC Dock. 2775 (2003) (adoption). Investment Company Act Rule 38a-1 requires fund boards to take a similar approach with respect to violations of the federal securities laws.

# CHAPTER 10

# MANIPULATION

## D. MANIPULATION OF THE OVER-THE-COUNTER MARKET UNDER THE SEC STATUTES

***P. 1137, end carryover par.***    In Rockies Fund v. SEC, 428 F.3d 1088 (D.C. Cir. 2005), the court held that the Commission failed to show requisite scienter in a manipulation case under either §9(a)(1) or Rule 10b-5. With respect to the different scienter standards, the court explained:

> Whereas Section 9(a)(1) requires a showing of specific intent, Rule 10b-5 generally requires only "extreme recklessness." SEC v. Steadman, 967 F.2d 636, 641 (D.C. Cir. 1992). Extreme recklessness is an "extreme departure from the standards of ordinary care, ... which presents a danger of misleading buyers or sellers that is either known to the defendant or is so obvious that the actor must have been aware of it." Id. at 642 (internal quotations omitted) (alteration in original). In other words, extreme recklessness requires a stronger showing than simple recklessness but does not rise to the level of specific intent. The difference between the standards could potentially have significant effects on the interplay between Section 10(b) and Section 9(a)(1) and SEC actions under each provision. Because we conclude that the SEC has not met its burden of proving scienter under either standard, we need not reach the question of what standard of intent should be applied to matched orders and wash sales under Section 10(b) and Rule 10b-5.

Id. at 1093.

# E.  STABILIZATION

## 2.  ACTIVITIES BY DISTRIBUTION PARTICIPANTS
### [Rule 101]

### a.  Basic Prohibitions

***P. 1141 n.17, end note.***    After bringing three enforcement actions alleging abuses in the offering process under Regulation M, the Commission in 2005 issued an interpretative Release with respect to book building and the process for allocating IPO shares. Sec. Act Rel. 8565, 85 SEC Dock. 266 (2005). The Release highlighted prohibited activities that underwriters should avoid during restricted periods, including:

- Inducements to purchase in the form of tie-in agreements or other solicitations of aftermarket bids or purchases prior to the completion of the distribution.
- Communicating to customers that expressing an interest in buying shares in the immediate aftermarket (aftermarket interest) or immediate aftermarket buying would help them obtain allocations of hot IPOs.
- Soliciting customers prior to the completion of the distribution regarding whether and at what price and in what quantity they intend to place immediate aftermarket orders for IPO stock.
- Proposing aftermarket prices to customers or encouraging customers who provide aftermarket interest to increase the prices that they are willing to place orders in the immediate aftermarket.
- Accepting or seeking expressions of interest from customers that they intend to purchase an amount of shares in the aftermarket equal to the size of their IPO allocation ("1 for 1") or intend to bid for or purchase specific amounts of shares in the aftermarket that are pegged to the allocation amount without any reference to a fixed total position size.

- Soliciting aftermarket orders from customers before all IPO shares are distributed or rewarding customers for aftermarket orders by allocating additional IPO shares to such customers.
- Communicating to customers in connection with one offering that expressing an interest in the aftermarket or buying in the aftermarket would help them obtain IPO allocations of other hot IPOs.

Id. at 267.

With respect to book building, the interpretative Release elaborated:

Book-building refers to the process by which underwriters gather and assess potential investor demand for an offering of securities and seek information important to their determination as to the size and pricing of an issue. When used, the IPO book-building process begins with the filing of a registration statement with an initial estimated price range. Underwriters and the issuer then conduct road shows to market the offering to potential investors, generally institutions. The road shows provide investors, the issuer, and underwriters the opportunity to gather important information from each other. Investors seek information about a company, its management and its prospects, and underwriters seek information from investors that will assist them in determining particular investors' interest in the company, assessing demand for the offering, and improving pricing accuracy for the offering. Investors' demand for an offering necessarily depends on the value they place, and the value they expect the market to place, on the stock, both initially and in the future. In conjunction with the road shows, there are discussions between the underwriter's sales representatives and prospective investors to obtain investors' views about the issuer and the offered securities, and to obtain indications of the investors' interest in purchasing quantities of the underwritten securities in the offering at particular prices. As the IPO Advisory Committee Report stated: "[C]ollecting information about investors' long-term interest in, and valuation of, a prospective issuer is an essential part of the book-building process. By aggregating information obtained during this period from investors with other information, the underwriters and the issuer will agree on the size and pricing of the offering, and the underwriters will decide how to allocate the IPO shares to purchasers...."

While we recognize the importance of the book-building process in obtaining and assessing demand for an offering and in pricing the securities, we remind market participants that there is no "book-building exception" to Regulation M for inducing or attempting to induce aftermarket bids or purchases. Although a distribution participant's obtaining and assessing information about demand for an offering during the book-building process would not, by itself, constitute an inducement or attempt to induce, accompanying conduct or communications, including one or more of the activities described below, may cause the collection of information to be part of conduct that violates Regulation M.

Id. at 271.


### 6.   SHORT SALES IN CONNECTION WITH AN OFFERING [RULE 105]

*P. 1168, new text after 2d full par.*   In 2004, the Commission proposed amendments to Regulation M. Sec. Ex. Act Rel. 50,831, 84 SEC Dock. 1118 (2004) (proposal), citing the text. The proposal Release summarized the proposed amendments:

- Amend Rule 100's definition of restricted period with respect to IPOs and to expressly reflect the Commission's long-standing application of the definition in the context of mergers, acquisitions, and exchange offers;
- Amend Rule 101's "*de minimis* exception" to require recordkeeping;
- Amend Rules 100, 101, and 102 to update the average daily trading volume (ADTV) value and public float value qualifying thresholds for purposes of the *restricted period* definition and the *actively-traded* securities and *actively-traded* reference securities exceptions;
- Amend Rule 104 to require disclosure of syndicate covering bids and to prohibit penalty bids;

- Amend Rule 104(j)(2) to include reference securities in the exception for transactions in securities eligible for resale under Rule 144A; and
- Adopt new Rule 106 to expressly prohibit conditioning the award of allocations of offered securities on the receipt of consideration in addition to the stated offering consideration.

As a consequence of these proposals, we are also recommending amendments to Rule 481 and Item 508 of Regulations S-K and S-B under the Securities Act concerning disclosure, and Rules 17a-2 and 17a-4 with respect to recordkeeping.

Id. at 1121.

The proposals were intended to address misconduct in connection with IPOs identified in recent SEC, SRO, and private actions. Id. at 1120.

New proposed Rule 106 was intended to explicitly prohibit distribution participants, including underwriters, and issuers and their affiliates, directly or indirectly, from demanding, soliciting, or attempting to induce, or accepting an offer from their customers of any payment or other consideration in addition to the security's stated consideration. For example, this rule would prohibit distribution participants, issuers and their affiliated persons, in connection with allocating an offered security, from inducing, soliciting, requiring or otherwise accepting an offer from a potential purchaser to purchase any other security to be sold or proposed to be offered or sold by such person. Similarly, Rule 106 would also prohibit distribution participants, issuers and their affiliated persons, in connection with allocating an offered security, from inducing, soliciting, requiring (or accepting an offer from) prospective customers to effect any other transaction or refrain from any of the foregoing, other than as stated in the registration statement or applicable offering document for the offer and sale of such offered security. Rule 106 would apply to any distribution of securities, whether a public offering or private placement of securities, and would apply to initial as well as secondary offerings.

Id. at 1133.

CHAPTER 11

# CIVIL LIABILITY

## B. BLUE SKY LAWS AND THE SECURITIES LITIGATION UNIFORM STANDARDS ACT OF 1998

**P. 1192 n.13, end note.**   In Enron Corp. Sec., Deriv. & ERISA Litig., 284 F. Supp. 2d 511 (S.D. Tex. 2003), the court held that SLUSA preempts cases based on the purchase or sale of a security, but does not apply to claims that solely address the retention of securities, id. at 632–642, and state claims including negligence that do not meet the §10(b) scienter requirement, id. at 642–644, 682–683.

An appeals court concluded it lacked jurisdiction to review a District Court order remanding a case to a state court. 28 U.S.C. §1447(d) has been interpreted to preclude appellate review based on lack of subject matter jurisdiction or to remove procedural irregularities. The Ninth Circuit concluded that the District Court reached its decision on the basis of lack of subject matter jurisdiction. United Investors Life Ins. Co. v. Waddell & Reed, Inc., 360 F.3d 960 (9th Cir. 2004).

After Spielman v. Merrill Lynch, Pierce, Fenner & Smith, Inc., 332 F.3d 116 (2d Cir. 2003), "it is now clear that the courts must probe the plaintiff's pleading to determine whether SLUSA preemption applies." Xpedior Creditor Trust v. Credit Suisse First Boston (USA) Inc., 341 F. Supp. 2d 258, 265–266 (S.D.N.Y. 2004) (discussing other cases, and adopting *necessary component* test: whether the state law claim relies on misstatements or omissions as a *necessary component* of a claim). Id. at 266–269. In the immediate case none of the plaintiff's claims were banned by SLUSA:

> None of the state law claims asserted by Xpedior—breach of contract, breach of the implied covenants of good faith and fair dealing, breach of fiduciary duty, or unjust enrichment—require misrepresentations or omissions as a necessary element.

Id. at 269. See also Breakaway Solutions, Inc. v. Morgan Stanley & Co., Inc., 2004 Del. Ch. LEXIS 125 (Del. Ch. 2004) (citing *Spielman* and *Xpedior* and similarly declining to preempt after applying *necessary component* test to state contract case); Finance & Trading LTD v. Rhodia S.A., 2004 Fed. Sec. L. Rep. (CCH) ¶93,046 (S.D.N.Y. 2004) (declining to remove state case to federal court when no substantial federal question was presented).

In Kircher v. Putnam Funds Trust, 373 F.3d 847 (7th Cir. 2004), the court held that suits that a district court finds to have been properly removed are unaffected by 28 U.S.C. §1447(d) and can be appealed. In a later decision in this case, the court held: "Every court of appeals to encounter SLUSA has held that its language has the same scope as its antecedent in Rule 10b-5." Kircher v. Putnam Funds Trust, 403 F.3d 478, 482 (7th Cir. 2005), *cert. denied*, 126 S. Ct. 979, citing cases.

In Dabit v. Merrill Lynch, Pierce, Fenner & Smith, Inc., 395 F.3d 25, 28 (2d Cir. 2005), the court held:

> (i) the meaning of "in connection with" under SLUSA is coterminous with the meaning of the nearly identical language of §10(b) of the Securities Exchange Act of 1934 . . . , and its corresponding Rule 10b-5 . . . and (ii) the purchaser-seller rule of *Blue Chip Stamps v. Manor Drug Stores*, 421 U.S. 723, 95 S. Ct. 1917, 44 L. Ed. 2d 539 (1975), applies as a limit on SLUSA's "in connection with" requirement such that SLUSA does not preempt claims that do not allege purchases or sales made by the plaintiff or the alleged class members.

In Merrill Lynch, Pierce, Fenner & Smith, Inc. v. Dabit, 126 S. Ct. 1503 (2006), the Supreme Court rejected the Second Circuit decision and adopted language in Kircher v. Putnam

Funds Trust, 403 F.3d 478 (7th Cir. 2005), which held that SLUSA also preempts state law class actions for which the federal securities law provides no remedy. The Court explained in part:

> Respondent urges that the operative language must be read narrowly to encompass (and therefore preempt) only those actions in which the purchaser-seller requirement of *Blue Chip Stamps* is met. Such, too, was the Second Circuit's view. But insofar as the argument assumes that the rule adopted in *Blue Chip Stamps* stems from the text of Rule 10b-5 — specifically, the "in connection with" language, it must be rejected. Unlike the *Birnbaum* court, which relied on Rule 10b-5's text in crafting its purchaser-seller limitation, this Court in *Blue Chip Stamps* relied chiefly, and candidly, on "policy considerations" in adopting that limitation. 421 U.S., at 737. The *Blue Chip Stamps* Court purported to define the scope of a private right of action under Rule 10b-5 — not to define the words "in connection with the purchase or sale." *Id.* at 749. . . . Any ambiguity on that score had long been resolved by the time Congress enacted SLUSA. . . .
>
> Moreover, when this Court *has* sought to give meaning to the phrase in the context of §10(b) and Rule 10b-5, it has espoused a broad interpretation. A narrow construction would not, as a matter of first impression, have been unreasonable; one might have concluded that an alleged fraud is "in connection with" a purchase or sale of securities only when the plaintiff himself was defrauded into purchasing or selling particular securities. After all, that was the interpretation adopted by the panel in the *Birnbaum* case. See 193 F.2d at 464. But this Court, in early cases like *Superintendent of Ins. of N.Y. v. Bankers Life & Casualty Co.*, 404 U.S. 6 (1971), and most recently in *SEC v. Zandford*, 535 U.S. 813, 820, 822 (2002), has rejected that view. Under our precedents, it is enough that the fraud alleged "coincide" with a securities transaction — whether by the plaintiff or by someone else. See *O'Hagan*, 521 U.S., at 651. The requisite showing, in other words, is "deception 'in connection with the purchase or sale of any security,' not deception of an identifiable purchaser or seller." *Id.*, at 658. Notably, this broader interpretation of the statutory language comports with the longstanding views of the SEC. See *Zandford*, 535 U.S., at 819–820.
>
> Congress can hardly have been unaware of the broad construction adopted by both this Court and the SEC when it imported the key phrase — "in connection with the purchase or sale" — into

SLUSA's core provision. And when "judicial interpretations have settled the meaning of an existing statutory provision, repetition of the same language in a new statute indicates, as a general matter, the intent to incorporate its ... judicial interpretations as well." *Bragdon v. Abbott*, 524 U.S. 624, 645 (1998); see *Cannon v. University of Chicago*, 441 U.S. 677, 696–699 (1979). Application of that presumption is particularly apt here; not only did Congress use the same words as are used in §10(b) and Rule 10b-5, but it used them in a provision that appears in the same statute as §10(b). Generally, "identical words used in different parts of the same statute are ... presumed to have the same meaning." *IBP, Inc. v. Alvarez*, [126 S. Ct. 514] (2005) (slip op., at 11).

The presumption that Congress envisioned a broad construction follows not only from ordinary principles of statutory construction but also from the particular concerns that culminated in SLUSA's enactment. A narrow reading of the statute would undercut the effectiveness of the 1995 Reform Act and thus run contrary to SLUSA's stated purpose, viz., "to prevent certain State private securities class action lawsuits alleging fraud from being used to frustrate the objectives" of the 1995 Act. SLUSA §2(5), 112 Stat. 3227. As the *Blue Chip Stamps* Court observed, class actions brought by holders pose a special risk of vexatious litigation. 421 U.S., at 739. It would be odd, to say the least, if SLUSA exempted that particularly troublesome subset of class actions from its preemptive sweep. See *Kircher*, 403 F.3d at 484.

Respondent's preferred construction also would give rise to wasteful, duplicative litigation. Facts supporting an action by purchasers under Rule 10b-5 (which must proceed in federal court if at all) typically support an action by holders as well, at least in those States that recognize holder claims. The prospect is raised, then, of parallel class actions proceeding in state and federal court, with different standards governing claims asserted on identical facts. That prospect, which exists to some extent in this very case, squarely conflicts with the congressional preference for "national standards for securities class action lawsuits involving nationally traded securities." SLUSA §2(5), 112 Stat. 3227.

In concluding that SLUSA preempts state-law holder class-action claims of the kind alleged in Dabit's complaint, we do not lose sight of the general "presum[ption] that Congress does not cavalierly preempt state-law causes of action." *Medtronic, Inc. v. Lohr*, 518 U.S. 470, 485 (1996). But that presumption carries less force here than in other contexts because SLUSA does not actually preempt any state cause of action. It simply denies plaintiffs the right to use the class action device to vindicate certain claims. The Act does not deny any individual plaintiff, or indeed any group of fewer than 50 plaintiffs, the right to enforce any state-law cause of action that may exist. . . .

Finally, federal law, not state law, has long been the principal vehicle for asserting class-action securities fraud claims. . . . More importantly, while state-law holder claims were theoretically available both before and after the decision in *Blue Chip Stamps*, the actual assertion of such claims by way of class action was virtually unheard of before SLUSA was enacted; respondent and his *amici* have identified only *one* pre-SLUSA case involving a state-law class action asserting holder claims. This is hardly a situation, then, in which a federal statute has eliminated a historically entrenched state-law remedy.

Id. at 1512–1515.

In Kircher v. Putnam Funds Trust, 74 USLW 4325 (2006), the Supreme Court subsequently held that an order remanding a case removed under SLUSA is not appealable.

Cf. Rowinski v. Salomon Smith Barney, Inc., 398 F.3d 294 (3d Cir. 2005), in which the court concluded at 299–300:

The misrepresentation issue is straightforward. Plaintiff's complaint is replete with allegations that Salomon Smith Barney disseminated biased and materially misleading investment research. Plaintiff alleges Salomon Smith Barney "provides customers with biased investment research and analysis"; "artificially inflates the ratings and analysis of its investment banking clients"; was fined by the NASD "for issuing materially misleading research reports"; and "provided biased and misleading analysis that was intended to curry favor with Defendant's existing and potential investment banking clients." These allegations, which are incorporated by reference in every count in the complaint, readily satisfy the misrepresentation requirement under SLUSA.

Plaintiff responds that the "breach of contract claim does not involve a misrepresentation or omission." In other words, plaintiff contends that because "misrepresentation" is not an essential legal element of his claim under Pennsylvania contract law, the factual allegations of misrepresentation included in the complaint are irrelevant to the SLUSA inquiry.

We disagree. Plaintiff's suggested distinction—between the legal and factual allegations in a complaint—is immaterial under the statute. SLUSA preempts any covered class action "alleging" a material misrepresentation or omission in connection with the purchase or sale of securities. 15 U.S.C. §78bb(f)(1). Under this provision, preemption does not turn on whether allegations are characterized as facts or as essential legal elements of a claim, but rather on whether the SLUSA prerequisites are "alleged" in one form or another. A contrary approach, under which only essential legal elements of a state law claim trigger preemption, is inconsistent with the plain meaning of the statute. Furthermore, it would allow artful pleading to undermine SLUSA's goal of uniformity—a result manifestly contrary to congressional intent.

The court relied on *Zandford* for a broad reading of the *in connection with* element of §10(b) and Rule 10b-5. Id. at 300–305.

But see Blaz v. Belfer, 368 F.3d 501 (5th Cir. 2004), *cert. denied*, 543 U.S. 874, where the Court applied SLUSA retroactively to preenactment conduct. "The application is permitted because SLUSA governs why secondary conduct—procedural requirements for filing certain state law securities claims—and not the primary conduct that is the subject of these claims." Id. at 502.

The Class Action Fairness Act of 2005 precludes a federal district court from exercising original jurisdiction over any class action that solely involves a claim concerning a covered security as defined under §16(f)(7) of the Securities Act or §28(f)(5)(b) of the Securities Exchange Act. 28 U.S.C. §1332(d)(9)(A).

## C.  SEC STATUTES

### 2.  SECURITIES ACT OF 1933

#### b.  Section 12(a)(2)

(iv)  *Secondary Trading*

***P. 1216 n.51, end note.***   See also Yung v. Lee, 432 F.3d 142, 149 (2d Cir. 2005) ("We now join ... courts in holding that *Gustafson's* definition of a prospectus ... compels the conclusion that a Section 12(a)(2) action cannot be maintained by a plaintiff who acquires securities through a private transaction, whether primary or secondary"); Faye L. Roth Revocable Trust v. UBS PaineWebber, Inc., 323 F. Supp. 2d 1279, 1290, n.1 (S.D. Fla. 2004), quoting the text. On the other hand, several courts have now held that whether a claimed §4(2) private offering, Rule 144A or Regulation S is subject to §12(a)(2) involves a fact question whether the claimed exemption, in fact, involved a public offering. Enron Corp., Sec., Derivative & ERISA Litig., 310 F. Supp. 2d 819, 859–866 (S.D. Tex. 2004) (declining to resolve issue on pretrial motion before discovery). See also Fisk v. Superannuities, Inc., 927 F. Supp. 718, 729–731 (S.D.N.Y. 1996) (§12(a)(2) claim can be successfully pled if defendants could not establish entitlement to §4(2) private placement exemption); Steed Fin. LDC v. Nomura Sec. Int'l, Inc., 2001 Fed. Sec. L. Rep. (CCH) ¶91,552 (S.D.N.Y. 2001) (declining to dismiss §12(a)(2) claim when defendants claimed §4(2) private placement and plaintiff pled that securities were offered to the public), citing cases.

### d. Section 11: Misstatements or Omissions in Registration Statement

*(i) Elements of the Action*

***P. 1228 n.84, end note.***    In Krim v. PC Order.Com, Inc., 402 F.3d 489 (5th Cir. 2005), the Fifth Circuit addressed statistical methodology in a tracing case, explaining in part:

> In *Rosenzweig*, we further held that this traceability requirement is satisfied, as a matter of logic, when stock has only entered the market via a single offering. We did not speculate on what other methods might be available to satisfy the traceability requirement for aftermarket purchases, but we were careful to note the Supreme Court's concern "that the Securities Act remain anchored to its original purpose of regulating only public offerings."
>
> Appellants, as aftermarket purchasers, assert that they can also demonstrate standing by showing a very high probability that they each have at least one PO share. Appellants argue that their statistical determinations, being over 50%, demonstrate by a preponderance of the evidence, that it is "more likely than not," that their shares are traceable to the public offerings in question.
>
> We are persuaded that accepting such "statistical tracing" would impermissibly expand the statute's standing requirement. Because any share of pcOrder.com stock chosen at random in the aftermarket has at least a 90% chance of being tainted, its holder, according to Appellants' view, would have Section 11 standing. In other words, *every* aftermarket purchaser would have standing for every share, despite the language of Section 11, limiting suit to "any person acquiring *such* security." As the district court found, it is "likely that any street name shareholder can make a similar claim with regard to *one* share." This cannot be squared with the statutory language — that is, with what Congress intended. We decline the invitation to reach further than the statute. . . .
>
> However, as we have explained, Section 11 *is* available for anyone who purchased directly in the offering and any aftermarket purchasers who can demonstrate that their shares are traceable to the registration statement in question — *e.g.*, when, as with Beebe, there had only been one offering at the time of purchase. When Congress enacted the Securities Act of 1933 it was not confronted

with the widespread practice of holding stock in street name that Appellants describe as an impediment, absent our acceptance of statistical tracing, to invoking Section 11. That present market realities, given the fungibility of stock held in street name, may render Section 11 ineffective as a practical matter in some after-market scenarios is an issue properly addressed by Congress. It is not within our purview to rewrite the statute to take account of changed conditions. In the words of one court, Appellants' arguments may "have the sound ring of economic reality but unfortunately they merely point up the problems involved in the present scheme of statutory regulation."

It is, therefore, perhaps not surprising that we failed to locate any court, nor did Appellants point to any, that found Section 11 standing based solely on the statistical tracing theory espoused today. Given that the statute has been in existence for over 70 years and such elementary statistical calculations have been around for centuries, it is difficult to conclude that this is a coincidence. We note that a handful of lower courts have rebuffed similar attempts by plaintiffs. [Citing cases.]

Id. at 495–498.

***P. 1232 n.105, end note.*** In WorldCom, Inc. Sec. Litig., 346 F. Supp. 2d 628 (S.D.N.Y. 2004), quoting the text, Judge Cote addressed the underwriters' due diligence obligations with respect to the financial statements that were incorporated into two WorldCom bond offerings. Both were prepared by Arthur Andersen.

First, with respect to accountants as expert, the court wrote:

Not every auditor's opinion, however, qualifies as an expert's opinion for purposes of the Section 11 reliance defense. To distinguish among auditor's opinions, some background is in order. While financial statements are prepared by the management of a company, an accountant serving as the company's auditor may give an opinion as to whether the financial statements have been presented in conformity with GAAP. This opinion is given after the accountant has performed an audit of the company's books and records. Audits are generally completed once a year, in connection with a company's year-end financial statements. There are ten audit standards with which an auditor must comply in performing its annual audit. They are known as Generally Accepted Auditing Standards ("GAAS"). If an auditor signs a consent to have its opinion on financial statements incorporated into a company's public filings, the opinion may be shared with the public through incorporation.

Public companies are also required under the Exchange Act to file quarterly financial statements, which are referred to as interim financial statements. While not subject to an audit, interim financial statements included in Form 10-Q quarterly reports are reviewed by an independent public accountant using professional standards and procedures for conducting such reviews, as established by GAAS. The standards for the review of interim financial statements are set forth in Statement of Auditing Standards No. 71, Interim Financial Information ("SAS 71"). When a public company files a registration statement for a sale of securities, the auditor is customarily asked by underwriters to provide a comfort letter. The comfort letter will contain representations about the auditor's review of the interim financial statements. Guidance about the content of comfort letters is contained in the Statement on Auditing Standards No. 72, Letters for Underwriters and Certain Other Requesting Parties ("SAS 72"). There is frequently more than one comfort letter for a transaction: an initial comfort letter, and a second or "bringdown" comfort letter issued closer to the time of closing.

In order for an accountant's opinion to qualify as an expert opinion under Section 11(b)(3)(C), there are three prerequisites. First, it must be reported in the Registration Statement. Second, it must be an audit opinion. Finally, the accountant must consent to inclusion of the audit opinion in the registration statement.

In an effort to encourage auditor reviews of interim financial statements, the SEC acted in 1979 to assure auditors that their review of unaudited interim financial information would not subject them to liability under Section 11. [Citation omitted.] The SEC addressed the circumstances in which an accountant's opinion can be considered an expert's opinion for purposes of Section 11(b) and made it clear that reviews of unaudited interim financial statements do not constitute such an opinion. Under Rule 436, where the opinion of an expert is quoted or summarized in a registration statement, or where any information contained in a registration statement "has been reviewed or passed upon" by an expert, the written consent of the expert must be filed as an exhibit to the registration statement. [Rule] 436(a), (b). Yet written consent is not sufficient to convert an opinion or review into an expertised statement. Rule 436 provides that notwithstanding written consent, "*a report on unaudited interim financial information* ... by an independent accountant who has conducted a review of such interim financial information *shall not be considered a part of a registration statement prepared or certified by an accountant* or a report prepared or certified by an accountant within the meaning of sections 7 and 11" of the Securities Act. [Rule] 436(c) (emphasis supplied).

Rule 436 also defined the term "report on unaudited interim financial information." It consists of a report that contains the following five items:

(1) A statement that the review of interim financial information was made in accordance with established professional standards for such reviews;

(2) An identification of the interim financial information reviewed;

(3) A description of the procedures for a review of interim financial information;

(4) A statement that a review of interim financial information is substantially less in scope than an examination in accordance with generally accepted auditing standards, the objective of which is an expression of opinion regarding the financial statements taken as a whole, and, accordingly, no such opinion is expressed; and

(5) A statement about whether the accountant is aware of any material modifications that should be made to the accompanying financial information so that it conforms with generally accepted accounting principles.

Rule 436(d).

In promulgating Rule 436, the SEC contrasted accountants' review of year-end financial statements with those of interim financial data, remarking that

*The objective of a review of interim financial information differs significantly from the objective of an examination of financial statements in accordance with generally accepted auditing standards.* The objective of an audit is to provide a reasonable basis for expressing an opinion regarding the financial statements taken as a whole. A review of interim financial information does not provide a basis for the expression of such an opinion, because the review does not contemplate a study and evaluation of internal accounting control; tests of accounting records and of responses to inquiries by obtaining corroborating evidential matter through inspection, observation, or confirmation; and certain other procedures ordinarily performed during an audit. A review may bring to the accountant's attention significant matters affecting the interim financial information, but it does not provide assurance that the accountant will become aware of all significant matters that would be disclosed in an audit.

Id. at 664–666.

Second, the court highlighted that underwriters ability to rely on accountants as experts is correlatively limited:

Rule 436 underscores that SAS 71 reports and SAS 72 letters are not expertised statements within the meaning of the Section 11 reliance defense. Specifically, in finalizing Rule 436, the SEC directed that

[i]n any suit for damages under Section 11(a), the directors and *underwriters should not be able to rely on SAS No. [71] reports on interim financial data included in a registration statement* as statements "purporting to be made on the authority of an expert ... which they had no ground to believe ... were untrue ..." under Section 11(b)(3)(C). Rather, *underwriters* and directors *should be required*, as has previously been the case whenever unaudited financials are included in a registration statement, *to demonstrate affirmatively* under Section 11(b)(3)(A) *that, after conducting a reasonable investigation, they had reasonable ground to believe, and did believe, that the interim financial data was true....*

Given this, the SEC expects that "underwriters will continue to exercise due diligence in a vigorous manner with respect to SAS No. [71] reports." ...

In sum, underwriters can rely on an accountant's audit opinion incorporated into a registration statement in presenting a defense under Section 11(b)(3)(C). Underwriters may not rely on an accountant's comfort letters for interim financial statements in presenting such a defense. Comfort letters do not "expertise any portion of the registration statement that is otherwise non-expertised."

Id. at 666.

Third, the court reiterated that in spite of Rule 176 "current law continues to place a burden upon an underwriter to conduct a reasonable investigation of non-expertised statements in a registration, including an issuer's interim financial statements." Id. at 671. See generally id at 674–678.

Fourth, an underwriter's reliance on audited financial statements may not be blind, but must respond to red flags. Id. at 672-673, citing cases.

In EBC I v. Goldman Sachs & Co., 832 N.E.2d 26 (N.Y. 2005), citing the text, the highest court in New York held that a cause of action for breach of fiduciary duty may survive when the plaintiff alleges that the underwriter and issuer created a relationship of higher trust than would arise from the underwriting agreement itself. The underwriting agreement itself normally would not create a fiduciary relationship, but an advisory relationship independent of the underwriting agreement could create a fiduciary relationship.

### 3. SECURITIES EXCHANGE ACT OF 1934: EXPRESS LIABILITIES

*P. 1240 n.125, end note.* In Suprema Specialties, Inc. Sec. Litig., 438 F.3d 256, 283 (3d Cir. 2006), the Court held that plaintiffs must prove actual reliance on specific statements in SEC filings in a §18 case.

### 4. SECURITIES EXCHANGE ACT OF 1934: IMPLIED LIABILITIES

#### a. Theory and Scope

*P. 1264, new text, end page.*     In Alexander v. Sandoval, 532 U.S. 275 (2001), Justice Scalia, writing for the Supreme Court majority, addressed a private right of action to enforce regulations issued under Title VI of the Civil Rights Act of 1964:

> Respondents would have us revert in this case to the understanding of private causes of action that held sway 40 years ago when Title VI was enacted. That understanding is captured by the Court's statement in *J. I. Case Co. v. Borak*, 377 U.S. 426, 433 (1964), that "it is the duty of the courts to be alert to provide such remedies as are necessary to make [effectuate] the congressional purpose" expressed by a statute. We abandoned that understanding in *Cort v. Ash*, 422 U.S. 66, 78 (1975)—which itself interpreted a statute enacted under the *ancien regime*—and have not returned to it since. Not even when interpreting the same Securities Exchange Act of 1934 that was at issue in *Borak* have we applied *Borak's* method for discerning and defining causes of action. See *Central Bank of Denver, N.A. v. First Interstate Bank of Denver, N.A., supra,* at 188; *Musick, Peeler & Garrett v. Employers Ins. of Wausau*, 508 U.S. 286, 291–293 (1993); *Virginia Bankshares, Inc. v. Sandberg, supra,* at 1102–1103; *Touche Ross & Co. v. Redington, supra,* at 576–1578. Having sworn off the habit of venturing beyond Congress's intent, we will not accept respondents' invitation to have one last drink.
>
> Nor do we agree with the Government that our cases interpreting statutes enacted prior to *Cort v. Ash* have given "dispositive weight" to the "expectations" that the enacting Congress had formed "in light of the 'contemporary legal context.'" Brief for United States 14. Only three of our legion implied-right-of-action cases have found this sort of "contemporary legal context" relevant, and two of those involved in Congress's enactment (or reenactment) of the verbatim statutory text that courts had previously interpreted to create a private right of action. See *Merrill Lynch, Pierce, Fenner & Smith, Inc. v. Curran*, 456 U.S. 353, 378–379 (1982); *Cannon v. University of Chicago*, 441 U.S. at 698–699. In the

third case, this sort of "contemporary legal context" simply buttressed a conclusion independently supported by the text of the statute. See *Thompson v. Thompson*, 484 U.S. 174 (1988). We have never accorded dispositive weight to context shorn of text. In determining whether statutes create private rights of action, as in interpreting statutes generally, see *Blatchford v. Native Village of Noatak*, 501 U.S. 775, 784 (1991), legal context matters only to the extent it clarifies text.

We therefore begin (and find we can end) our search for Congress's intent with the text and structure of Title VI.

Id. at 287–288.

### c.   Tender Offers

(i)   *Standing*

***P. 1272 n.232, end note.***   Edelson v. Ch'ien, 405 F.3d 620 (7th Cir. 2005), the court concluded that Congress intended to recognize a private cause of action under §13(d) but "only in the context of a tender offer or other contest for control." Id. at 634.

### d.   Rule 10b-5

(i)   *Reliance and Causation*

***P. 1281 n.265, end note.***   In a fraud on the market case when a plaintiff made both statements that suggested he did not rely on a market price and other statements that suggested he did rely, a reasonable jury could find that the defendant has not established that the plaintiff did not rely on the market price. The Second Circuit accordingly reversed a District Court judgment as a matter of law that has overturned a jury verdict for the plaintiff. Black v. Finantra Capital, Inc., 418 F.3d 203 (2d Cir. 2005).

The Fifth Circuit joined several other circuits in requiring a rigorous, though preliminary, standard of proof to the market efficiency determinations. See Bell v. Ascendant Solutions,

Inc., 422 F.3d 307 (5th Cir. 2005). The Court set forth specific rules
to determine whether a stock trades in an efficient market. Cf. n.10:

(1) the average weekly trading volume expressed as a percentage of total outstanding shares;

(2) the number of securities analysts following and reporting
on the stock;

(3) the extent to which market makers and arbitrageurs trade
in the stock;

(4) the company's eligibility to file SEC registration Form S-3
(as opposed to Form S-1 or S-2);

(5) the existence of empirical facts "showing a cause and
effect relationship between unexpected corporate events
or financial releases and an immediate response in the
stock price";

(6) the company's market capitalization;

(7) the bid-ask spread for stock sales; and

(8) float, the stock's trading volume without counting insider-
owned stock.

**P. 1285, new text after carryover par.**      In Broudo v. Dura Pharmaceuticals, Inc., 339 F.3d 933 (9th Cir. 2003), the court quoted
earlier Ninth Circuit cases for the proposition that "loss causation is satisfied where 'the plaintiff shows that the misrepresentation touches upon the reasons for the investment decline in
value.'" Id. at 937–938. While acknowledging that the "touches
upon language is admittedly ambiguous," id. at 938, the court
held: "loss causation does not require pleading a stock price drop
following a corrective disclosure or otherwise. It merely requires
pleading that the price at the time of purchase was overstated and
sufficient identification of the cause." Ibid. See also Gebhardt v.
ConAgra Foods, Inc., 335 F.3d 824, 831 (8th Cir. 2003) (similar
loss causation standard).

The Eleventh Circuit, in contrast, did require "proof of a causal
connection between the misrepresentation and the investment's
subsequent decline in value." Robbins v. Koger Prop., Inc., 116
F.3d 1441, 1448 (11th Cir. 1997). *Robbins* was explicitly followed
by the Third Circuit, Semerenko v. Cendant Corp., 223 F.3d 165,

185 (3d Cir. 2000), *cert. denied*, 531 U.S. 1149; similar holdings also have been reached in the Second and Seventh Circuits, Emergent Capital Inv. Mgmt., LLC v. Stonepath Group, Inc., 343 F.3d 189, 198–199 (2d Cir. 2003) (plaintiff must demonstrate a causal connection between the alleged misstatements or omissions and "the harm actually suffered"); Bastian v. Petren Resources Corp., 892 F.2d 680, 682–683 (7th Cir. 1990) *cert. denied*, 496 U.S. 906 (similar).

The United States Solicitor General and SEC filed an amicus brief with the United States Supreme Court in Dura Pharmaceuticals, Inc. v. Broudo, No. 03-932 (May 2004), urging the Court to grant certiorari and reverse the Ninth Circuit. The SEC brief stated in part:

> 1. In a Rule 10b-5 action brought by a private party, the plaintiff must prove that he suffered an injury that was caused by the defendant's misrepresentations. As the court of appeals correctly recognized, the causation requirement encompasses both transaction causation — "that the violations in question caused the plaintiff to engage in the transaction" — and loss causation — "that the misrepresentations or omissions caused the harm." [citation omitted.] Loss causation had long been a judicially inferred element of a Rule 10b-5 claim, see *Bastian*, 892 F.2d at 683–685, and for nearly a decade it has been a statutory element by virtue of the Private Securities Litigation Reform Act of 1995 (PSLRA), Pub. L. No. 104-67, 109 State. 737. As amended by the PSLRA, the Exchange Act, in a provision titled "Loss causation," requires a plaintiff in a private action to prove that "the [challenged] act or omission of the defendant ... caused the loss for which the plaintiff seeks to recover damages." 15 U.S.C. 78u-4(b)(4). Under the court of appeals' view of loss causation, an investor's loss in a fraud-on-the-market case "occurs at the time of the transaction," when he is harmed by paying too much for the security, and a causal link exists because the defendant's misrepresentation inflated the price. [citation omitted.] That holding is incorrect.

> A material misrepresentation that reflects an unduly favorable view of a company, when disseminated to the investing public, will typically raise the price of the company's stock, because the price of a security taded in an efficient market ordinarily reflects all publicly available information. See *Basic Inc. v. Levinson*, 485

U.S. at 241–249. The artificial inflation will not be reduced or eliminated until the market price reflects the true facts that had been concealed by the fraud. This will most commonly occur when the truth is reveled in whole or in part through a corrective disclosure. That, however, is not the only way the fraud may be revealed. Events may also effectively disclose the truth. [Citation omitted.]

Because "the cost of the alleged misrepresentation" will be "incorporated into the value of the security" until that time, the investor who purchased the security will be able to recoup part or all of his overpayment "by reselling the security at the inflated price." *Semerenko*, 223 F.3d at 185. For that reason, it cannot be said that an investor in a fraud-on-the-market case who purchases a security at an inflated price has suffered *any* loss at the time of purchase, much less one caused by the defendant's misrepresentation. See *Robbins*, 116 F.3d at 1448. Measuring the loss in such a case as of the time of purchase, and not requiring any allegation of a subsequent loss of value attributable to the fraud, would grant a windfall to investors who sold before the reduction of elimination of the artificial inflation, because they would recover the portion of the purchase price attributable to the fraud on resale, and then would be entitled to recover that same amount again in damages.

Id. at 9–11.

The Supreme Court adopted the logic of the SEC-Solicitor General brief in Dura Pharmaceuticals, Inc. v. Broudo, 125 S. Ct. 1627 (2005), citing this text and stating in part:

Private federal securities fraud actions are based upon federal securities statutes and their implementing regulations. Section 10(b) of the Securities Exchange Act of 1934 forbids (1) the "use or employ[ment ... of any ... deceptive device,"] "in connection with the purchase or sale of any security," and (3) "in contravention of" Securities and Exchange Commission "rules and regulations." [Citation omitted.] Commission Rule 10b-5 forbids, among other things, the making of any "untrue statement of material fact" or the omission of any material fact "necessary in order to make the statements made ... not misleading." [Citation omitted.]

The courts have implied from these statutes and Rule a private damages action, which resembles, but is not identical to, common law tort actions for deceit and misrepresentation. [Citations omitted.] And Congress has imposed statutory requirements on that private action. [Citation omitted.]

In cases involving publicly traded securities and purchases or sales in public securities markets, the action's basic elements include:

(1) *a material misrepresentation (or omission)*, see *Basic Inc. v. Levinson*, 485 U.S. 224, 231–232 (1988);

(2) *scienter, i.e.*, a wrongful state of mind, see *Ernst & Ernst, supra*, at 197, 199;

(3) *a connection with the purchase or sale of a securities*, see *Blue Chip Stamps, supra*, at 730–731;

(4) *reliance*, often referred to in cases involving public securities markets (fraud-on-the-market cases) as "transaction causation," see *Basic, supra*, at 248–249 (nonconclusively presuming that the price of a publicly traded share reflects a material misrepresentation as long as they would not have bought the share in its absence);

(5) *economic loss*, 15 U.S.C. §78u–4(b)(4); and

(6) *"loss causation," i.e.*, a causal connection between the material misrepresentation and the loss, *ibid.*; . . .

*Dura* argues that the complaint's allegations are inadequate in respect to these last two elements . . . .

We begin with the Ninth Circuit's basic reason for finding the complaint adequate, namely, that at the end of the day plaintiffs need only "establish," *i.e.*, prove, that "the price *on the date of purchase* was inflated because of the misrepresentation." 339 F.3d at 938 (internal quotation marks omitted). In our view, this statement of the law is wrong. Normally, in cases such as this one (*i.e.*, fraud-on-the-market cases), and inflated purchase price will not itself constitute or proximately cause the relevant economic loss.

For one thing, as a matter of pure logic, at the moment the transaction takes place, the plaintiff has suffered no loss; the inflated purchase payment is offset by ownership of a share that *at that instant* possesses equivalent value. Moreover, the logical link between the inflated share purchase price and any later economic loss is not invariably strong. Shares are normally purchased with an eye toward a later sale. But if, say, the purchaser sells the shares quickly before the relevant truth begins to leak out, the misrepresentation will not have led to any loss. If the purchaser sells later

273

after the truth makes its way into the market place, an initially inflated purchase price *might* mean a later loss. But that is far from inevitably so. When the purchaser subsequently resells such shares, even at a lower price, that lower price may reflect, not the earlier misrepresentation, but changed economic circumstances, changed investor expectations, new industry-specific or firm-specific facts, conditions, or other events, which taken separately or together account for some or all of that lower price. (The same is true in respect to a claim that a share's higher price is lower than it would otherwise have been—a claim we do not consider here.) Other things being equal, the longer the time between purchase and sale, the more likely that this is so, *i.e.,* the more likely that other factors caused the loss.

Given the tangle of factors affecting price, the most logic alone permits us to say is that the higher purchase price will *sometimes* play a role in bringing about a future loss. It may prove to be a necessary condition of any such loss, and in that sense one might say that the inflated purchase price suggests that the misrepresentation (using language the Ninth Circuit used) "touches upon" a later economic loss. *Ibid.* But, even if that is so, it is insufficient. To "touch upon" a loss is not to *cause* a loss, and it is the latter that the law requires. 15 U.S.C. §78u-4(b)(4).

For another thing, the Ninth Circuit's holding lacks support in precedent. Judicially implied private securities-fraud actions resemble in many (but not all) respects common-law deceit and misrepresentation actions. See *Blue Chip Stamps, supra,* at 744; see also L. Loss & J. Seligman, Fundamentals of Securities Regulation, 910–918 (5th ed. 2004) (describing relationship to common-law deceit). The common law of deceit subjects a person who "fraudulently" makes a "misrepresentation" to liability "for pecuniary loss caused" to one who justifiably relies upon that misrepresentation. Restatement (Second) of Torts §525, p. 55 (1977) (hereinafter Restatement of Torts); see also *Southern Development Co. v. Silva,* 125 U.S. 247, 250 (1988) (setting forth elements of fraudulent misrepresentation). And the common law has long insisted that a plaintiff in such a case show not only that had he known the truth he would not have acted but also that he suffered actual economic loss. See, *e.g., Pasley v. Freeman,* 3 T.R. 5:1, 100 Eng. Rep. 450, 457 (1789) (if "no injury is occasioned by the lie, it is not actionable; but if it be attended with a damage, it then becomes the subject of an action"); *Freeman v. Venner,* 120 Mass. 424, 426 (1876) (a mortgagee cannot bring a tort action for damages stemming from a fraudulent note that a misrepresentation led him to execute unless and until the note has to be paid); see also M. Bigelow, Law of Torts 101 (8th ed. 1907) (damage "must already have been suffered before the bringing of the suit"); 2 T. Cooley, Law of Torts §348, p. 551 (4th ed. 1932) (plaintiff must show that he "suffered damage" and that the "damage followed proximately the deception"); W. Keeton, D. Dobbs, R. Keeton, & D. Owen, Prosser and Keeton on Law of Torts §110, p. 765 (5th ed. 1984) (hereinafter Prosser and Keeton) (plaintiff "must have suffered substantial damage" not simply nominal damages, before "the cause of action can arise").

Given the common-law roots of the securities fraud action (and the common-law requirement that a plaintiff show actual damages), it is not surprising that other courts of appeals have rejected the Ninth Circuit's "inflated purchase price" approach to proving causation and loss. See, *e.g.*, *Emergent Capital*, 343 F.3d at 198 (inflation of purchase price alone cannot satisfy loss causation); *Semerenko*, 223 F.3d, at 185 (same); *Robbins*, 116 F.3d, at 1448 (same); cf. *Bastian*, 892 F.2d, at 685. Indeed, the Restatement of Torts, in setting forth the judicial consensus, says that a person who "misrepresents the financial condition of a corporation in order to sell its stock" becomes liable to a relying purchase "for the loss" the purchaser sustains "when the facts … become generally known" and "as a result" share value "depreciate[s]." §548A, Comment b, at 107. Treatise writers, too, have emphasized the need to prove proximate causation. Prosser and Keeton §110, at 767 (losses do "not afford any basis for recovery" if "brought about by business conditions or other factors").

We cannot reconcile the Ninth Circuit's "inflated purchase price" approach with these views of other courts. And the uniqueness of its perspective argues against the validity of its approach in a case like this one where we consider the contours of a judicially implied cause of action with roots in the common law.

Finally, the Ninth Circuit's approach overlooks an important securities law objective. The securities statutes seek to maintain public confidence in the marketplace. See *United States v. O'Hagan*, 521 U.S. 642, 658 (1997). They do so by deterring fraud actions. *Randall v. Loftsgaarden*, 478 U.S. 647, 664 (1986). But the statutes make these latter actions available, not to provide investors with broad insurance against market losses, but to protect them against those economic losses that misrepresentations actually cause. Cf.

275

*Basic*, 485 U.S., at 252 (White, J., joined by O'CONNOR, J., concurring in part and dissenting in part) ("[A]llowing recovery in the face of affirmative evidence of nonreliance—would effectively convert Rule 10b-5 into a scheme of investor's insurance. There is no support in the Securities Exchange Act, the Rule, or our cases for such a result" (internal quotation marks and citations omitted)).

The statutory provision at issue here and the paragraphs that precede it emphasize this last mentioned objective. Private Securities Litigation Reform Act of 1995, 109 Stat. 737. The statute insists that securities fraud complaints "specify" each misleading statement; that they set forth the facts "on which [a] belief" that a statement is misleading was "formed"; and that they "state with particularity facts giving rise to a strong inference that the defendant acted with the required state of mind." 15 U.S.C. §§78u-4(b)(1), (2). And the statute expressly imposes on plaintiffs "the burden of proving" that the defendant's misrepresentations "caused the loss for which the plaintiff seeks to recover." §78u-4(b)(4).

The statute thereby makes clear Congress' intent to permit private securities fraud actions for recovery where, but only where, plaintiffs adequately allege and prove the traditional elements of causation and loss. We need not, and do not, consider other proximate cause or loss-related questions.

Id. at 1630–1633.

The Supreme Court decision in *Dura* was notable for its close reliance on common law concepts and for how limited its impact is likely to be on future securities class actions. While the courts rarely, if ever, have so linked the federal securities laws to common law precedents, the result here is unexceptional. The question is not must the plaintiff plead and prove that the defendant was responsible for the plaintiff's loss. But rather, how, does the plaintiff plead and prove such responsibility. Here *Dura* is strikingly limited in its significance.

At its core *Dura* is largely a case about pleading. The Court concluded its analysis by highlighting how little would have been necessary by the plaintiffs to have effectively pled this cause of action:

> Our holding about plaintiffs' need to *prove* proximate causation and economic loss leads us also to conclude that the plaintiffs' complaint here failed adequately to *allege* these requirements. We

concede that the Federal Rules of Civil Procedure require only "a short and plain statement of the claim showing that the pleader is entitled to relief." Fed. Rule Civ. Proc. 8(a)(2). And we assume, at least for argument's sake, that neither the Rules nor the securities statutes impose any special further requirement in respect to the pleading of proximate causation or economic loss. But, even so, the "short and plain statement" must provide the defendant with "fair notice of what the plaintiff's claim is and the grounds upon which it rests." *Conley v. Gibson*, 355 U.S. 41, 47 (1957). The complaint before us fails this simple test.

As we have pointed out, the plaintiffs' lengthy complaint contains only one statement that we can fairly read as describing the loss caused by the defendants' "spray device" misrepresentations. That statement says that the plaintiffs "paid artificially inflated prices for Dura's securities" and suffered "damage[s]." App. 139a. The statement implies that the plaintiffs' loss consisted of the "artificially inflated" purchase "prices." The complaint's failure to claim that Dura's share price fell significantly after the truth became known suggests that the plaintiffs considered the allegation of purchase price inflation alone sufficient. The complaint contains nothing that suggests otherwise.

For reasons set forth in Part II-A, *supra*, however, the "artificially inflated purchase price" is not a relevant economic loss. And the complaint nowhere else provides the defendants with notice of what the relevant economic loss might be or of what the causal connection might be between that loss and the misrepresentation concerning Dura's "spray device."

We concede that ordinary pleading rules are not meant to impose a great burden upon a plaintiff. *Swierkiewicz v. Sorema N.A.*, 534 U.S. 506, 513–515 (2002). But it should not prove burdensome for a plaintiff who has suffered an economic loss to provide a defendant with some indication of the loss and the causal connection that the plaintiff has in mind. At the same time, allowing a plaintiff to forgo giving any indication of the economic loss and proximate cause that the plaintiff has in mind would bring about harm of the very sort the statutes seek to avoid. Cf. H.R. Conf. Rep. No. 104-369, p. 31 (1995) (criticizing "abusive" practices including "the routine filing of lawsuits ... with only a faint hope that the discovery process might lead eventually to some plausible cause of action"). It would permit a plaintiff "with a largely groundless claim to simply take up the time of a number of other people, with the right to do so representing an *in terrorem* the settlement value, rather than a reasonably founded hope that the [discovery] process will reveal relevant evidence." *Blue Chip Stamps*, 421 U.S., at 741. Such a rule would tend to transform a private securities action into a partial downside insurance policy.

Id. at 1634.

In other words, a few appropriately pled paragraphs identifying what the plaintiff's economic loss "might be" and the causal connection between that loss and the defendant's fraud will suffice.

(ii) *Damages and Rescission*

***P. 1286 n.289, end note.***    A finding of liability can be found without an award of damages. Miller v. Asensio & Co., Inc., 364 F.3d 223 (4th Cir. 2004).

# D.   GENERAL PROVISIONS

## 1.   Secondary Liability

### a.   Controlling Persons

***P. 1310 n.16, end note.***    In Suprema Specialties, Inc. Sec. Litig., 438 F.3d 256, 284–286 (3d Cir. 2006), the court held that in a §15 or §20 case there is no requirement that the controlled person be named as a defendant to impose liability upon the controlling persons. The plaintiff need only establish the controlled person's liability in order to bring suit against the controlled person.

In SEC v. J.W. Barclay & Co., Inc., 442 F.3d 834, 841 (3d Cir. 2006), the court ruled:

> The plain language of §20(a) supports our holding that the SEC had a claim for payment from Bruno under §20(a) because Bruno was

jointly and severally liable to the SEC for a debt in the amount of Barclay's unpaid penalty. In order for Bruno to be jointly and severally liable to the SEC under §20(a): (1) the SEC has to be a person; (2) to whom the controlled person, Barclay, was liable; (3) as a result of some act or acts constituting a violation or cause of action under any provision of the Exchange Act or any rule or regulation thereunder.

## c.   Aiding and Abetting

*P. 1332 n.43, end note.*   Substantial participation as proof of a primary violation under Rule 10b-5 is narrower than substantial assistance in an aiding and abetting case in two important respects. First, while the difference between substantial participation and substantial assistance may be a matter of degree, substantial participation, after *Central Bank* must cover a narrower category of misconduct or it would be impermissible. If the only difference between substantial participation and substantial assistance is a name change, then substantial participation will not stand. How much of a difference is required is unaddressed by *Central Bank*. But reasonably, if the theory is permitted, it will have to be a substantial difference.

In Judge Harmon's analysis Vinson & Elkins could be held liable because it was "in league" with Enron and others in structuring several illicit partnerships and off-the-book SPEs. Among other steps, Vinson & Elkins drafted formation documents and legal opinions and gave advice regarding nondisclosure of an Enron executive's role that collectively were essential to a fraudulent transaction. As Judge Harmon put it in a damning sentence; "In other words [Vinson & Elkins] effected the very deceptive devices and contrivances that were the heart of the alleged Ponzi scheme." In contrast, Kirkland & Ellis was dismissed when it represented and performed routine legal services for specified illicit entities. Kirkland was not alleged to have drafted documents that either were the heart of a fraud or relied upon by public investors. If Judge Harmon's analysis is affirmed the type of conduct that a defendant would have to engage in presumably would require scienter, conduct roughly equivalent to being a co-conspirator, and reliance by the plaintiff on the device or contrivance, in part, created by the defendant. This is considerably narrower than aiding and abetting substantial assistance that, for example, presumably could reach the type of conduct performed by Kirkland & Ellis if a defendant knew or was reckless in not knowing about a primary violation. Cf. Carter & Johnson, 47 SEC 471, 503 (1981): "The second element — substantial assistance — is generally satisfied in the context of a securities lawyer performing professional duties, for he is inevitably deeply involved in his client's disclosure activities and often partici- pates in the drafting of the documents, as was the case with Carter."

Second, even when a plaintiff could demonstrate a permissible form of substantial participation, the plaintiff would also have to prove reliance on the substantial participation itself. In an aiding and abetting case, the plaintiff only had to show that the aider and abetter provided substantial assistance to a primary violation on which the plaintiff relied. The absence of reliance from aiding and abetting signifies a major conceptual difference between that doc- trine and primary violation under Rule 10b-5. Aiding and abetting is, in essence, a deterrence theory. By broadening potential liability, aiding and abetting also increases the legal actors with an incentive to prevent legal misconduct. Reliance in a primary Rule 10b-5 claim is a compensatory concept. It limits liability to a class of plaintiffs who can prove a loss that was caused by the defendant's misconduct.

Cf. Hamdani, Gatekeeper Liability, 77 S. Cal. L. Rev. 53 (2004):

> Recent corporate scandals, most notably the collapse of Enron, Worldcom, and Global Crossing, have highlighted the importance of enlisting various gatekeepers — auditors, lawyers, underwriters, lenders and stock analysts — to prevent corporate fraud. It is thus not surprising that the goal of harnessing gatekeepers to the task of ensuring the accuracy of corporate disclosure has occupied a central role on the post-Enron regulatory agenda.

Id. at 55–56.

In Enron Corp. Sec., Derivative & ERISA Litig., 310 F. Supp. 2d 819 (S.D. Tex. 2004), Judge Harmon concluded that plaintiffs had adequately pled a primary violator claim under §10(b) against Merrill Lynch with respect to allegations of a "purported Ponzi scheme" in a Nigerian barge deal that involved purchasing barges from Enron to create sham earnings of $12 million in return for a secret, oral agreement that Enron would repurchase them within six months with a lucrative profit to Merrill Lynch.

## 2. DEFENSES

### a. Statutes of Limitations

#### (i) *Express Liabilities*

***P. 1335 n.50, end note.*** In P. Stolz Family Partnership L.P. v. Daum, 355 F.3d 92 (2d Cir. 2004), quoting and citing the text, the court followed the vast majority of courts and concluded that the §13 three year statute of limitations begins when a security is first bona fide offered. Id. at 100–106.

***P. 1338 n.63, end note.*** In Litzler v. CC Inv., L.D.C., 362 F.3d 203 (2d Cir. 2004), the court concluded "that the two-year limitations period of Section 16(b) is subject to equitable tolling when a covered party fails to comply with Section 16(a) and that such tolling ends when a potential claimant otherwise receives sufficient notice that short-swing profits were realized by the party covered by Section 16(a)." Id. at 205.

#### (ii) *Implied Liabilities*

***P. 1346 n.92, end note.*** See also New Eng. Health Care Employees Pension Fund v. Ernst & Young, LLP, 336 F.3d 495 (6th Cir. 2003) (joining at least seven other circuits in adoption of inquiry notice standard); Newman v. Warnaco Group, Inc., 335 F.3d 187 (2d Cir. 2003) (earnings restatements did not place plaintiff on inquiry notice of fraud); Caprin v. Simon Transp. Serv., Inc., 2003–2004 Fed. Sec. L. Rep. (CCH) ¶92,692 (10th Cir. 2004) (following *Sterlin*); Grippo v. Perazzo, 357 F.3d 1218 (11th Cir. 2004) (inquiry notice required); LaGrasta v. First Union Sec., Inc., 358 F.3d 840 (11th Cir. 2004) (disagreeing that investor put on inquiry notice when article on Smart

Money was published); Lentell v. Merrill Lynch & Co., Inc. 396 F.3d 161 (2d Cir. 2005), *cert. denied*, 126 S. Ct. 421 (declining to dismiss on inquiry notice grounds when there was no "manifest indication that plaintiffs 'could have learned' the facts underpinning their allegations more than a year prior to filing"); Benak v. Alliance Capital Mgmt. L.P., 435 F.3d 396 (3d Cir. 2006) (comparing mutual fund investing to direct investing for purposes of inquiry notice and concluding on facts in this case that even mutual fund investor was on inquiry notice).

For a definitive judgment that inquiry notice began when a specific *Fortune* magazine article was published, see Shah v. Meeker, 435 F.3d 244 (2d Cir. 2006).

Inquiry notice is also relevant to the question of whether a claim filed after November 15, 2002, will be barred because the class was sufficiently on notice before the effective date of the Sarbanes-Oxley Act. Tello v. Dean Witter Reynolds, 410 F.3d 1275 (11th Cir. 2005). The Act does not apply retroactively to revive stale claims. See, e.g., ADC Telecomms., Inc. Sec. Litig., 409 F.3d 974 (8th Cir. 2005).

(iii)    *Sarbanes–Oxley Act Amendments*

***P. 1347, new n.92.1, after indented quotation.***    The new statute of limitations, however, has been held not to apply to §§11 and 12 of the Securities Act since these provisions do not sound in "fraud, deceit manipulation or contrivance" as is required under §804. See WorldCom, Inc. Sec. Litig., 294 F. Supp. 2d 431, 443 (S.D.N.Y. 2003); Global Crossing, Ltd. Sec. Litig., 2003–2004 Fed. Sec. L. Rep. (CCH) ¶92,654 (S.D.N.Y. 2003).

In Enterprise Mortgage Acceptance Co., LLC, Sec. Litig., 391 F.3d 401(2d Cir. 2004), the Second Circuit held that §804 of the Sarbanes-Oxley Act did not revive plaintiffs' expired securities fraud cases. Enterprise relied on Landgraf v. USI Film Prod., 511 U.S. 244 (1994) and declined to apply §804 retroactively. *Accord*: Foss v. Bear, Stearns & Co., Inc., 394 F.3d 540, 542 (7th Cir. 2005) (§804 does not apply retroactively).

### c. Failure to Plead Fraud with Particularity

***P. 1357 n.121, new par., next to last par.*** See also Ottmann v. Hanger Orthopedic Group, Inc., 353 F.3d 338, 345 (4th Cir. 2003), the court adopted "a flexible, case-specific analysis":

> We agree that a flexible, case-specific analysis is appropriate in examining scienter pleadings. Both the absence of any statutory language addressing particular methods of pleading and the inconclusive legislative history regarding the adoption of Second Circuit pleading standards indicate that Congress ultimately chose not to specify particular types of facts that would or would not show a strong inference of scienter. [Citations omitted.] We therefore conclude that courts should not restrict their scienter inquiry by focusing on specific categories of facts, such as those relating to motive and opportunity, but instead should examine all of the allegations in each case to determine whether they collectively establish a strong inference of scienter. And, while particular facts demonstrating a motive and opportunity to commit fraud (or lack of such facts) may be relevant to the scienter inquiry, the weight accorded to those facts should depend on the circumstances of each case.

***P. 1359 n.120, end note.*** In Rombach v. Chang, 355 F.3d 164 (2d Cir. 2004), the Second Circuit, following several circuits, held that the heightened pleading standards of Rule 9(b) apply to §§11 and 12(a)(2) when they are premised on claims of fraud.

Following Shapiro v. UJB Fin. Corp., 964 F.2d 272, 288 (3d Cir. 1992), the court in California Pub. Employees Retirement Sys. v. Chubb Corp., 394 F.3d 126, 160–163 (3d Cir. 2004) dismissed §11 claims under Rule 9(b) when the claims "sounded in fraud." Judge Sloviter dissented on this point. Id. at 166.

See also Knollenberg v. Harmonic, Inc., 2005–2006 Fed. Sec. L. Rep. (CCH) ¶93,554, at 97,342–97,343 (9th Cir. 2005) ("Claims brought under Sections 11 and 12 of the 1933 Act are *not* subject to the heightened pleading requirements of the PSLRA"); Suprema Specialties, Inc., Sec. Litig., 438 F.3d 256, 269–270 (3d Cir. 2006) (following *CALPERS*).

A subsequent circuit split has concerned the endurance of group pleading after the 1995 Act. See Financial Acquisition Partners LP v. Blackwell, 440 F.3d 278, 281 (5th Cir. 2006) (the PSLRA abolished the group pleading doctrine, following Southland Sec. Corp. v. Inspire Ins. Solutions, Inc., 365 F.3d 353, 364–365 (5th Cir. 2004)).

Insider trading will only support an inference of scienter by revealing a motive and opportunity for profiting from a fraud if the timing and amount are "unusual or suspicious." PEC Solutions, Inc., Sec. Litig., 418 F.3d 379, 390 (4th Cir. 2005). Here sales between 1.17 and 13 percent of defendant's holdings were characterized as *de minimis*. The court further noted that some of the individual defendants simultaneously exercised and did not sell stock options and lost money on their stock sales. Ibid.

In Makor Issues & Rights Ltd. v. Tellabs, Inc., 437 F.3d 588 (7th Cir. 2006), the Seventh Circuit agreed with several other circuits that a complaint could proceed under the Private Securities Litigation Reform Act relying on confidential sources, but a complaint must describe its sources with sufficient particularity "to support the probability that a person in the position occupied by the source would possess the information alleged." Id. at 596.

Plaintiffs are not required to name witnesses, but can rely on confidential witnesses if appropriate in the circumstance of a case. Metawave Communications Corp. Sec. Litig., 298 F. Supp. 2d 1056, 1068 (W.D. Wash. 2003), citing Novak v. Kasaks, 216 F.3d 300, 314 (2d Cir. 2000). The court in *Metawave* amplified:

> "To contribute meaningfully toward a 'strong inference' of scienter, however, allegations attributed to unnamed sources must be accompanied by enough particularized detail to support a reasonable conviction in the informant's basis of knowledge." [Citations omitted.] Plaintiffs must plead "with substantial specificity" how confidential witnesses "came to learn of the information they provide in the complaint." [Citation omitted.] The court must be able to tell whether a confidential witness is speaking from personal knowledge, or "merely regurgitating gossip and innuendo." [Citation omitted.] The court can look to "the level of the detail provided by the confidential witnesses, the

corroborative nature of the other facts alleged (including from other sources), the coherence and plausibility of the allegations, the number of sources, the reliability of the sources, and similar indicia." [Citation omitted.]

The Third Circuit, in California Pub. Employees Retirement Sys. v. Chubb Corp., 394 F.3d 126 (3d Cir. 2004), followed Novak v. Kasaks, 216 F.3d 300, 314 (2d Cir. 2000), cert. denied, 531 U.S. 1012, as well as ABC Arbitrage Plaintiffs Group v. Tchuruk, 291 F.3d 336, 351–354 (5th Cir. 2002); and Cabletron Sys., Inc., 311 F.3d 11, 29–31 (1st Cir. 2002) in not requiring disclosure of confidential sources as a general matter. Plaintiffs are only required to "plead with particularly *sufficient* facts to support those beliefs." *Chubb* at 146. However, in this case when confidential sources were not described with sufficient particularity, plaintiffs failed to state a claim. Id. at 156. See also Daou Sys., Inc. Sec. Litig., 411 F.3d 1006, 1015–1016 (9th Cir. 2005) (plaintiffs description of confidential witnesses pled with sufficient particularity).

See also McMulen v. Fluor Corp., 2003–2004 Fed. Sec. L. Rep. (CCH) ¶92,665 (9th Cir. 2004) (allowing leave to amend when court concluded that further amendment would not be futile); Miller v. Champion Enter., Inc., 346 F.3d 660, 689–692 (6th Cir. 2003) (denying motion to amend pleadings as futile).

## 3.   ARBITRATION AND NONWAIVER PROVISIONS

*P. 1376 n.198, end note.*   In Credit Suisse First Boston Corp. v. Grunwald, 400 F.3d 1119 (9th Cir. 2005), the court held that the Securities Exchange Act of 1934 preempted application of California's Ethics Standards to NASD appointed arbitrators. The court relied on Merrill Lynch, Pierce, Fenner & Smith v. Ware, 414 U.S. 117, 125, 130–131 (1973) to determine when SRO rules would preempt state law. The court also noted that the 1975 Securities Acts Amendments requires the SEC to determine that proposed SRO rule changes must be consistent with the purposes of the Securities Exchange Act. Id. at 1128-1130.

In Buckeye Check Cashing v. Cardegna, 126 S. Ct. 1204 (2006), the Supreme Court held that the arbitrator, rather than the court, should consider the claim that a contract containing an arbitration provision is void for illegality. The Court relied on Southland Corp. v. Keating, 465 U.S. 1 (1984), and Prima Paint Corp. v. Flood & Conklin Mfg. Co., 388 U.S. 395 (1967), to generalize:

> *Prima Paint* and *Southland* answer the question presented here by establishing three propositions. First, as a matter of substantive federal arbitration law, an arbitration provision is severable from the remainder of the contract. Second, unless the challenge is to the arbitration clause itself, the issue of the contract's validity is considered by the arbitrator in the first instance. Third, this arbitration law applies in state as well as federal courts. The parties have not requested, and we do not undertake, reconsideration of those holdings. Applying them to this case, we conclude that because respondents challenge the Agreement, but not specifically its arbitration provisions, those provisions are enforceable apart from the remainder of the contract. The challenge should therefore be considered by an arbitrator, not a court.

126 S. Ct. at 1209.

## 4. CLASS ACTIONS

*P. 1384 n.222, end note.*     In Merck & Co. Sec. Litig., 432 F.3d 261 (3d Cir. 2005), lead plaintiff retained appellate counsel without court approval. The Third Circuit permitted this counsel to prosecute this appeal but held that future lead plaintiffs must obtain court approval for any new counsel, including appellate counsel.

*P. 1391, 3d full par. & nn. 242–243.*     *Substitute:* §21D(f) for §21D(g). [In 1998 §21D(g) was renumbered §21D(f).]
The Class Action Fairness Act of 2005 generally enables defendants to remove class actions when (1) they aggregate claims of all plaintiffs exceed $5 million and (2) at least one plaintiff is diverse from at least one defendant. 28 U.S.C. §1332(d).

## 7. INDEMNIFICATION, CONTRIBUTION, AND INSURANCE

***PP. 1397–1398.*** *Substitute*: §21D(f) for §21D(g). [In 1998 §21D(g) was renumbered §21D(f).]

***P. 1398 n.281, end note.*** In Gerber v. MTC Elec. Tech., 329 F.3d 297 (2d Cir. 2003), *cert. denied sub nom.* Daiwa Sec. Am., Inc. v. Kayne, 124 S. Ct. 432, the trial court followed a "capped proportionate rule" under which the credit given for a settlement will be the greater of the settlement amount for common damages (a "pro tanto" rule) or the "proportionate share" of the settling defendants as proven at fault. Id. at 302–303. On appeal the Court of Appeals generally approved this approach for limiting its application to common damages. Id. at 304. This was a pre-PSLRA Act case, but the court remanded the District order approving a nonmutual bar order for further consideration and balancing of competing fairness issues. Id. at 307–309. See also BankAmerica Sec. Litig., 350 F.3d 747 (8th Cir. 2003) (affirming approval of global settlement over objections after fairness hearing).

***P. 1403 n.300, end note.*** Cf. AAL High Yield Bond Fund v. Deloitte & Touche LLP, 361 F.3d 1305 (11th Cir. 2004), in which the court vacated a ban of all related present and future claims by Deloitte and a nonsettling defendant, and also banned claims against officers and agents of a nonparty. The lower court made no findings of fact and expressed no rationale or authority for barring claims without a settlement credit or set off.

## 8. ATTORNEYS' FEES AND SECURITY FOR COSTS

***P. 1408 n.318, end note.*** In Professional Mgmt. Assoc. Inc. Employees' Profit Sharing Plan v. KPMG LLP, 345 F.3d 1030 (8th Cir. 2003), the court of Appeals reversed and remanded a District Court opinion declining to award Rule 11 sanctions when the well settled law of res judicata establishes the frivolousness of a plaintiff seeking to relitigate a claim he has been denied leave to serve against the same party in a earlier lawsuit.

In De la Fuente v. OCI DCI Telecommunications, Inc., 2003–2004 Fed. Sec. L. Rep. (CCH) ¶92,646 (2d Cir. 2003), the court affirmed sanctions when all arguments made by a plaintiff in response to a motion to dismiss were considered frivolous.

***P. 1409, 1st full par., 1st line.***   *Substitute*: Securities Act §20(f) [not §21(f)].

# CHAPTER 12

# GOVERNMENT LITIGATION

## B. CRIMINAL PROSECUTION

### 1. SEC PENAL PROVISIONS

***P. 1420, end 3d full par.*** In SEC v. Gemstar-TV Guide Int'l Inc., 401 F.3d 1031 (9th Cir. *en banc* 2005), *cert. denied sub nom.* Yuen v. SEC, 126 S. Ct. 416, the court reversed and concluded that the $37.4 million paid to Yuen and Levy were extraordinary payments under §1103. The court explained:

> "Extraordinary" means, in plain language, out of the ordinary. In the context of a statute aimed at preventing the raiding of corporate assets, "out of the ordinary" means a payment that would not typically be made by a company in its customary course of business. The standard of comparison is the company's common or regular behavior. Thus, the determination of whether a payment is extraordinary will be a fact-based and flexible inquiry. Context-specific factors such as the circumstances under which the payment is contemplated or made the purpose of the payment, and the size of the payment may inform whether a payment is extraordinary, as the district court properly noted in this case. For example, a payment made by a company that would otherwise be unremarkable may be rendered extraordinary by unusual circumstances. . . .
>
> A nexus between the suspected wrongdoing and the payment itself may further demonstrate that the payment is extraordinary,

although such a connection is not required. Evidence of the company's deviation from an "industry standard"—or the practice of similarly situated businesses—also might reveal whether a payment is extraordinary.

Id. at 1045.

## 3. RELEVANT PROVISIONS OF THE CRIMINAL CODE

***P. 1423, end carryover par.***    In May 2005 the United States Supreme Court reversed and remanded the conviction of Arthur Andersen because "the jury instructions failed to convey properly the elements of a 'corrupt persuas[ion]' conviction under [18 U.S.C.] §1512(b)." Arthur Andersen LLP v. United States, 125 S. Ct. 2129 (2005).

CHAPTER 13

# SEC ADMINISTRATIVE LAW

## A. SECURITIES LAWYERS

### 2. THE SECURITIES LAWYER IN GENERAL

*P. 1458 n.29, end note.* In August 2003 the ABA House of Delegates approved both the Task Force proposed amendments to Rule 1.13 and to Rule 1.6. ABA Amends Rule on Client Confidentiality to Allow Lawyers to Disclose Financial Fraud, 35 Sec. Reg. L. Rep. (BNA) 1357 (2003); ABA Amends Model Ethics Rules to Permit Up the Ladder Reports of Corporate Wrongs, 35 id. 1358.

## B. INVESTIGATION

### 1. THE STATUTORY PROVISIONS AND THE COMMISSION'S PROCEDURES

*P. 1484 n.21, end note.* In 2003 the Commission announced that it would no longer permit defendants who settle civil injunctive cases to subsequently contest the factual allegations in later administrative proceedings. SEC Outlines New Enforcement Policy Based on Use of Facts in Settled Cases, 35 Sec. Reg. & L. Rep. (BNA) 1322 (2003).

In April 2004 Stephen Cutler, Director of the SEC Division of Enforcement, noted that "all but three of the 12 penalties of $50 million or more obtained in Commission settlements since 1986 were obtained in the last twelve months." Speech, 24th Ann. Ray Garrett Jr. Corporate and Securities Law Inst., Apr. 29, 2004, Chicago, Ill.

In February 2006, SEC Chair Cox reacted swiftly to media reports that the Commissioner had ordered two journalists to provide information to the SEC about conversations they had with stock traders and analysts, stating:

> The issuance of a subpoena to a journalist which seeks to compel production of his or her notes and records of conversations with sources is highly unusual. Until the appearance of media reports this weekend, neither the Chairman of the SEC, the General Counsel, the Office of Public Affairs, nor any Commissioner was apprised of or consulted in connection with a decision to take such an extraordinary step. The sensitive issues that such a subpoena raises are of sufficient importance that they should, and will be, considered and decided by the Commission before this matter proceeds further.

SEC Press Rel. 2006-24 (Feb. 27, 2006). See also Labaton & Norris, Crime and Consequences Still Weigh on Corporate World, N.Y. Times, Jan. 5, 2006, at C1; Ferrara, Clark, & Chang, The SEC's Newly Announced Standards for the Imposition of Corporate Monetary Penalties: An Overdue Step Toward Predictability, 38 Sec. Reg. & L. Rep. (BNA) 170 (2006).

In 2006 the Commission issued a Statement Concerning Financial Penalties in the context of an announcement of the settled actions against corporate issuers, SEC v. McAfee, Inc., and Applix, Inc. The Statement explained in part:

> The question of whether, and if so to what extent, to impose civil penalties against a corporation raises significant questions for our mission of investor protection. The authority to impose such penalties is relatively recent in the Commission's history, and the use of very large corporate penalties is more recent still. Recent cases have not produced a clear public view of when and

how the Commission will use corporate penalties, and within the Commission itself a variety of views have heretofore been expressed, but not reconciled. . . .

In 1990, Congress passed the Securities Enforcement Remedies and Penny Stock Reform Act (the "Remedies Act"), which gave the Commission authority generally to seek civil money penalties in enforcement cases. The penalty provisions added by the Remedies Act expressly authorize the Commission to obtain money penalties from entities, including corporate issuers. . . .

. . . [A] key question for the Commission is whether the issuer's violation has provided an improper benefit to the shareholders, or conversely whether the violation has resulted in harm to the shareholders. Where shareholders have been victimized by the violative conduct, or by the resulting negative effect on the entity following its discovery, the Commission is expected to seek penalties from culpable individual offenders acting for a corporation. . . .

In addition to the benefit or harm to shareholders, the statute and its legislative history suggest several other factors that may be pertinent to the analysis of corporate issuer penalties. For example, the need for effective deterrence is discussed throughout the legislative history of the Remedies Act. The Senate Report also notes the importance of good compliance programs and observes that the availability of penalties may encourage development of such programs. The Senate Report also observes that penalties may serve to decrease the temptation to violate the law in areas where the perceived risk of detection of wrongdoing is small. Other factors discussed in the legislative history include whether there was fraudulent intent, harm to innocent third parties, and the possibility of unjust enrichment to the wrongdoer.

The Sarbanes-Oxley Act of 2002 changed the ultimate disposition of penalties. Section 308 of Sarbanes-Oxley (the Fair Funds provision) allows the Commission to take penalties paid by individuals and entities in enforcement actions and add them to disgorgement funds for the benefit of victims. Penalty moneys no longer always go to the Treasury. Under Fair Funds, penalty moneys instead can be used to compensate the victims for the losses they experienced from the wrongdoing. If the victims are shareholders of the corporation being penalized, they will still bear the cost of issuer penalty payments (which is the case with any penalty against a corporate entity). When penalty moneys are ultimately returned to all or some of the investors who were victims of the violation, the amounts returned are less the administrative costs of the distribution. While the legislative history of the Fair Funds provision is scant, there are two general points that can be discerned. First, the purpose of the provision is to provide an additional source of compensation to victims of securities law violations. Second, the provision applies to all penalties and makes no distinction between penalties against individuals or entities. . . .

We proceed from the fundamental principle that corporate penalties are an essential part of an aggressive and comprehensive program to enforce the federal securities laws, and that the availability of a corporate penalty, as one of a range of remedies, contributes to the Commission's ability to achieve an appropriate level of deterrence through its decision in a particular case.

With this principle in mind, our view of the appropriateness of a penalty on the corporation in a particular case, as distinct from the individuals who commit a securities law violation, turns principally on two considerations:

*The presence or absence of a direct benefit to the corporation as a result of the violation.* The fact that a corporation itself has received a direct and material benefit from the offense, for example through reduced expenses or increased revenues, weighs in support of the imposition of a corporate penalty. If the corporation is in any other way unjustly enriched, this similarly weighs in support of the imposition of a corporate penalty. Within this parameter, the strongest case for the imposition of a corporate penalty is one in which the shareholders of the corporation have received an improper benefit as a result of the violation; the weakest case is one in which the current shareholders of the corporation are the principal victims of the securities law violation.

*The degree to which the penalty will recompense or further harm the injured shareholders.* Because the protection of innocent investors is a principal objective of the securities laws, the imposition of a penalty on the corporation itself carries with it the risk that shareholders who are innocent of the violation will nonetheless bear the burden of the penalty. In some cases, however, the penalty itself may be used as a source of funds to recompense the injury suffered by victims of the securities law violations. The presence of an opportunity to use the penalty as a meaningful source of compensation to injured shareholders is a factor in support of its imposition. The likelihood a corporate penalty will unfairly injure investors, the corporation, or third parties weighs against its use as a sanction.

In addition to these two principal considerations, there are several additional factors that are properly considered in determining whether to impose a penalty on the corporation. These are:

*The need to deter the particular type of offense.* The likelihood that a corporate penalty will serve as a strong deterrent to others similarly situated weighs in favor of the imposition of a corporate penalty. Conversely, the prevalence of unique circumstances that render the particular offense unlikely to be repeated in other contexts is a factor weighing against the need for a penalty on the corporation rather than on the responsible individuals.

*The extent of the injury to innocent parties.* The egregiousness of the harm done, the number of investors injured, and the extent of societal harm if the corporation's infliction of such injury on innocent parties goes unpunished, are significant determinants of the propriety of a corporate penalty.

*Whether complicity in the violation is widespread throughout the corporation.* The more pervasive the participation in the offense by responsible persons within the corporation, the more appropriate is the use of a corporate penalty. Conversely, within this parameter, isolated conduct by only a few individuals would tend not to support the imposition of a corporate penalty. Whether the corporation has replaced those persons responsible for the violation will also be considered in weighing this factor.

*The level of intent on the part of the perpetrators.* Within this parameter, the imposition of a corporate penalty is most appropriate in egregious circumstances, where the culpability and fraudulent intent of the perpetrators are manifest. A corporate penalty is less likely to be imposed if the violation is not the result of deliberate, intentionally fraudulent conduct.

*The degree of difficulty in detecting the particular type of offense.* Because offenses that are particularly difficult to detect call for an especially high level of deterrence, this factor weighs in support of the imposition of a corporate penalty.

*Presence or lack of remedial steps by the corporation.* Because the aim of the securities laws is to protect investors, the prevention of future harm, as well as the punishment of past offenses, is a high priority. The Commission's decisions in particular cases are

295

intended to encourage the management of corporations accused of securities law violations to do everything within their power to take remedial steps, from the first moment that the violation is brought to their attention. Exemplary conduct by management in this respect weighs against the use of a corporate penalty; failure of management to take remedial steps is a factor supporting the imposition of a corporate penalty.

*Extent of cooperation with Commission and other law enforcement.* Effective compliance with the securities laws depends upon vigilant supervision, monitoring, and reporting of violations. When securities law violations are discovered, it is incumbent upon management to report them to the Commission and to other appropriate law enforcement authorities. The degree to which a corporation has self reported an offense, or otherwise cooperated with the investigation and remediation of the offense, is a factor that the Commission will consider in determining the propriety of a corporate penalty.

## C. QUASIJUDICIAL PROCEEDINGS

*P. 1499 n.39, end note.* In Rule 161(b) the Commission adopted a policy to strongly disfavor requests to extend time limits or grant postponements, adjournments, and extensions, but the Commission or the hearing offer can extend the time limits. Rule 161(c)(2) permits an extension to consider an offer of settlement. Under Rule 360 the deadlines will be 120, 210, and 300 days. Other temporal amendments were made to Rules 230(d) and 450. Sec. Ex. Act Rel. 48,018, 80 SEC Dock. 1266 (2003) (adoption).

## D. STATUTORY REMEDIES

### 2. CEASE AND DESIST ORDERS

*P. 1510 n.18, end note.* See also WHX Corp. v. SEC, 362 F.3d 854 (D.C. Cir. 2004), citing *KPMG* standard, but reversing cease and desist order; Geiger v. SEC, 363 F.3d 481 (D.C. Cir. 2004), affirming cease and desist order, and observing, "under Commission precedent, the existence of a violation raises an inference that it will be repeated." Id. at 489.

### 3. CORPORATE BAR ORDERS

***P. 1511 n.24, end note.***    In Vernazza v. SEC, 327 F.3d 851, 862–863 (9th Cir. 2003), the court agreed with the SEC that a six month bar from association with other investment advisers was reasonable after the investment adviser was deceived by a fraudulent scheme that spanned several years. See also Lowry v. SEC, 340 F.3d 501 (5th Cir. 2003) (similar).

***P. 1511, new text, end page.***    In SEC v. Smyth, 420 F.3d 1225 (11th Cir. 2005), the court vacated a disgorgement order when the District Court refused to hold an evidentiary hearing to determine the amount that should have been disgorged. The amount was in dispute. The case was remanded for further proceedings.

# TABLE OF CASES

*References are to page numbers of main volume.*